ENGLISH CORE LINGUISTICS

Cornelia Tschichold
(Ed.)

ENGLISH CORE LINGUISTICS

Essays in honour of
D. J. Allerton

PETER LANG
Bern · Berlin · Bruxelles · Frankfurt am Main · New York · Oxford · Wien

Bibliographic information published by Die Deutsche Bibliothek
Die Deutsche Bibliothek lists this publication in the Deutsche National-
bibliografie; detailed bibliographic data is available on the Internet at
‹http://dnb.ddb.de›.

British Library and Library of Congress Cataloguing-in-Publication Data:
A catalogue record for this book is available from The British Library,
Great Britain, and from The Library of Congress, USA

Cover design: Thomas Jaberg, Peter Lang AG

ISBN 3-906770-98-2
US-ISBN 0-8204-6259-4

© Peter Lang AG, European Academic Publishers, Bern 2003
Hochfeldstrasse 32, Postfach 746, CH-3000 Bern 9, Switzerland
info@peterlang.com, www.peterlang.com, www.peterlang.net

All rights reserved.
All parts of this publication are protected by copyright.
Any utilisation outside the strict limits of the copyright law, without the
permission of the publisher, is forbidden and liable to prosecution.
This applies in particular to reproductions, translations, microfilming, and
storage and processing in electronic retrieval systems.

Printed in Germany

Contents

Preface 9

Phonetics and Phonology

RICHARD J. WATTS (BERNE)
Was the Great Vowel Shift really 'great'? A reappraisal
of research work on an elusive linguistic phenomenon 13

MARTINA HÄCKER (CONSTANCE)
From linking [h] to glottal stop:
changes in the phonotactic system of 20th-century Cockney 31

PETER TRUDGILL (FRIBOURG)
Linguistic changes in pan-world English 55

RICHARD MATTHEWS (FREIBURG)
English vowel phonology
and the quest for the 'fourth dimension' 69

ALAN CRUTTENDEN (MANCHESTER)
A two-tone approach to urban North British 93

SARAH EBNER (BASEL)
A dynamical systems approach to speech and language 107

Morphology

MARTIN DURRELL (MANCHESTER)
From regularity to irregularity in morphology:
Ablaut in the West Germanic Languages 125

CLIVE GREY (EDGE HILL)
Well I'll be verbed: "walksorted" and conversion
as a lexical process in contemporary British English 147

DOROTA A. SMYK (ZÜRICH)
On unintentionality in morphological productivity.................167

PIUS TEN HACKEN (SWANSEA)
Phrases in words 185

Phraseology

ANTHONY COWIE (LEEDS)
Some aspects of the treatment of phraseology in the OED 205

JUDITH WIESER (BASEL)
Opening and closing eyes:
a corpus-based study of a set of idioms....................................225

ALEXANDRA PUSCH & MICHAEL STUBBS (TRIER)
Frequent terms in linguistics:
A pilot corpus study for a pedagogical word-list.....................247

NADJA NESSELHAUF (BASEL)
Transfer at the locutional level: an investigation of
German-speaking and French-speaking learners of English.....269

CORNELIA TSCHICHOLD (NEUCHÂTEL)
Error analysis and lexical errors...287

Syntax

ALLAN TURNER (NEWCASTLE)
Fronting in Tolkien's archaising style and its translation 301

KEVIN MCCAFFERTY (TROMSØ)
Language contact in Early Modern Ireland:
the case of be after V-ing as a future gram 323

PAUL SKANDERA (INNSBRUCK)
Start doing or *start to do:*
Is the gerund spreading in American English? 343

LYNDON HIGGS (STRASBOURG)
Has *shall* become extinct? 353

Preface

The nineteen papers in this volume deal with four core areas of English linguistics, covering phonetics and phonology, morphology, syntax and phraseology. They have been collected as a tribute to D. J. Allerton, to be presented to him on the occasion of his retirement from the chair of Modern English Linguistics at the University of Basel, Switzerland. D. J. Allerton began his career in linguistics at the University of Manchester, as Lecturer, later as Senior Lecturer, in General Linguistics. In 1980, he was appointed to the chair at Basel University where he still teaches today. In his more than twenty years as professor at Basel, he has continued to publish widely and supervised a growing number of PhD students (several of whom are among the contributors to this volume). He has helped institutionalize the subject of general linguistics at the University of Basel and also (co-)established a number of linguistic organizations known today by their acronyms (JASGIL, the Joint Advanced Study Group In Linguistics, a Franco-Swiss cooperation; SWELL, the linguistic subgroup of SAUTE (Swiss Association of University Teachers of English), and CURL, the Circle of Upper Rhine Linguists). While he has had very wide-ranging interests in all fields of linguistics, as reflected in his publications and in the topics of the PhD theses that he supervised in the course of his career, in his teaching he has always put the emphasis firmly on what he calls 'core linguistics', a term borrowed for the title of the present volume.

The order of the contributions in this tribute to D. J. Allerton roughly follows the order of topics in any classic introductory lecture on core linguistics, and thus we start with papers on phonetic and phonological issues. The first three contributions in this section take a diachronic perspective. In the opening chapter, R. Watts challenges the greatness of the Great Vowel Shift and calls for an enlargement of the perspective to include sociolinguistic aspects, linking this to questions on the discursive construction of the Great Vowel Shift and 'standard' English. In the second contribution, looking at the changes within Modern English, M. Häcker examines h-dropping and h-insertion in Cockney, calling into question previous interpretations of the data. P. Trudgill then looks at the most recent changes in the pronunciation of vowels in World Englishes, suggesting that certain drift phenomena found in the Great Vowel Shift can be observed again today, seemingly independently, in a number of varieties of English around the world.

R. Matthews' topic, too, is the English vowel system, but he takes a synchronic and more theoretical viewpoint. He proposes to drop the 'tense vs. lax' distinction in favour of a fourth dimension better suited to the system of English vowels. In a paper on intonation in the variety of English spoken in Manchester, A. Cruttenden also suggests replacing certain theoretical models that have been applied to the data by another, originally older, model that can better account for the data at hand. In the final contribution in this first section, S. Ebner suggests taking an entirely different point of view by applying the theory of dynamical systems to questions in the domain of speech in particular and of language in general.

The second section, on morphology, opens with a paper by M. Durrell, who argues that even irregular verb patterns in the Germanic languages show signs of (limited) productivity, attracting previously regular verbs into their class. C. Grey then shows the extraordinarily high productivity of conversion in English, illustrating his argument with some recent examples. D. Smyk's paper continues the thread on the topic of productivity. She investigates unintentionality as one of the criteria for productivity as documented by recent neologisms, and comes to the conclusion that – despite its intuitive appeal – it cannot be considered a viable criterion. In the last contribution on morphology, P. ten Hacken considers the interaction of syntax and morphology in exocentric compounds. He shows a number of cases where phrases seem to be involved in word formation and how they can be accommodated in line with the Chomskyan Lexicalist Hypothesis.

The third group of papers all examine some aspect of phraseology, one of D. J. Allerton's most long-lasting areas of interest. In the first contribution in this section, A. Cowie scrutinizes a number of entries in the OED for traces of phraseologisms. This is followed by an equally meticulous, corpus-based study on expressions containing the word *eye*, by J. Wieser, who provides a comparative analysis in her paper. The contribution by A. Pusch and M. Stubbs shows a practical application of a small corpus study, revealing gaps in published glossaries of linguistic terminology. N. Nesselhauf's paper gives some interesting results of a corpus study on learner language and provides empirical evidence for the problems non-native speakers have with a particular type of phraseologisms. The last paper in this section on the lexicon is also concerned with learner language and tries to assess the role of error analysis with respect to learners' lexical and phraseological problems.

The final group of papers deals with topics in syntax. It opens on A. Turner's discussion of Tolkien's archaising style, making heavy use of fronting, and the syntactic problems this causes for translators. The next contribution, by P. Skandera, asks whether the gerund is becoming more frequent in Modern English and provides evidence in favour of (slow) change. The volume is rounded off with a paper by L. Higgs, who shows that despite being well alive in dialectal forms of English, the use of *shall* seems to be on its way to extinction in standard English.

The authors of the contributions to the present volume hope to provide some interesting reading in the field of English core linguistics to D. J. Allerton and to students and scholars of English linguistics. In a time of increasing fragmentation of the subject of linguistics, it can have beneficial effects to focus on the common core of one's discipline, even if only for a moment. Certainly D. J. Allerton has never lost the overview of the important developments in linguistics and can always be counted on to have read the seminal works, even if they are still unpublished. I am sure that he will be sorely missed at the

English Seminar in Basel and at the regular meetings on linguistic topics he helped establish, not least because of his talent to ask the right question after any presentation, sometimes actually making clear both the topic and the main argument of somewhat obscure papers by asking that question.

Finally, I would like to thank all those who made this volume possible: I am deeply grateful to the contributors, who were all very cooperative, and to M. Lehner at Lang for her swift and thorough work. I would also like to thank B. Engler and P. ten Hacken for their help and encouragement. The printing of this book has been made possible thanks to the financial contribution by the James Fenimore Cooper Fund.

Cornelia Tschichold
April 2003

Richard J. Watts

Was the Great Vowel Shift really 'great'? A reappraisal of research work on an elusive linguistic phenomenon

The title of my contribution to the present volume is intended to sound provocative, although readers should not imagine that I consider the Great Vowel Shift (GVS) to be unimportant in explaining the historical development of the present-day phonological structure(s) of English (or should I perhaps say 'Englishes'?). I have not previously entered the lists to joust on the subject of the GVS, and my argument in this contribution might thus appear somewhat heretical to seasoned jousters like Roger Lass and the formidable team of Bob Stockwell and Donka Minkova. I shall nevertheless conclude the argument with the thought that, if we conceptualise the GVS as a unitary phenomenon and restrict ourselves to purely phonetic/phonological aspects of the vowel shift, it might indeed turn out to be a historical red herring, as Stockwell and Minkova have claimed.

Let's start off by considering a few other 'greats' in order to get a feeling for the awe felt by scholars in the presence of the GVS, a feeling that emerges through reading the literature from Ellis onwards, but particularly in Jespersen and Wyld's work. We could start off with old chestnuts like 'Great Britain', the 'Great Western Railway', etc. and go as far as the 'Great Train Robbery' or even the 'Great Eskimo Vocabulary Hoax', coined by linguist Geoffrey Pullum as the title of a collection of brilliant satirical squibs written by him for the journal *Natural Language and Linguistics*. Greatness in each case extends further than simply denoting large size, although that denotation is still present. There is a sense of uniqueness, unitariness, of grandiose proportions and perhaps even of historical significance in the term 'great'.

This, of course, contributes towards the note of irony in the Great Train Robbery and the Great Eskimo Vocabulary Hoax, although I hesitate to attribute irony to the term the 'Great Vowel Shift'.

The vigorous debate between Stockwell and Minkova and their jousting opponent Roger Lass over the past 15 years has engendered a more cautious approach to the phonological/ phonetic phenomena encompassed by the term 'Great Vowel Shift' than was the case as late as the early 1980s. Most serious researchers in English historical linguistics since the beginning of the 90s have become very sceptical about most of the arguments put foward to explain those phenomena, and they doubt the 'greatness' of the GVS. Stockwell and Minkova themselves tend to stop short of explaining why any vowel shift in the varieties of native-speaker English across the world would fail to merit the ascription of greatness, and it is precisely the point at which they stop which needs to be transcended if we want to achieve a more realistic account of vowel shifts in English.

This has in part already been attempted by meticulous researchers like Paul Johnston (1992) with the overall result that the GVS does indeed appear to disintegrate into a number of smaller shifts whose importance is not thereby weakened, but certainly more realistically contextualised. I shall argue here that we need to enter the world of sociolinguistics and discourse analysis, in addition to researching into the phonetic conditions that trigger off the phenomenon of vowel shifting, to give this research a more solid explanatory foundation.

What was the GVS and how has it been presented?

The GVS is a term used to refer to a series of phonological changes affecting the long vowel system of Middle English stretching from around the middle of the 14th century to the beginning of the 18th. The term itself is usually attributed to Otto

Jespersen, who gave Chapter VIII in the first volume of his monumental *A Modern English Grammar on Historical Principles* (1909-1949) the title 'The Great Vowel-shift', but Karl Luick in his *Historische Grammatik der englischen Sprache* (1914-21) also mentions 'die grosse Lautverschiebung', possibly having borrowed the term from Jespersen. In his earlier work on English phonetics, however, it is clear that Luick was aware of the details of the vowel shift, since these had already been amply documented by both Alexander Ellis (1869) and Henry Sweet (1874).

The period during which the GVS is assumed to have taken place thus covers almost 400 years, so it is hardly surprising to find researchers who, following Jespersen and Luick, have attempted to restrict it to the period from the end of the 15th to the 17th centuries. Johnston's research, however, places some of the first shifts back into the 13th century, thus lengthening the period of the GVS to around 500 years.

If we ask why the attempt has been made to restrict the GVS to a period of just 200 years, a number of significant answers present themselves, all of which are interlinked. As Giancarlo (2001) points out, it creates a convenient borderline between the outgoing Middle Ages in the literary shape of Chaucer and the period of early 'modernism' in the shape of Shakespeare. It allows us to claim Shakespeare as 'one of us' and, while not disclaiming his greatness, to place Chaucer into the camp of those who did not speak 'English' as we do. It allows us to define the language of Shakespeare as 'modern English', even if it is 'early modern English', and to locate the 'beginning' of standard English in the 16th century. This, of course, leads to a funnel view of the history of the language in which, from the 16th century on, standard English becomes the narrow focus of attention to the detriment of the dialects and of other related Germanic languages (Milroy 2002). It allows the researcher to present the GVS as a uniform linguistic phenomenon crucially affecting the structure of the modern English phonological system. In the standard view of the GVS, it is presented as a systematically near-perfect construct. This lends support to what Milroy & Milroy (1985) call the 'ideology of the standard', but it assumes an absurd teleology, in which speakers within those 200 years were striving to bring about the creation of standard English. After all, 200 years represent roughly ten generations of speakers! The counter question might very well be: "Once the GVS was completed, why did they stop? Because they 'knew' that standard English had been achieved, or because the GVS had exhausted itself?"

It would be relatively easy to show how all these points are interlinked and how this tendency in what we can only call the 'conventional' way of teaching the history of English leads to the fiction of *an* English language to the complete disregard of other varieties of English. Indeed, the collection of contributions in Watts & Trudgill (2002) is aimed at counteracting precisely this tendency. The 'conventional' way of presenting *the* history of English is clearly revealed at other places in Jespersen's work, e.g. in the following quotation from *Essentials of English Grammar* (1933: 16):

> In old (sic!) times, when communication between various parts of the country was not easy and when the population was, on the whole, very stationary, a great many local *dialects* arose which differed very considerably from one another; the divergencies naturally (sic!) became greater among the uneducated than among the educated and richer classes, as the latter moved more about and had more intercourse with people from other parts of the country. In recent times the enormously increased facilities of communication have to a great extent counteracted the tendency towards the splitting up of the language into dialects – class dialects and local dialects. [...] Our chief concern will be with the normal (sic!) speech of the educated class, what may be called Standard English [...]

The message comes through clearly enough, even though it is a rather contradictory message when one considers Jespersen's earlier interest in dialects. Dialects are out-of-date (a thing of 'old times'); they are spoken by the 'uneducated'; they 'split up' and hence endanger the unity of *the* language; and they are not 'normal' speech, which in any case is only attributed to the 'educated class'.

Conceptualising the GVS as 'great', as a unifying movement, as the impulse towards the inevitable development of standard

English, and as a way of somehow 'overcoming' the disruptive effect of dialects on efficient communication lent philological and, later, linguistic support to the ideology of the standard, which, if we look at matters from a Bourdieuan perspective, is none other than the exercise of symbolic power to legitimise the standard language. What, after all, could be better than finding as 'pure' a justification of standard speech as the coherent, unitary system of phonological changes represented by the GVS?

But what exactly did the GVS consist of? Conventional wisdom maintains that it was series of phonological changes affecting the long vowel system of Middle English, in which the high front vowel [iː] was shifted (eventually, of course) to the modern diphthong [aɪ] and the high back vowel [uː] was shifted to the modern diphthong [aʊ]. The mid-high long vowels [eː] and [oː] were shifted to [iː] and [uː], and the mid-low long vowels [ɛː] and [ɔː] were shifted firstly to [eː] and [oː] were then diphthongised to [eɪ] and [oʊ]. The low long vowel [aː] was shifted to [ɛː] and then moved along with [ɛː] to [eː] and then to [eɪ]. There are of course several irregularities that can be observed even in standard British English, and the stages that these shifts went through before they reached their modern positions in the vowel trapezoid are a matter of continual dispute. Disregarding those irregularities and disputes, however, the GVS, when seen in this light, does indeed give all the appearances of being a unified phonetic movement taking us from late Middle English to modern standard English and, as a heuristic principle, serves its purpose in teaching 'the history of English'.

But suppose we were to challenge the argument that there *is* such a thing as the English language? After all, as a pluricentric language (Clyne 1992), there are by now a number of different 'standard Englishes' (standard British English, the existence of which Trudgill (1999) disputes, standard American English, possibly also standard Australian English), and there are plenty of candidates waiting in the wings to receive the accolade of 'standardness' (e.g. standard Scottish English, which is not the same thing as Scots, standard Irish English, and even standard Indian English). And suppose the very unifying factor that has, along with other powerful arguments, allowed this particular kind of symbolic power to be constructed, can be shown to be, if not a chimera, then at the very least a much more complicated set of vowel shifts that is always potentially part and parcel of varieties of English and is as active today as it always has been? Would we then not lose the beauty, the simplicity of that heuristic principle? Would we not lose the ability to present the history of English as a series of coherent developmental steps? This, in fact, is precisely what it does imply.

GVS disputes

Giancarlo (2001) shows how the GVS has been represented in diagrammatic and tabular form as a way of simplifying, visualising and generally making palatable to the uninitiated student the phonetic complexities of the shifts that it covers. His overall point is that it is a way of telling 'the story'. However, he admits that it is the story of the development of standard English that is ultimately at stake rather than the story of the GVS itself. The dispute that the diagrams have generated – possibly precisely *because* they have been represented as diagrams – is whether we have a chain reaction in the whole of the vowel system and whether the set of movements was sparked off by the shift of the long high vowels [iː] and [uː], i.e. whether this movement 'dragged' or 'pulled' the mid-high vowels [eː] and [oː] into the places vacated in the vowel trapezoid by the diphthongisation of the long high vowels, or whether the initial movement was the raising of the mid-high vowels [eː] and [oː] and/or the mid-low vowels [ɛː] and [ɔː] into the upper slots, 'pushing' the occupants of those slots out. This dispute can still be found in literature on the GVS today.

The other major issue concerns the process of diphthongisation of the high vowels. Did [iː] move to a more central position, say, something like [ɨ] and thence to [əɪ], or did it move to [eɪ] first? Did [uː] move to something like [ʉʊ] and thence to [əʊ], or did it move to [oʊ] first? In addition, there are varieties of English within Northern England and Scotland in which certain parts of the 'chain' shifts did not occur, a point, which is not lost either on Stockwell and Minkova or on Lass. The classic example is the failure of [uː] to shift to [aʊ] in Lowland Scottish English and Northumberland.

The explanation for this failure neatly exemplifies the kind of arguments that are used to bolster the 'drag-chain' or 'push-chain' theories. 'Push-chainers' like Lass maintain that because [oː] was fronted to [øː] in these Northern dialects, it did not come under pressure to diphthongise. But it's easy to imagine a 'drag-chainer' claiming that, if a dialect could be found in which [oː] was fronted and [uː] nevertheless diphthongised, the push-chainer's argument disintegrates.

Further dispute revolves around the nature of the evidence used to support different interpretations of what, how and when the shifts in the GVS took place. Wolfe (1972) and Lass (1989) both rely on the real-time evidence of orthoëpists like Hart, Gil, and Bullokar in the 16th century and Cooper, Daines and Wallis in the 17th, whereas Stockwell and Minkova challenge the phonetic accuracy of the orthoëpists' observations and instead rely on spellings and rhymes. This leads them to posit much earlier datings of the first shifts in the GVS, and it also leads them to challenge the push-chain theory. In order to find orthographic evidence of this kind, Stockwell and Minkova need to examine texts that are written in localised varieties of English. But even Lass's argument on the partial failure of [uː] to shift forces him to consider Northern varieties of English. Several varieties of English, both within Great Britain and in the wider English-speaking world, also show different end-points in the diphthongisation process, [əɪ], [ɑɪ] or [ɔɪ] for [aɪ] and [əʊ] and [ɑʊ] for [aʊ]. If we add to this the fact that since the GVS a number of shortening and lengthening processes have taken place together with the fact that certain dialects in the USA and in New Zealand are currently undergoing shifts in the short back and front vowels, then it is time to start reconsidering the significance of the GVS and to give up the simple teaching heuristic as a simplistic justification of the development of the standard.

In the following section I shall indicate how conventional representations of the GVS have been challenged and how this leads to the need for much more careful analysis of the phonetic processes involved in vowel shifting in general. The final link in my argumentative chain concerns the producers of the vowels themselves. After all, even if we believe with Weinreich, Labov & Herzog (1968) that languages do not change, but people change languages, we still need to fix the dialectological and phonetic evidence to a theory of how interactants perceive innovations, of how they adopt them and of how those newly adopted innovations are diffused through space and time. This problem will be tackled in the final section.

Challenging the GVS

The work of dismantling the traditional conceptualisation was begun by Stockwell and Minkova and during the 1980s it has been continued in a number of significant articles, e.g. Johnston (1992), Smith (1993), Guzman (1994). Since Johnston's argument is the most detailed and also the most plausible, I shall focus on it almost uniquely in this section.

Before we examine Johnston's argument, however, we need to consider a few hard facts about standard languages. In effect, standard languages are nothing more or less than 'synecdochic dialects' (Joseph 1987), i.e. they are dialects which are 'chosen' – generally, but not always, by chance – to 'represent' all the others in the construction of the 'language' itself. During the process of standardisation a synecdochic dialect is also prey to the introduction into its lexical, grammatical and phonological system of elements from other dialects and other 'languages'. In this sense a standard language (or, as I would prefer to say, dialect) is never free from innovations introduced either naturally or by force of codification processes that are often controlled institutionally by language academies.

In addition, standard dialects begin life as written variants representing synecdochically the dialect varieties, both social and geographical, which exist within the territory in which they are destined to become a socio-political 'standard'. The final stage in the standardisation process is often, but not always, the construction of an oral standard, and this final stage can lead to divisive dispute over what is or is not part of that oral standard. This has been the case within the last thirty years in Britain, and it is a dispute that has by no means reached a settlement (Bex & Watts 1999). In the case of English, the beginnings of a concern with the oral standard can be traced back to the second half of the 18th century (Sheridan 1762, Walker 1791), although much of the groundwork had already been laid by the orthoëpists in the late 16th and 17th centuries.

If we accept this brief sketch of the standardisation of English, it follows that, even if we were to restrict the GVS to the 16th and 17th centuries, we would need to look closely at the dialects to find evidence of vowel shifts, since there was no standard *oral* English at all till, at the very earliest, the latter half of the 18th century. We also find evidence in the present-day dialects that vowel shifts are still continuing, and if we consider some of the currently more prestigious varieties of English in the UK (the 'infamous' Estuary English) and the USA (parts of the Midwest), it is noticeable that they are exerting a significant influence on the shifting of vowels in oral standard English English (to use Trudgill's term) and oral standard American English. If we carry this argument back into the past beyond the 16th century, which is what we need to do to identify the beginnings of the GVS, the only place in which we will ever be able to locate those vowel changes will be in localised forms of writing, i.e. in the dialects. This, in turn, means accepting the validity of occasional spellings as evidence for vowel shifting, which is what Wolfe (1972: Chapter 4) rejects in favour of a close study of the orthoëpists. Johnston (1992), on the other hand, argues that, if we seriously intend to look for the beginnings of the GVS, "orthoëpic evidence is, in fact, too late" (1992: 205). He supports his argument by locating the likely areas of vowel shifting in the dialects through a close study of important sources of evidence such as the *Survey of English Dialects*, Anderson's *A Structural Atlas of the English Dialects* (1987), Kristensson's *Survey of Middle English Dialects* (1967, 1988) and McIntosh, Samuels and Benskin's *A Linguistic Atlas of Late Mediaeval English* (1986).

Johnston is well aware of the vagaries of relying on occasional spellings. The first difficulty in interpreting possible phonological realisations from graphological evidence is the limited representational power of the Roman alphabet, complicated after the Conquest by the adoption of Norman-based spelling conventions. Middle English length interchange processes followed by short vowel raisings make it almost impossible to differentiate between long vowels that have gone through this process and those that may have been raised without shortening during the GVS. If we add to these difficulties in using occasional spellings the simple fact that what we are looking for is spellings that are "necessarily 'occasional' and sporadic" (Johnston 1992: 206), it is not difficult to appreciate the unwillingness of researchers like Wolfe (1972) to consider this sort of evidence.

Indeed, even Johnston suggests that occasional spellings are hard to distinguish from 'simple errors'. But this is a distinctly odd comment to make. Surely an 'error' in spelling presupposes a well established set of conventions for spelling. Even Wolfe's refusal to take spellings into account on the grounds that "anyone who has corrected many high school essays will be reluctant to ascribe much [...] phonetic accuracy to occasional spellings" (1972: 115) becomes vacuous if we consider that most of those 'incorrect' spellings are an attempt to represent graphologically the way the speller pronounces the word. I would argue that precisely because they are 'errors' – a point which in any case has little substance in the absence of a generally accepted set of spelling conventions – they are the kind of evidence we should be looking for. Attempts by local scribes to find a way of representing graphologically what they say provide invaluable insights into the earlier phonological structure of the dialects.

Johnston's careful analysis of occasional spellings from all parts of the country (see his Table 2) reveals the need to reinterpret the GVS as two (possibly more) smaller chain shifts that must have taken place in different parts of the country at different periods of time. In general, he is able to differentiate a shift in the high front and back vowels in two areas that would hardly warrant the assumption of frequent sociolinguistic contact among their speakers, the Midlands and/or East Anglia and the Southwest. For these areas the focus of attention in terms of trade, migration, prestige, etc. must have been, primarily, local centres such as Norwich, Exeter, Chester, Stafford, etc. and, secondarily, London. The second chain shift affects the bottom half of the vowel trapezoid and overlaps the shift in the high vowels in the area of the North Midlands. The focus of attention here becomes Yorkshire and in particular the Plain of York, which lay outside the area of overlap. Evidence from occasional spellings from this area allow Johnston to surmise that "at least on the Plain of York, low-vowel raising occurred so early that it not only precedes the high-vowel raising chain but also Open Syllable Lenthening" (1992: 214), i.e. the shifting can be located temporally in at least the early 13th century, possibly even earlier.

This is strong evidence to support Stockwell and Minkova's rejection of the GVS as a coherent, unitary phenomenon. It is also strong evidence on which to base a rejection of interpretations of the GVS that effectively see it as an element in the process of the standardisation of English, even if, as in the case of Jespersen, Wolfe and also Chomsky and Halle in *The Sound Pattern of English* (1968), this is not their explicit averred purpose. Johnston, however, goes further than this. In support of the following statement:

> Vowel shifting, then, can be described as a continuous process rather than as something unique to a specific, long-past period, and the consequent reduction in the number of explanations needed to account for all the data is a gain in simplicity rather than a loss. (1992: 219)

he suggests that studying the phonetic processes involved in any vowel-shifting in the present can help us to gain a fuller picture of vowel-shifting in the past. Some of this work has already been done by Labov, Yeager & Steiner (1972) in their discussion of the connections between peripherality (or tensing) of vowels and raising, on the one hand, and deperipheralisation (laxing) of long vowels resulting in double-mora nuclei and consequent diphthongisation, on the other. Johnston suggests that more attention should be paid to phonetic environments such as final or prepausal position, added stress (often for emphasis) and slower speech rate, all of which tend to produce an increase in vowel length rather than peripherality. Lengthening 'pure' vowels is likely to produce an increase in sonority. In the case of the high vowels this opens up one mora of the vowel to produce nuclei such as [ɪi] and [ɷu].

All of these processes are involved in the apparent, and in all likelihood necessary, instability of vowel systems. They might induce us to suggest that, no matter how we try to explain the GVS, we are ultimately forced to admit that it really was not quite as 'great' has been assumed in the traditional literature on the history of the language. Johnston's work provides strong evidence of at least two partially independent, but at some stage interlocking small vowel shifts, and it is quite possible that further research of this kind will necessitate the introduction of more small vowel shifts. At this point, however, the option that this leaves us of denying that the GVS ever took place at all makes me a little uneasy, and this will be the final step in my argument.

Sociolinguistic aspects of the GVS

Denying that the GVS ever took place is a dangerous step to take if it involves denying that there was ever an ideology of the GVS that formed part of Milroy and Milroy's ideology of the standardisation of English. It is important to recognise the existence of certain powerful discourses and to investigate how they could have come into existence. If we carry out such an investigation, we are automatically involved in prising open the historicity of those discourses, and, in the case of the GVS discourse, this ultimately takes us into the realm of historical sociolinguistics.

The major aspect of the GVS that is consistently ignored, although often mentioned briefly by researchers as a desideratum, is the question of the actuation of the changes that took place in the vowel systems of the varieties of English from around the 13th century (if Johnston's analysis is sound) to the end of the 18th century. This is not to say, of course, that vowel shifts were not occurring prior to the 13th century or that they have not occurred since the end of the 18th and are still in progress today. Weinreich, Labov & Herzog's (1968) actuation problem concerns the mechanisms involved in the introduction into a language variety of an innovative structure, its adoption by members of the speech community and its diffusion to other communities, and although we know that it is almost impossible to observe these processes historically, we do know enough about what happens in present-day speech communities to be sure that they are always active (Milroy 1992). From sociolinguistic work, we also know that the slenderest of differences in the quality of a vowel can operate as a salient marker of social and geographical differentiation between speakers.

Let us now apply these insights to a possible scenario of text types and everyday communicative situations on the Plain of York in the 13th century, on the well-founded assumption that Johnston's occasional spellings are indeed signs of a shift in the low vowels that had already taken place before Open Syllable Lengthening. We obviously need to know more about the kind of texts that would have been produced locally in English in that area and for what purpose. But even without access to Johnston's sources, we can be reasonably certain that 'official' texts would have been produced in Anglo-Norman French and possibly Latin. Writing a text in English would thus have been aimed primarily at an English-speaking audience. Literacy in the 13th century is not likely to have been common in the English-speaking community, so those texts would have been produced for oral performance of some kind. It is therefore highly likely that a scribe would introduce spellings that reflected the phonological structures of the language in his local area. But that scribe will have been privileged enough to be one of the few who were literate. If the texts were largely for oral communciation, why were there not more spellings that reflected the vowel shifts? It is here that we begin to see the tensions between oral communication and communication through writing. The scribe must have been writing within the framework of orthographic conventions regulating the ways in which English was to be represented in written form and at the same time within the framework of patterns of oral communication within the English-speaking community. Producing the 'mis-spelling' of a word by reflecting the oral quality of the vowel may thus be interpreted as a way of – unconsciously – documenting membership in the speech community at the same time as documenting membership in the community of 'writers in English'.

Tensions such as these become more obvious, the more closely the texts approach oral communication, e.g. in the case of personal letters. This is well documented in the Paston letters, the problem here being that they date from the 15th century. If the beginnings of one of the shift chains of the GVS are locatable in the 13th century, then evidence of the social tensions between a writer and her/his reading public in terms of whether or not s/he documents identity in a speech community through written texts becomes even harder to find. On the assumption that the salience of vowel shifts may mark social distinctions of various kinds and that these distinctions frequently lead to accommodation to the language of socially more prestigious speakers (Smith 1993), the area in which the two shifts overlapped, the Northeast Midland area, suddenly becomes crucial in investigating the geographical diffusion of the shifts, particularly in the direction of East Anglia and London.

The major problem in dealing with written texts from the 15th century on is that the orthographic conventions, haphazard as they often are, generally reflect the language of areas prior to the vowel shifts that go under the nomenclature of the GVS, which Chomsky & Halle (1968) make abundantly clear. There are two points that we can derive from this fact. Firstly, we desperately need to access texts prior to the 15th century that were written in those areas in which we know the shifts associated with the GVS were either already completed or were well underway. The introduction of the printing press in the last few decades of the 15th century focused the orthographic conventions of printing on the phonologically more conservative varieties of London and the Southeast. Secondly, precisely because of this intensified focus on the language of the capital, the work of the orthoëpists takes on a radically new significance. Orthoëpists like Hart, Gil, Cooper, Daines, Wallis, etc., however good or deficient they were as phoneticians, were primarily concerned with standardising the orthographic conventions of written English. Their comments on how various vowels were pronounced were prompted by an acute awareness of the discrepancy between phonological structures and the graphology with which they were represented, not by a desire to standardise pronunciation. In striving to promote a standardised orthography, they were simultaneously promoting the language variety of London and the area around London as their model and thereby taking the first steps towards making that variety the synecdochic dialect that ultimately became 'standard English English'. Unwittingly, therefore, they began the funnel vision of equating the history of English with the history of the standard variety.

Let us now turn the wheel full circle. In the first section I suggested that the adjective 'great' with reference to the vowel shifts that are generally subsumed under the GVS refer to the assumed grandiose proportions, the uniqueness, the coherence and the historical significance of those shifts. Stockwell & Minkova, Giancarlo, Johnston and others would probably not want to admit the term 'great' to the vowel shift for the simple reason that it was not one vowel shift and that vowels, in any case, are always shifting. If we are interested in researching into how the traditional discourse of the history of English has been constructed, however, the GVS loses none of its compulsive power. It certainly does become something of a chimera, but one that we reject at our peril if we are at all interested in putting a number of records straight in the history – and here I would in fact prefer to say 'histories' – of English. One thing is certain in my mind: we need to shift to an examination of the GVS from two other perspectives than the purely linguistic. We need to look more closely at the discursive construction of the GVS and link it to the discursive construction of the standard, and we need to consider speakers of the many varieties of English within England and Scotland in the period from the 13th to the 18th centuries and what they were actually doing with language, i.e. we need to look at vowel shifts from a more sociolinguistic perspective.

One final point is worth making here. Our colleague David Allerton, in whose honour this volume has been prepared, has worked, as I have, for much of his professional life in Switzerland. I am sure that he will agree with me that despite the fact that Switzerland is a small country, that its public transportation system is one of the best, if not the best, in Europe, and that social contact at all social levels and in all walks of life is brisk and relatively harmonious, it harbours in its German-speaking majority of roughly 64% of the overall population the perfect rejoinder to Otto Jerspersen's all too hasty rejection of dialects. We live and work in a speech community in which dialects are more prestigious than the standard, in which dialect differences do not present serious problems in communication, in which accommodation among speakers is the rule rather than the exception, and in which vowels are still merrily being shifted.

References

Anderson, P. M. (1987). *A Structural Atlas of the English Dialects*. London: Croom Helm.

Bex, T. & R. J. Watts (1999). *Standard English: The widening debate*. London: Routledge.

Chomsky, N. & M. Halle (1968). *The Sound Pattern of English*. New York; Harper and Row.

Clyne, M. (ed.) (1992). *Pluricentric Languages*. Berlin: Mouton de Gruyter.

Ellis, A. J. (1969 [1869-89]). *Early English Pronunciation*. New York: Maskell House.

Giancarlo, M. (2001). 'The rise and fall of the Great Vowel Shift? The changing ideological intersections of philology, historical linguistics, and literary history', *Representations* 76, 27-60.

Guzman, T. (1994). 'The Great Vowel Shift revisited', in Fernández, Francisco, Fuster, Miguel and Calvo, Juan José (eds.), *English Historical Linguistics 1992: Papers from the 7th International Conference on English Historical Linguistics*. Amsterdam: Benjamins, 81-89.

Jespersen, O. (1922). *A Modern English Grammar on Historical Principles*, Vol. I: Sounds and Spellings. Heidelberg: Carl Winter.

Jespersen, O. (1933). *Essentials of English Grammar*. London: George Allen and Unwin.

Johnston, P. A., Jr. (1992). 'English vowel shifting: One Great Vowel Shift or two small vowel shifts?', *Diachronica* IX, 189-226.

Joseph, J. E. (1987). *Eloquence and Power: The Rise of Language Standards and Standard Languages*. London: Pinter.

Kristensson, G. (1967). *A Survey of Middle English Dialects, 1290-1350: The Six Northern Counties and Lincolnshire*. Lund: Gleerup.

Labov, W., M. Yeager, & R. Steiner (1972). *A Quantitative Study of Sound Change in Progess*. Philadelphia: U.S. Regional Survey.

Lass, R. (1988) 'Vowel shifts, great and otherwise; remarks on Stockwell and Minkova', in Kastovsky & Bauer (eds.), *Luick Revisited: Papers read at the Luick-Symposium at Schloss Liechtenstein*, 15-18.9.85. Tübingen: Gunter Narr, 395-410.

Lass, R. (1989) 'How early does English get modern? Or, what happens if you listen to orthoëpists and not to historians', in *Diachronica* 6, 75-110.

Lass, R. (1992). 'What, if anything, was the Great Vowel Shift?', in Rissanen, Ihalainen, Nevalainen & Taavitsainen (eds.). *History of Englishes: New Methods and Interpretations in Historical Linguistics*. Berlin: Mouton de Gruyter, 144-155.

Luick, K. W. (1964 [1898]). *Studien zur englischen Lautgeschichte*, 2 vols. Oxford, Blackwell; New York: Johnson.

Luick, K. W. (1914-1921). *Historische Grammatik der englischen Sprache*.

McIntosh, A., M.L. Samuels & M. Benskin (1986-7). *The Linguistic Atlas of Late Middle English*, with the assistance of M. Laing and K. Williamson, Aberdeen: Aberdeen University Press.

Milroy, J. (2000). 'Historical description and the ideology of the standard language', in Wright, L. (ed.), *The Development of Standard English, 1300-*

1800: Theories, Decsriptions, Conflicts. Cambridge: Cambridge University Press, 11-28.

Milroy, J. (2002). 'The legitimate language: Giving a history to English', in Watts and Trudgill (eds.), 7-28.

Milroy, J. & L. Milroy (1985). *Authority in Language*. London: Routledge.

Orton, H. et al. (1933-1966). *The Survey of English Dialects*. Leeds: Arnold.

Sheridan, T. (1762). *A Course of Lectures on Elocution: Together with Two Dissertations on Language; and Some Tracts Relative to those Subjects*. London.

Smith, J. (1993). 'Dialectal variation and the actuation of the Great Vowel Shift', in *Neuphilologische Mitteilungen* 94, 259-77.

Stockwell, R. & D. Minkova (1988). 'The English Vowel Shift: Problems of coherence and explanation', in Kastovsky & Bauer (eds.), *Luick Revisited: Papers read at the Luick-Symposium at Schloss Liechtenstein, 15-18.9.85*. Tübingen: Gunter Narr, 355-393.

Stockwell, R. & D. Minkova (1990). 'The Early English modern vowels: More o' Lass', in *Diachronica* 7, 199-214.

Stockwell, R. & D. Minkova (1999). 'Explanations of sound change: Contradictions between dialect data and theories of chain shifting', in *Leeds Studies in English* 30, 83-111.

Sweet, H. (1874). *A History of English Sounds*. London:

Trudgill, P. (1999). 'Standard English: What it isn't', in Bex and Watts (eds.), *Standard English: The Widening Debate*. London: Routledge, 117-128.

Walker, J. (1791). *A Critical Pronouncing Dictionary*. Reprinted Menston: Scolar Press.

Watts, R. J. & Trudgill, P. (eds.) (2002). *Alternative Histories of English*. London: Routledge.

Weinreich, U., W. Labov & M. Herzog (1968). 'Empirical foundations for a theory of language change', in Lehmann & Malkiel (eds.). *Directions for Historical Linguistics*. Austin, TX: University of Texas Press, 97-195.

Wolfe, P. (1972). *Linguistic Change and the Great Vowel Shift in English*. Berkeley: University of California Press.

Wolfram, W. (1991). *Dialects and American English*. Englewood Cliffs, N.J.: Prentice-Hall.

Wyld, H. C. (1953). *A History of Modern Colloquial English*. 3rd edition. Oxford: Blackwell.

Martina Häcker

From linking [h] to glottal stop: changes in the phonotactic system of 20th-century Cockney[1]

The phenomenon referred to as [h]-dropping is perhaps the most widespread and certainly one of the most stigmatised features of British English regional accents. The term is used for the omission for word-initial [h] in stressed syllables of lexical words. This habit was first criticised by Sheridan in 1762, but appears to have been resistent to the efforts of those who tried to oust it. Wells (1982: 254) reports a London school teacher as saying that he had "only to look sternly at any child who drops an /h/, and that child will say the word again, this time correctly." Despite the fact that it is such a well-known phenomenon, we know comparatively little about the history of [h]-dropping. Traditional descriptions of the history of English pronunciation generally agree that [h]-dropping was not widespread before the eighteenth century.[2] Earlier omissions of an etymological <h> are usually blamed on scribal errors, to which Anglo-Norman scribes were said to be particularly prone. This view was first expressed by Skeat (1897: 415), and seems to have become the default explanation, as it is repeated by Brunner (1963: 5), Luick (1964: 871) and Wyld (1920: 295). The Anglo-Norman scribe has, how-

---

[1] I am grateful to Professor Elizabeth Couper-Kuhlen (University of Konstanz) for helpful comments on an earlier version of the manuscript. Any remaining errors are, of course, mine.

[2] An exception is the first editor of the OED, James A. Murray (1901), who states in his entry on the letter *h*: 'During the Middle-English period, and down to the 17th c., we find numerous instances of the non-etymological absence or (more often) presence of initial *h* in native words.'

ever, since been shown to be one of the great myths of English philology (Clarke 1992).

In contrast to earlier scholarship, Lass (1987: 96) argues that the beginning of the process of [h]-loss goes back to the eleventh century, while Milroy (1983) claims that a large part of Eastern England was /h/-less in the Middle English period and that the /h/-less variety may well have enjoyed high prestige. The date of first mention in orthoepic literature would, according to Milroy, not indicate that the phenomenon was new, but that attitudes towards it had shifted and that it had begun to be stigmatised.

Unlike <h>-omission, the addition of unetymological <h> has received comparatively little attention. It is typically mentioned in passing and referred to as hypercorrection, the assumption being that *h*-insertion in medieval texts is a reflection of /h/-loss in the scribe's speech. Here Milroy is in full agreement with earlier scholarship. He even takes Wyld to task for treating /h/-loss and /h/-omission separately:

> Wyld's lists for omission of *h* and addition of *h* are kept entirely separate, and his negative conclusions on /h/-loss are based entirely on loss of *h* in spelling with no account being taken of hypercorrect insertion of *h*. (1983: 42)

What are the implications if the insertion of <h> in medieval texts is interpreted as a reflection of /h/-loss? It is assumed that (a) /h/-loss is generally accompanied by unetymological insertions of [h], and that (b) the grapheme <h> corresponds to the phone [h] in speech. This may, but need not be the case. Two other functions have been suggested for the grapheme <h> in the literature: (a) that it may be used as a diacritic marking a hiatus, probably realised as a glottal stop (Scragg 1970), and (b) that it corresponds to the "devocalised version of any segment with which it is contiguous" (Jones 1989: 270). The latter description is given for insertions of <h> between a verb stem ending in a vowel and *-ing*, i.e. word-internal <h>-insertion, in the mid-sixteenth-century diary of Henry Machyn (Nichols 1847),[3] while the analysis as a diacritic representing a glottal stop was advanced by Scragg (1970) in his study of initial <h> in Old English texts.

In addition, we need to consider that the phone [h] may not be added by mistake in an attempt to avoid [h]-dropping, as the term 'hypercorrection' suggests, but may be utilised deliberately. Such a view is tentatively expressed for present-day English varieties by Wells (1982: 253), who states that the sound change leading to the deletion of /h/ may have led to an additional rule "which variably adds [h] before initial vowel as a mark of emphasis." Besides the functionless interpretation of [h]-insertion as hypercorrection, any research on the history of [h]-dropping will therefore need to consider at least three possible functions for unetymological <h>: (a) that of a hiatus filler in form of a glottal stop, (b) that of a transitional sound in form of a devocalised vowel, and (c) that of a marker of emphasis.

It is the purpose of the present paper to contribute to the research into [h]-dropping by looking at its more accessible recent history and to take a fresh look at the underresearched area of [h]-insertion. The paper investigates whether any systematic relationship between [h]-dropping and [h]-insertion can be established and to what extent changes in the use of [h] can be related to other phonological changes.

The scope of the present paper is largely restricted to one accent, with only a few glimpses at others. The variety chosen for analysis is Cockney. Both [h]-dropping and [h]-insertion are well-

---

[3] The geographical origin of Henry Machyn has been the subject of considerable scholarly debate. The editor of the text, Nichols, believed him to be of London origin, possibly because London was where Machyn lived and worked as a tailor, as is evident from the diary. This was the accepted view until Wijk (1937) argued for a South-Eastern Yorkshire origin on the basis of Machyn's spelling. Britton (2000), using the fitting technique, places Machyn in South-West Yorkshire. The fact that the Cockney origin of Machyn was a rather persistent myth may well reflect the extent to which [h]-dropping and [h]-insertion were associated with that variety.

known features of modern Cockney. The earliest issues of *Punch*, dating from the middle of the nineteenth century, and Shaw, whose plays were written half a century later, both present Cockneys as using inverse pronunciations (Saxe 1936: 10-14; 47-48). This presentation may not correspond to reality, as caricatures tend to exaggerate, but it suggests that [h]-insertion was as noticeable to contemporaries as was [h]-dropping.

A further reason for choosing Cockney for this investigation is the fact that [h]-dropping in Cockney is a comparatively recent phenomenon. Despite the fact that [h]-dropping is frequently assumed to have spread from Cockney to other accents, there is evidence to the contrary. The Cockney pronunciations that Sheridan castigates in 1762 (1970: 33-34) are [w] for [v] and the pronunciation of words ending in -*ow* as

> er – as feller for fellow – beller, holler, foller, winder, – for bellow, hollow, follow, window. As also adding the letter r to all proper names ending in *a* unaccented, as Belindar, Dorindar, for Belinda, Dorinda.

Sheridan does not indicate <h>-omission in *hollow*, which he certainly would have done if an [h]-less pronunciation had been common among Cockneys in his days. When he criticises [h]-dropping he does not refer to Cockneys:

> With respect to the rustic pronunciation, prevailing in the several counties, I mean amongst the gentry, and such as have a liberal education, there does not seem to be any general errour of this sort [the two Cockney pronunciations just mentioned]; [...] But there is one defect which more generally prevails in the counties than any other, and indeed is daily gaining ground amongst the politer part of the world, I mean the omission of the aspirate in many words by some, and in most by others. [...] But let no one imagine, that because he would not pronounce many successive words, or a whole sentence in this manner, he is therefore entirely free from defect in this point; for I have met with but few instances in the course of my experience, and those only in the most correct speakers, of persons who have not been guilty of omitting the aspirate from some words, or giving it too faintly to others.

This clearly suggests that [h]-dropping must have spread into Cockney, unless it developed there independently, in the twenty years between the publication of Sheridan's *A course of lectures on elocution* in 1762 and Walker's (1781) *A rhetorical grammar*, who "censures [h]-loss as a 'vice' of the Cockneys" (Mugglestone 1995: 118).

A third reason for investigating [h]-omission and [h]-insertion in Cockney is the fact that phonetically transcribed data are available. The transcripts used for the present study are from Sivertsen's (1960) study of Cockney and from Leith's (1973) study[4] of North London speech. Sivertsen recorded predominantly female Cockneys in the years 1949 to 1956, while Leith recorded both male and female informants in 1972 from several North-London[5] boroughs. The informants of both studies were from the working class with little education (Sivertsen 1960: 3; Leith 1973: 5) and over fifty-five at the time of recording, with the exception of four members of a youth club recorded by Sivertsen. Leith (1973: 171) states that in his data women's vowels tended to be more fronted than men's and that women tended to substitute nonstandard consonant realisations less frequently than men, such as [ʔ] for [t], [f] for [θ], and [v] for [ð]. It is therefore unfortunate that Leith's transcripts contain no female speaker from the central areas of the inner East End (Bethnal Green, Poplar and Hackney), while Sivertsen's main speakers are female, which makes it difficult to decide whether differences result from gender differences or linguistic change. To allow a comparison between male and female speakers, two female speakers are included who are not from the East End, one from Canning Town and one from Victoria (borough of Westminster), the two districts closest to the East End for which transcripts of the speech of women are available in Leith (1973). Canning Town is one of the newer boroughs east of the Lea, while

---

4   Citations from the transcripts have been adapted to the current IPA system, and Leith's slashes have been replaced by vertical lines in order to use the same symbol for tone unit boundaries in both transcripts.
5   Notting Hill, Notting Dale, Victoria (in the borough of Westminster), Clerkenwell, Islington, Tottenham, Hackney, Bethnal Green, Poplar, Canning Town, Dagenham, and Deptford.

Victoria is an old working class area south of the Houses of Parliament, at the eastern edge of West London. An overview of the data selected for analysis is given in Table 1.

speaker	date of birth[6]	date of recording	gen-der	locality	source
EC	1874	1949-1956	f	Bethnal Green	Sivertsen
AP	1876	1949-1956	f	Bethnal Green	Sivertsen
EE	ca. 1890	1949-1956	f	Bethnal Green	Sivertsen
MM	1892	1949-1956	f	Bethnal Green	Sivertsen
A	1930-45	1949-1956	m	Bethnal Green	Sivertsen
B	1930-45	1949-1956	m	Bethnal Green	Sivertsen
C	1930-45	1949-1956	m	Bethnal Green	Sivertsen
D	1930-45	1949-1956	m	Bethnal Green	Sivertsen
Harry	1890-91	1972	m	Poplar	Leith
Earnie	1896-97	1972	m	Hackney	Leith
Jim	1901-02	1972	m	Bethnal Green	Leith
Lucy	1888-89	1972	f	Victoria	Leith
Kate	1896-97	1972	f	Canning Town	Leith

Table 1: Database of Cockney speakers

The transcripts were checked by the author of the present paper for [h]-omission and [h]-replacement, as well as for [h]-insertion. This yielded the following results: All speakers drop [h] in the

---

6   Sivertsen does not give any dates of birth for the members of the youth club. It is, however, clear from the context that they are teenagers at the time of recording, which puts their dates of birth between 1930 and 1945. Two possible years of birth are given for Leith's informants, as he gives the age of the respective speaker at the date of recording, but not his or her date of birth. The earlier year would be correct for speakers whose birthday is later in the year than the day and month of recording; for those whose birthdays were before the day and month of recording the later year would apply.

majority of cases, but [h] is retained in some cases and in a few instances added unetymologically. A comparison of the phonetic contexts shows that [h]-retention and [h]-insertion do not occur randomly, but are restricted to certain phonetic contexts. Neither [h]-retention nor [h]-insertion are, however, obligatory in these contexts. All instances of [h]-retention and [h]-insertion in the data are listed below, for completeness' sake also including those where [h] is retained in an unstressed syllable and the absence of [h] would be normal in RP and therefore not considered as [h]-dropping (example (3)). The examples are given in orthographic spelling. Phonetic transcriptions are added in cases where the phonetic realisation is unclear (e.g. realisation of plosives as glottal stops). The transcripts are Sivertsen's and Leith's but have been adapted to the current IPA system.

The contexts for [h]-retention are:

a) after a voiceless plosive:[7]

(1) just 'past that '**public 'house** (EC)
(2) 'only on a '**bank 'holiday** (EC)
(3) (h)e 'used to '**sweep his** 'hut (AP)
(4) 'quite 'six '**feet 'high** (EE)
(5) be'cause the 'music '**got** (/t/ is realised as [ʔ])'**hold** of them (D)
(6) 'water was 'right **up** 'high (Lucy)
(7) 'do any'thing a'bout **it** '**help** us 'out (Lucy)

b) after [s] and [z]:

(8) (h)e 'used to '**sweep his** [hɪz]'**hut** (AP)
(9) '**that's 'how** they 'got a 'living (AP)
(10) and '**that's 'how** they 'used to 'be (MM)

---

7 Parentheses are used to indicate that the sound corresponding to the letter is not pronounced.

(11) 'five to 'six 'hundred a 'day   (Ernie)

(12) we 'wondered oh what was 'happening   (Lucy)

c)   after [ɪ] and [ə]:

(13) it 'seems to (realised as [tʰə])'hypno'tize *you*   (A)

(14) it 'makes you 'feel well 'not 'actually 'happy   (C)

(15) who it 'does 'really 'get a 'hold of   (D)

(16) 'one 'fell 'over the (realised as [ðə])'whole 'fall [sic] 'over (Jim)

(17) course I had a 'big 'cellar 'underneath the 'house ['ɐnnɪiθ ðë hɤ̈s]   (Lucy)

d)   at the beginning of a tone unit:[8]

(18) They' used to' come 'out'side the 'door | and 'cut them 'out | 'hold them | — I 'seen (th)em   (AP)

(19) 'So I said, "Yes | 'come and '(h)ave a 'look | 'quick!' |'So (h)e 'looked. | He 'didn't 'say 'nothing   (EE)

(20) we 'borrowed a 'penny | 'halfpenny 'here and '(h)alfpenny there ['hæ̱ɪbn̩ɪi 'ɪən 'ä̱ɪpnɪ ðę̈·ə̧] and we (h)ad a 'penny 'cup o(f) 'tea   (Kate)

(21) was all 'sodden it 'was |' had to 'buy a 'new 'oil-'cloth | and 'all 'that   (Lucy)

Certain contexts appear to favour the retention of initial [h]: This is the case if etymological /h/ is preceded by voiceless consonants, the fricatives [s] and [z], schwa or a word boundary. The single

---

8   In the instances where [h] is retained at the beginning of a tone unit the preceding sound is one of those that also precede [h] if no preceding tone unit boundary is present. This is, however, in all probability coincidence, as Leith's criterion for inserting marks for tone unit boundaries in his transcripts are pauses (Leith 1973: 66). We do not know what exactly Sivertsen's criteria were for inserting marks of tone unit boundaries, as the only information she gives is "A vertical line, [|], shows the end of an intonation (macrosegment)" (Sivertsen 1960: 232).

instance of a preceding [ɪ] does not allow any conclusions. In the instances where initial [h] is retained after a word boundary, we do not have a single semantic or pragmatic relationship between the unit preceding and following the word boundary but a variety of relationships: a temporal sequence (18) and (19), an instance of rephrasing (20), and a causal relationship (21).

How do these contexts compare to the contexts in which [h]-insertions are found? Four instances of [h]-insertion occur in the transcripts:

(22) they 'put them 'all on **their** 'arm (realised as [ðeə 'hɑːm]) (AP)

(23) can't tell them '**nothing** (realised with [-ŋ]) [**h**]**and** 'that was 'that (Harry)

(24) 'started a '**job** | [**h**]**and** 'all we ' (h)ad er we (h)ad 'no 'money (Kate)

(25) 'all I had was a '**farthing** (realised with [-ṇ]) | [**h**]**and** er / 'went to 'work (Kate)

Sivertsen (1960: 141-2) lists the following additional instances that occurred in her data, but are not part of the transcripts in the appendix.[9]

(26) '*no I* '[h]*aint*

(27) 'time to **get** '[h]**up**

(28) '*te* '[h]*aitch* (the letter sequence) [10]

---

9   Sivertsen gives orthographic and phonemic transcriptions of her additional examples. As in particular the use of /h/ in her phonemic system is confusing in the present context, the additional examples are given in orthographic spelling but [h]-insertion is indicated phonetically. Sivertsen's orthographic spelling *th* (example 28), has been replaced by the more explicit *te aitch*.

10 The pronunciation [heɪtʃ] of the letter <h> is extremely frequent throughout England. The reason may be that it seems illogical to many people that the sound symbolised by the letter should be absent in the pronunciation of its name.

(29) (h)er ˌ[h]errands
(30) fo(r) 'her '[h]anyway
(31) I'll '[h]en(d) that 'story
(32) I 'like '[h]eels [ɑɪ 'lɑɪʔ 'hɨɹz]

Unfortunately Sivertsen gives no information on the speakers of her additional examples, which are only transcribed orthographically and phonemically, with the exception of (32). In her phonemic system [ʔ] is generally given as /t/, and /l/-vocalisation as /l/. Therefore we do not know how /t/ in *get* in (27) and /l/ in *I'll* in (31) are realised. Despite these uncertainties the majority of the examples follow the same pattern as AP's realisation of *their arm*, where [h] is inserted between a word-final and a word-initial vowel. In all of Sivertsen's examples the words that have [h]-insertions are stressed. In contrast, in (23) to (25) [h] is inserted before unstressed *and*, which is preceded in two cases by a tone unit boundary.

While there are not enough examples to exclude other contexts, the examples do not suggest that the contexts for [h]-insertion and [h]-retention are identical. This poses problems for phoneme theory. If [h] has no phoneme status in Cockney, as is claimed in the literature, we might expect one of the following distributions: (a) [h] appears only in stressed words, which would suggest that it is a mark of emphasis and should be treated as a suprasegmental feature; (b) [h]-insertion and [h]-retention are found in the same phonetic context, in which case [h] would be utilised for ease of pronunciation and the same lexeme would have two phonologically conditioned allomorphs; (c) [h] shows random distribution, which would suggest that an effort to avoid [h]-dropping is partially successful but results also in the utilisation of hypercorrect [h], a case that phoneme theory cannot really deal with.

On the basis of the comparatively regular pattern of [h]-retention we can dismiss the last hypothesis. Stress seems to play a role, as with the exception of examples (3) and (19) [h]-retention is found in stressed syllables and for Sivertsen's informants the same holds for [h]-insertion. But even in stressed syllables [h]-retention and [h]-insertion do not occur freely, but are restricted to certain phonetic contexts. The question why these contexts rather than others favour [h]-retention and [h]-insertion respectively is a difficult one and one that cannot be answered on the basis of phonetic transcripts alone.

The three instances of [h]-insertion in unstressed [h]*and* (examples (23), (24) and (25)) appear to fall into a different category. They are found in the speech of Kate and Harry, who are both fast speakers according to Leith, which suggests that many of the tone unit boundaries, which according to Leith correspond to pauses, are not pauses used to take breath but are short pauses that separate idea units. Therefore it seems possible that the [h]-additions in [h]*and* are delayed breathy releases of the preceding voiced plosive in (24) or nasal in (25) which function at the same time as vowel onsets for the following word. The same explanation would hold for (23), where [h]*and* according to Leith's transcript is not preceded by a pause, but where the content suggests that the preceding text belongs to a different idea unit, as it contains a citation in direct speech of what Harry said to the foreman, while [h]*and that was that* is no longer direct speech but the idiomatic expression with which Harry closes the topic. It is also worth noting that neither Kate nor Harry have any instances of [h]-retention.

The data suggest that the transcripts reflect the later stages of a transitional period from an [h]-ful accent to an [h]-less one. The use of [h] falls into three categories: (a) [h]-retention which optionally occurs in certain phonetic contexts and which is found predominantly in the speech of Sivertsen's speakers, who were recorded some twenty-five years earlier than Leith's (examples (1) to (21)), (b) [h]-insertion with a linking function, which is likewise restricted to Sivertsen's speakers (examples (22), (26), (28) to (30) and possibly (31) if /l/ is vocalised), and (c) [h]-insertion which appears to be the result of a delayed breathy release of a closure which functions at the same time as vowel onset and which is restricted to two of Leith's speakers who do not have [h] of type (a) or (b) (examples (23) to (25)).

A further fact that complicates matters is that besides [h]-omission and [h]-insertion, we find replacement of [h] by [j] and [ʔ] in the data. The realisation [j] for RP /h/ occurs only in the speech of one speaker, Jim, the speaker from Bethnal Green, once in a stressed syllable word-internally and once in an unstressed syllable in a sequence of pronoun and verb, which is realised by the speaker without a marked word boundary:

(33) 'red 'light be'hind (realised as [bɪ'jə̈ːn]) (Jim)

(34) that's 'all they 'worry a'bout I **he had** (realised as [ɪjæd]) it all in a 'big 'safe (Jim)

Jim uses [j] after a close front vowel, a context in which [ʲ] is used as a linking vowel in RP (cf. Cruttenden & Gimson 1994: 264). This may suggest that [j] is inserted as a linking sound rather than constituting a replacement of etymological [h] in examples (33) and (34). It is, however, worth noting that the realisation of *behind* with an intervocalic voiced [ɦ] was standard in educated pronunciation at the turn of the 20th century. This is attested by Sweet's (1907: 56) description of intervocalic /h/:

> In most languages, when an aspirate comes between voiced sounds, it is formed with 'half-voice' or imperfect vocality. Thus in English *behold!* compared with *hold!* the chords vibrate throughout the whole word, but their vibration is so feeble during the **h** that the contrast of this weak vocality with the full vocality of the other sounds is enough to produce the effect of aspiration. In the emphatic *aha!*, on the contrary, the glottis is opened enough to let out a distinct puff of air, instead of merely relaxing its closure, as in half-voice. [Sweet's emphasis]

Half a century later the pronunciation described by Sweet had become a minority pronunciation in educated British English, according to A. C. Gimson (1962: 186):

> Although /h/ functions in English essentially as a voiceless syllable-initial margin [...], *a few speakers* [my emphasis; MH] use a voiced (or slightly voiced) allophone medially between voiced sounds, e.g. in such words as *anyhow, perhaps, behind*. In such pronunciations, the strong airstream of /h/ is accompanied by vocal cord vibration, the result being a kind of breathy vowel or voiced glottal fricative [ɦ].

Jim's pronunciation of *behind* could therefore alternatively be interpreted as a retention of /h/ that differs from the standard English pronunciation [ɦ] that was the norm when he was a young man only in the degree of assimilation to the preceding vowel.[11] Such an interpretation receives some support from the fact that the transcript of Jim's speech contains no instances of [j]-insertions between vowels where the second word does not begin with etymological /h/.

Unlike the realisation of RP /h/ as [j], [ʔ] for RP /h/ is used by several of the Cockney speakers. There is one instance in the speech of MM, but not in that of any other of Sivertsen's speakers. In Leith's data [ʔ] for RP /h/ occurs once in the speech of Jim, once in that of Harry, three times in that of Ernie, while Kate and Lucy have no [ʔ] replacements of RP /h/.

(35) *and 'say like a 'woman's 'husband* (realised as ['wʊmənz 'ʔʌzbən]) *was to 'die* (MM)

(36) *'round where 'I live only 'railway 'arches | 'here* (realised as ['ʔiːə]) *you 'got the 'tube* (Jim)

(37) *he 'got a | like a 'hook* (realised as [ə 'ʔʊk]) (Harry)

(38) *and your 'heap* (realised as [jə 'ʔɪip]) (Ernie)

(39) *a 'packet of 'Hudson's soap* (realised as [əf 'ʔa̱tsənz]) (Ernie)

(40) *I 'says to him | he* (realised as [ɪm | ʔɪ]) *'calls us in a 'ring* (Ernie)

---

11 Sweet and Gimson do not state whether they refer to citation forms or natural speech, but it seems nevertheless safe to assume on the basis of their descriptions that the majority pronunciation of medial /h/ between voiced sounds has shifted from a voiced realisation to an unvoiced one for RP speakers. Wells (1994: 199) does not mention the variant [ɦ] in words such as *behind* in his discussion of [h]-dropping, where he states that "H-dropping is the failure to pronounce [h] in positions where RP-speakers would pronounce it: thus ['æmə] for ['hæmə] *hammer*, ['edʒ] for ['hedʒ] *hedge*, [bɪ'aɪnd] for [bɪ'haɪnd] *behind*, [aɪ 'æv] for [aɪ 'hæv] *I have*."

MM, Jim and Harry have glottal stops for RP /h/ after [z], after [ə], and at the beginning of a tone unit, all contexts in which other speakers have [h], while Ernie has glottal stop replacements of [h] after [ə] and [f], and at the beginning of a tone unit. There is a noticeable difference in frequency of [ʔ] stop replacements of [h] between Sivertsen's and Leith's speakers. At first sight this may suggest a gender difference. If, however, date of birth is taken into consideration, linguistic change is a more likely explanation. Sivertsen's speakers were on average born twenty years before those recorded by Leith, and MM, Sivertsen's youngest speaker, and Harry, Leith's oldest male speaker, who are approximately of the same age, have one instance each. Moreover, examples (37) and (38) show other features which point to a possible change in the phonotactic system of Cockney. Here [ʔ] not only replaces [h], but it is found where a linking consonant might be used instead to avoid a hiatus, namely linking [r] in (38), and linking [n] in (37). This may suggest that Cockney maintains in contexts where [h] was retained in earlier Cockney a difference in phonotactic rules between words beginning with etymological /h/ and words beginning with vowels. This would be comparable to the difference in liaison and elision rules between French words beginning with *ache aspiré* and those beginning with a vowel, including those beginning with *ache muet*. As recent changes in the phonotactics of *ache aspiré* words in French show (Tranel 1995), such a system is ultimately unstable. This would suggest for the subsequent development of Cockney that either glottal stop replacements of [h] will eventually be given up or that vowels will also be preceded by glottal stops.

If the use of a glottal stop to avoid a hiatus is a new feature in Cockney, we are faced with two questions: (a) How did earlier Cockney deal with the transition between words ending in a vowel and words beginning with a vowel, and (b) what caused the replacement of [h] by [ʔ] in Cockney? Present-day standard English uses predominantly linking consonants to avoid a hiatus, although this usage appears to be receding in recent formal English (Allerton 2000). Early Modern English dealt with hiatus at word boundaries by consonant retention and vowel elision. Consonant retention was available in sequences where nouns beginning with a vowel followed the indefinite article or possessive pronouns of the first and second persons singular. Here the older forms with final <n> were used before vowels. While the alternation in the indefinite article is still obligatory in present-day standard English, that of the possessive pronouns was given up in the eighteenth century and forms without <n> have become the norm. Linking [ɹ] is likewise an instance of consonant retention, although here, due to orthographic conventions, the alternation between forms with and without [ɹ] does not show up in the spelling.

In cases where consonant retention was not available, vowel elision was a common means of dealing with a hiatus at a word boundary. Common cases were sequences of the definite article and a following noun or adjective such as *thabbott* "the abbot", *thend* "the end" (Clark 1914: 131, 268) and the preposition *to* and a following noun phrase or infinitive such as *tabide* "to abide" (Clark 1914: 220). According to Dobson (1957: 877-78), the 16th-century spelling reformer John Hart shows in addition syncopes in *do (d')* and twice elisions of *-ow* in *borrow* before a vowel. This suggests that English was moving towards a system like the French or Italian one, where vowel elisions are frequent, as in French *l'ami* for *le ami* ('the friend') and *il m'a dit* for *il me a dit* ('he told me'), or Italian *l'immagine* for *la immagine* ('the image'), *nell'anno* for *nello anno* ('in the year'), *com'era bella!* for *come era bella!* ('how beautiful she was!') and *t'hanno chiamato* for *ti hanno chiamato* ('they've called you').[12] Early Modern English not only avoided vowel sequences in hiatus, but also phrase-initial vowels, as is attested by the frequent occurrences of *Tis* for *It is*. There is evidence that the latter usage continued in Cockney, as the following instances are found in the speech of Harry and Jim:

---

12   The Italian examples and glosses are Deugenio's (1982: 141).

(41) I 'said "(i)t is [ʔɪs] going to 'slip 'mate ..."   (Jim)
(42) cause they 'couldn('t) 'take the 'job their'selves | (i)t is [ʔɪs] 'too 'big a 'job for (th)em   (Harry)
(43) 'keep (h)im 'busy | (i)t is [ʔɪs] the 'muck they 'got (t)o 'keep 'getting up to them 'then   (Harry)
(44) an(d) 'we 'fire-'watchers | (i)t (w)as [ʔʌːz]'funny   (Harry)

All of these instances are found at the beginning of tone units or in (41) at the beginning of a citation of direct speech, while [ɪts] and [ɪʔ wəz] are used in other positions by the same speakers. The frequent realisation of *and* as [n̩] after tone unit boundaries in the Cockney data may be another instance of avoiding vocalic syllable onsets. In contrast, vowel elision in the definite article before words beginning with a vowel does not occur. There is, however, one instance in the speech of EC, Sivertsen's oldest speaker, where the initial vowel of the noun is elided after the definite article, the elision in the noun rather than the article probably being due to the Cockney preference for eliding unstressed initial syllables:

(45) an(d) the (A)mericans [ɛn ðə 'merɪkənz]   (EC)

The speakers follow the RP rules for the use of /ðɪ/- and /tʊ/-type variants of *the* and *to* before words beginning with vowels. These are realised as [ðɪ, ði, ðɪi] and [tü, tʊ, tˢü, tˢʊ, tʰü], but unlike in RP, they are realised as purely vocalic transitions without linking [ʲ] or [ʷ]. Before consonants the speakers predominantly use the /-ə/-variants of *the* and *to*, except for MM and Harry, who prefer /tʊ/-variants before place-names. In addition, in certain environments, /tʊ/- and /ðɪ/-variants are found beside /tə/ and /ðə/. This is the case before words beginning with [m, b, ð, ʃ, s, ɹ], i.e. bilabials and front to central fricatives as well as the palato-alveolar approximant. In all of these contexts the retention of the historically older /tʊ/- and /ðɪ/-variants could be accounted for by ease of pronunciation, as less tongue movement is required in the realisation with close vowels in these contexts.

As the Cockney informants are conservative in their retention of *the* and *to*, it might be expected that they are equally conservative in their use of linking [ɹ]. This is indeed the case with Sivertsen's speakers. In contrast, Leith's data show a steep decrease in the use of linking [ɹ], which seems to have become optional for speakers born after 1895. This change is not related to the avoidance of linking [ɹ] that is found in RP. According to Gimson (1962: 163), RP speakers tend to avoid linking [ɹ] in contexts in which intrusive [ɹ] is used, i.e. after [ə], [ɔː], and [ɑː], as most speakers seem to be unable to avoid one without avoiding the other. Unlike the RP speakers, Leith's informants do not avoid stigmatised pronunciations. The same speakers who have [ɹ]-less transitions frequently combine linking [ɹ] with [h]-omission, and they use linking [ɹ] in those contexts that are avoided by RP speakers, i. e. after schwa and sometimes also after open vowels. Moreover, they have almost exclusively vocalic transitions, whereas RP speakers who avoid linking [ɹ] vary between the insertion of a glottal stop and vocalic transitions (Gimson 1962: 163; Cruttenden & Gimson 1994: 155).

What then caused the change in Cockney? A closer look at the data shows that linking [ɹ] is generally used by both the older and the younger generation of speakers between the monophthongs [ə] and [ɪ], but is used less frequently by the younger generation if the vowel preceding a potential linking [ɹ] is [ɔː] or [ɑˑ] and the following word-initial vowel [ɪ] or [ə]. Sequences of words ending in centring diphthongs followed by words with initial vowel show that Sivertsen's informants generally retain both the diphthong and [ɹ] in such sequences, while Leith's informants to differing degrees elide both the schwa of the diphthong and [ɹ].[13] The development is illustrated in Table 2.

The elision of linking [ɹ] is most frequent between variants of [e, ɛ] and schwa, and it appears to be a characteristic of fast

---

13 Schwa elision in centring diphthongs was also noted by Beaken (1971, quoted in Wells 1982: 318).

speech. It is a typical feature of Kate's and Harry's speech, whose delivery is characterised by Leith as "very fast" (Kate) and "fast" (Harry). That the loss of linking [ɹ] is a gradual process in Cockney is suggested by Ernie's realisation of a'ware of [ə'wëˑə] and Lucy's realisation of our (h)ome [æˑ 'ɐüm],[14] where Leith chooses [ˑ] in his transcription. Intervocalic [ɹ]-elision is not restricted to word boundaries. Lucy has also one realisation of very as ['vɛˑɪ]. Moreover, the elision of [ɹ] is not an isolated phenomenon in Cockney. It needs to be seen in the context of a general weakening of sonorants, which also affected nasals and /l/, both of which may be vocalised in postvocalic position.

If word-internal intervocalic [h] was generally voiced between voiced sounds at the turn of the twentieth century, as Sweet's description suggests, it is highly probable that intervocalic [h] at word boundaries in Cockney was also voiced. Its decrease is then likely to have been caused by the same elision and vocalisation process that affected other sonorants. Why then did [h] not disappear completely as it did in French and Italian, but was replaced by a glottal stop in some contexts? The answer appears to be that the the rapid progression of consonant elision and vocalisation upset the balance between elision and liaison in Cockney and thus prepared the way for the rise of the glottal stop.

According to Leith (1973: 163-4), the *Survey of English Dialects* shows glottal stop replacements of [t] "in all positions in the east Midlands, particularly Buckinghamshire." In intervocalic position it is recorded in East Anglia, Essex, the counties north of London, but also Surrey, Berkshire and to a lesser degree in Kent, whereas in final position it is restricted to Buckinghamshire and Hertfordshire. The oldest of Sivertsen's speakers have no (AP) or very few (EC) realisations of /t/ as [ʔ] and none of her informants has more than fifteen, while Leith's informants Harry and Lucy have more than one hundred each. It is not only the overall frequency of the glottal stop that increases dramatically, but also

---

14 *Our* in Cockney has a centring diphthong, realised as [ɛə] or [ɛə].

	diphthong and [ɹ] retained	[ɹ]-insertion after diphthong	[ɹ] (partially) elided	[ə] (partially) elided	[ə] and [ɹ] (partially) elided
EC *1874		'(h)ow (h)e ['ɛ̈əɪi]			
AP *1876	'chair 'out ['tʃɛəˈɪɛ̈t] 'there (h)e ['ðeəɪi] where 'all [weəˈɪɒɫ]				
EE *c.1890				'sure it's ['ʃɔ̈ːɪts] 'sure it ['ʃɔːɪt]	
B *1930/45	there an(d) [ðɛəɹən]				
Harry *1890/91	'tear all ['tɛəɹ ɒɫ] 'share of it ['ʃɛəɹ əvɪʔ] 'flour or ['fɫɛɹəɹ ɔ] there and [ðɛəɹ ən] there is [ðɛ̈əɹ ɪz]	i'dea of [aɪ'dɪəɹəv] give you a ['gɪəɹə]	there and [ðɛ̈ə ən] there a [ðɛ̈ə] 'there 'early ['ðɛ̈ə ˈɜːlii] 'look here I ['lʊk ɪə ɑ̈ɪ]	'down 'there I ['dɐ̈n ˈnɛ̈ˑə̯ɹ ɑ̈ɪ] 'four or 'five ['fɔːɹ ɔ 'fɑ̈ɪv] 'more of ['mɒɹ ə]	
Earnie *1896/97			a'ware of [ə'we̝ˑə]	'door 'open [dɔːˑɹ 'ɔ̈ɪpən]	'more he ['mɔː ɪ]
Jim *1901/02	their 'own [ðɛəɹ ˈɔ̈ʊn]			for it [fɔːɪʔ]	an 'hour (h)e [ən 'ʌːˑə̯ ii] 'for he ['fɔː ɪ]
Lucy *1888/89	there and ['ðɛəɹənd]		'top there at ['tɒ̈p dˑə̯ɛ̈ə ɔʔ]	where I [weːɹɑ̈ɪ]	'there and we ['ðɛːə n̩ wɪ] (be)'fore I ['fɔ̈ː a]our '(h)ome [æˑ'tʊɨ̈m]
Kate *1896/97	'there of [ðɛəɹ əv]		there of [ðɛ̈ə əv]	'four o 'clock ['fɔ̈ɹ ɒ 'klɒk] 'for I ['fɔ̈ɹ ɑ̈ɪ]	chair an(d) [tʃe̝ˑə ən] there of [ðɛ̈ə əv]

Table 2: Loss of linking [ɹ] and [ə] in centring diphthongs

the environment in which a glottal stop may occur and the sound it can replace. Four major stages can be distinguished in the spread of [ʔ] as an allophone of /t/ in the data:

a) in monosyllabic words if preceded by a vowel and followed by a tone unit boundary or a word beginning with a consonant, including words consisting of [n̩],
b) in monosyllabic words if preceded by a vowel and followed by a word beginning with a vowel,
c) in intervocalic position in polysyllabic words,
d) in initial position and in clusters such as /ts/, /nt/.

From its use as an allophone of /t/, the use of [ʔ] is extended to first /k/ and then /p/, where the spread of the allophone [ʔ] likewise seems to proceed through stages a) to d). In addition, all speakers except EC and AP (born in 1874 and 1876 respectively) have [ʔ] replacements of /d/ before [n̩] in *didn't* and speakers Kate, Ernie, Jim and Harry also as a replacement of word-final /d/. Leith's speakers also have isolated instances of [ʔ] replacing a variety of fricatives, such as initial /j, ð, s/ and the cluster /ft/ in *after*. While stage (i) has no major effect on the phonotactic system, stages (ii) and (iii) produce sequences of vowel – glottal stop – vowel. With the extension of the use of the glottal stop to word-initial fricatives, the glottal stop offered itself as a replacement of [h] in those cases where a strong onset was desired either because the word was stressed or because it occurred at the beginning of a tone unit.

What caused the dramatic increase of the glottal stop in Cockney? Leith (1973: 163) argues for a process where postglottalised plosives were gradually replaced by glottal stops, as glottal reinforcement is frequent in the East Midlands and North London. Dobson (1957: 965) relates [ʔ] replacements of intervocalic /t/ to the loss of intervocalic [v] in Middle English:

> In present-day vulgar and dialectal speech intervocalic [t] has been lost, as far as dental articulation is concerned, though it is normally replaced by the glottal stop to preserve the separate identity of the preceding and

following vowels. The process (which is similar to the ME loss of intervocalic [v]) is not mentioned by the orthoepists.

Leith (1973: 151) adduces D'Orsey's 1882 report to the School Board for London as evidence that glottal stop replacements of consonants were current in the late 19th century. In this report D'Orsey has the following comments on consonant pronunciation: "The final consonants are so feebly uttered that it is sometimes impossible to tell whether the pupil says *life*, or *like*, or *light*." (cited in Matthews 1938: 63-4). While it is true that [ʔ] replacement might account for D'Orsey's difficulty in telling which of the three words in question a pupil actually said, our perception of a glottal stop is not that of a "feeble consonant", and it seems unlikely that D'Orsey's perception was very different from ours. Moreover, a replacement of word-final [f] by a glottal stop is a late development in the spread of the glottal stop. It is not described by Matthews, nor does it occur in the speech of Sivertsen's or Leith's Cockney speakers. It seems therefore more plausible to take D'Orsey's statement at face value and accept that the consonants were "feebly uttered", which suggests a weakening of word-final voiceless plosives and fricatives. Possible realisations that would obscure the distinction between /f/, /k/, and /t/ and could justly be described as "feeble" are unreleased consonants or plosives with incomplete closure and a bilabial realisation of /f/ with little intensity. Matthews (1938: 77) claims that "Cockneys avoid movement of the lips and jaw as far as possible, preserving a roughly half-open position of the lips." If there is any truth in this statement, incomplete closure of plosives would be a likely result of this habit. The sloppy release of plosives in Cockney (Wells 1982: 332) could easily develop into incomplete closure, as the lenition of /t/ in Irish English with its realisations [t̪, h] shows (Wells 1982: 429-30). It seems therefore probable that the process of consonant weakening that led to sonorant vocalisation or elision in Cockney also affected plosives. Reinforcement by a glottal plosive may then have put a literal stop to the rapid progression of consonant loss to avoid the elision of word-final postvocalic plosives and preserve intelligibility.

To sum up, the Cockney data show three distinct uses of [h]: [h]-retention, [h]-insertion with a linking function, and [h]-insertion which appears to be the result of delayed sloppy consonant release which at the same time functions as vowel onset. The data strongly suggests that [h]-insertion in Cockney is not the result of Cockneys' unsuccessful efforts to imitate speakers of standard English, but rather that it is an integral part of the phonotactic system of nineteenth- and early twentieth-century Cockney, while the loss of [h] in Cockney appears to be part of a lenition process which affected sonorants as well as plosives and which resulted in the well-known features of present-day Cockney such as [l]-vocalisation, [n]-vocalisation and the replacement of plosives as well as fricatives by the glottal stop.

References

Allerton, D. J. (2000). 'Articulatory inertia vs 'Systemzwang''. *English Studies* 6. 574-81.

Britton, D. (2000). 'Henry Machyn, Axel Wijk and the case of the wrong Riding: The south-west Yorkshire character of the language of Machyn's diary'. *Neuphilologische Mitteilungen* 101. 571-596.

Brunner, K. (1963). *An outline of Middle English grammar*. Oxford: Blackwell.

Clark, A. (ed.) (1914). *Lincolnshire diocese documents, 1450-1544*. London: EETS o. s. 149.

Clarke, C. (1992). 'The myth of 'the Anglo-Norman scribe''. *History of Englishes: new methods and interpretations in historical linguistics*. In: M. Rissanen, O. Ihalainen, T. Nervalainen & I. Taavitsainen (eds.). Berlin and New York: Mouton. 117-29.

Cruttenden, A. & A. C. Gimson (1994). *Gimson's pronunciation of English*. London: Arnold.

D'Eugenio, A. (1982). *Major problems of English phonology: with special reference to Italian-speaking learners*. Foggia: Atlantica.

Dobson, E. J. (1957). *English pronunciation 1500-1700*, 2 vols. Oxford: Clarendon.

Gimson, A. C. (1962). *An introduction to the pronunciation of English*. London: Arnold.

Jones, C. (1989). *A history of English phonology*. London and New York: Longman.
Lass, R. (1987). *The shape of English*. London: Dent.
Leith, R. (1973). 'The traditional phonology of North London speech'. Unpublished MA dissertstion, University of Leeds.
Luick, K. (1964). *Historische Grammatik der Englischen Sprache*. Stuttgart: Tauchnitz, reprint of first edition of 1929-40.
Matthews, W. (1938). *Cockney past and present: a short history of the dialect of London*. London: Routledge.
Milroy, J. (1983). 'On the sociolinguistic history of /h/-dropping in English'. *Current Topics in Historical Linguistics*. In: M. Davenport, E. Hansen & H. F. Nielsen (eds.). Odense: Odense University Press. 37-53.
Mugglestone, L. (1995). *"Talking proper": the rise of accent as a social symbol*. Oxford: Clarendon.
Nichols, J. G. (ed.) (1847). *The diary of Henry Machyn, citizen and merchant-taylor of London, from A.D. 1550 to A.D. 1563*. London: Camden Society, o.s. 42.
Saxe, J. (1936). *Bernhard Shaw's phonetics: a comparative study of Cockney sound-changes*. Copenhagen: Levin & Munksgaard and London: Allen & Unwin.
Scragg, D. G. (1970). 'Initial *H* in Old English'. *Anglia* 88. 165-196.
Sheridan, T. (1970). *A course of lectures on elocution*. Hildesheim and New York: Olms, 1970. Reprint of the original edition of 1762.
Sivertsen, E. (1960). *Cockney phonology*. Oslo: Oslo Universtity Press.
Skeat, W. W. (1897). 'The proverbs of Alfred'. *Transactions of the Philological Society*. 399-418.
Sweet, H. (1907). *The sounds of English: an introduction to phonetics*. Oxford: Clarendon.
Tranel, B. (1995). 'Current issues in French phonology: liason and position theories'. *The handbook of phonological theory*. In: J. A. Goldsmith (ed.). Cambridge, Massachusetts and Oxford: Blackwell. 798-816.
Wells, J. C. (1982). *Accents of English*, 3 vols. Cambridge: Cambridge University Press.
Wells, J. C. (1994). 'The Cockneyfication of R.P.?' *Nonstandard varieties of language: Papers from the Stockholm Symposium, 11-13 April 1991*. In: G. Melchers & N.-L. Johanneson (eds.). Stockholm: Almqvist & Wiksell. 198-205.
Wijk, A. (1937). *The pronunciation of Henry Machyn, the London diarist: a study of the south-east Yorkshire dialect in the early 16th century*. Uppsala: Appelberg.
Wyld, H. C. (1920). *A History of modern colloquial English*. London: Fisher Unwin.

PETER TRUDGILL

Linguistic changes in pan-world English

In an earlier paper (Trudgill 1998) I argued that the major native varieties of English around the world are currently converging lexically, most often in the direction of American English, but diverging phonologically.[1] The lexical convergence can be explained by the development during the last 100 years of the electronic media, and the dominant role played in these media by speakers of American English, who are also of course demographically dominant in the English-speaking world. This media-led lexical convergence is a very new type of phenomenon: for all of human history until extremely recently, spoken human communication was by means of face-to-face contact only.

The phonological divergence, on the other hand, can be accounted for by saying that what is happening now is, quite simply, what has always happened. All languages change through time, and, for reasons we do not altogether understand, they change in different ways in different places. This continues to occur in the case of English phonology, but not in the case of lexis, because, while lexis can quite readily diffuse through television and films – we all continue to acquire new vocabulary items throughout our lifetimes, and can do so from any source – the diffusion of phonological features from one speaker to another, and thus from one area to another, requires face-to-face contact and interaction (see Trudgill (1986) for a fuller discussion); and in spite of enormously increased possibilities for geographical mobility for some sections of the world's population in

---

1   I am grateful to a number of people who have commented on earlier versions of this paper and/or helped me to formulate the ideas contained in it, especially Lyle Campbell, Jan Terje Faarlund, and Brian Joseph.

the 20th and 21st centuries, the vast majority of, say, Australians spend far more of their lives in face-to-face contact with other Australians than they do with, say, anglophone Canadians. So, while younger New Zealanders are, on the one hand, increasingly saying and using in writing the originally American English form *truck* rather than *lorry*, their vowel in the lexical set of *dress* (in this paper I employ the key words introduced by Wells (1982)) is moving rapidly upwards in the direction of [i], while in the American English of the Northern Cities it is moving equally rapidly downwards and backwards in the direction of [ʌ]. (The position with respect to convergence or divergence at the level of syntax is much less clear).

This split development internationally as between changes in lexis and changes in phonology is paralleled by what is happening intranationally in individual anglophone polities. As I have suggested in Trudgill (1999), regional dialect vocabulary in England is disappearing at a very rapid rate. That is, homogenisation is taking place at the national level too. With phonology, on the other hand, while it is true that many phonological dialect boundaries in Britain are disappearing, i.e. dialect areas are becoming fewer in number and spatially larger, those dialect areas which still remain are becoming increasingly unlike one another – phonological divergence is taking place within Britain too, as it is in the United States (Labov 1994) and elsewhere. Just as the phonology of Canadian English is becoming more unlike the phonology of Australian English, so the phonology of English in Liverpool is diverging from that of English in London. And the phonology of English in Chicago is diverging from that of English in Birmingham, Alabama: for example, the first element of the /ei/ diphthong of *face* is becoming closer in the American northeast, but more open in the southeast (see Trudgill & Hannah 2002).

This is the general trend. In this paper, however, I point out that there are nevertheless a number of examples of identical or extremely similar phonological changes which have taken or are taking place in varieties of English around the world more or less simultaneously and, apparently, independently. This is an intriguing type of development and, at least in most cases, one which appears not to be susceptible to an explanation in terms of the diffusion of linguistic innovations from one place to another. In this paper, I cite five such cases.

(1) *The* NEAR/SQUARE *merger*

The vowels of the lexical sets of NEAR and SQUARE are currently undergoing a merger in modern New Zealand English. As reported in a number of papers by Gordon & Maclagan (1985, 1989, 2001), Maclagan & Gordon (1996, 2000), and others (e.g. Batterham 2000), more and more younger New Zealanders are increasingly failing to distinguish between pairs such as *pair – peer, hair – here, dare – deer,* and so on. Nearly all varieties of New Zealand English are non-rhotic; older, distinct pronunciations such as [ɛə] and [ɪə], respectively, are thus giving way to newer non-distinct forms such as [ɪə]. The merger, that is, seems to be on the vowel originally employed only for the NEAR set. The merger is now so widespread that it has led to the humorous advertising of, for example, hairdressers with slogans such as *Hair it is!*, and to beer advertising using pictures of bears.

We are able to date this change fairly precisely. Gordon and Maclagan (2001: 215) report that

> from about 1970 onwards, it became clear that some New Zealand university students studying linguistics were having difficulty distinguishing the diphthongs in word pairs such as *ear* and *air* when they wrote phonemic transcriptions.

It is therefore interesting to note that a very similar development has occurred in England, in northern East Anglia. Local accents in most parts of the county of Norfolk, including the main city Norwich, have also merged the lexical sets of NEAR and SQUARE. Fieldwork I carried out in Norwich in 1968 (Trudgill 1974) showed that the majority of speakers had merged these two vowels. The Norwich merger, unlike the New Zealand merger, is on the vowel originally employed only in the SQUARE set. Thus, *pair* and *peer* are both pronounced [pɛ:]. The merger has now gone to completion: I am a native of the area, born in 1943, and after a lifetime spent studying English phonology, I still have some doubts as to which lexical set words like *pear* and *tear* belong to. The Norwich development, too, seems to be a relatively recent, i.e. 20th-century phenomenon, but is probably earlier than the New Zealand development by two or three generations.

The merger also occurs in the English of Newfoundland. Newfoundland English is rhotic, and according to Wells (1982: 499), in broad Newfoundland accents, *beer* and *bear* are both pronounced [bɛr]. This is confirmed by Kirwin (2001: 447).

(2) /str/ > /ʃtr/

The second change involves the retraction of /s/ to /ʃ/ before /tr/ in words such as *street, straight, extraction* as well as across word-boundaries, as in *six trees*. For American English, this was first reported by Labov (1984: 50) for Philadelphia, but is certainly today found over a wider area than this – my own American informant for this phenomenon comes from Washington DC.[2] It has subsequently been discussed by Shapiro (1995), Lawrence (2000), and Janda et al. (1994). It is therefore remarkable to note that precisely the same phenomenon has been described for recent New Zealand English by Gordon and Maclagan (2000).

Janda and Joseph (forthcoming) also note its recent occurrence in Australian English:

> A readily available example of [ʃtr] can be heard in the pronunciation of *strong* as [ʃ]*trong* by a young Australian actor playing the role of the boy Lucius in the recent (2000) film *Gladiator* (a little more than halfway through the movie, when the title character is brought to the Colosseum in Rome).

---

2   I would like to thank Mercedes Durham very much for her help with this issue.

This pronunciation is now also beginning to occur in England. I have observed it informally from a number of people, including broadcasters, all of them apparently under 30, during the course of 2001.

(3) *th-fronting*

A well-known feature of the English of London has for many decades been th-fronting (Wells 1982) i.e. the mergers of /θ/ and /f/ on /f/, and of /ð/ and /v/ on /v/. Thus, *fin* and *thin* are homophonous, and *brother* and *lover* rhyme. However, as has been described many times in the last two decades, this feature is now spreading very rapidly to other parts of England (Trudgill 1988, Foulkes & Docherty 1999) and indeed now even to Scotland (Stuart Smith 1999). It is therefore of considerable interest that it is currently beginning to make an appearance in New Zealand English also (Campbell & Gordon 1996). It is, too, a feature of African American Vernacular English, although here it is typically confined to intervocalic and syllable-final position, e.g. *nothing* [nəfɪn], *bath* [bæf] (Wells 1982: 558).

(4) GOOSE-*fronting*

Wells (1982) discusses the fronting of the vowel of the lexical set of GOOSE as constituting a feature of what he terms *diphthong shift*. Diphthong shift is essentially the movement of the first elements of the upgliding diphthongs /iː, uː, eɪ, əʊ, aɪ, aʊ, ɔɪ/, as part of the continuing English Great Vowel Shift, to positions more innovative than those found in British RP e.g. /eɪ/ as in FACE as [æɪ] or [aɪ]. Diphthong shift is most typical of the accents of the south of England, of the southeastern United States, and of the Southern Hemisphere. It is clear, however, that there are a number of areas of the English-speaking world which have accents which have fronting of /uː/ to (for example) [ʉː] although they do not otherwise share in diphthong shift e.g. Scotland, northern Ireland, Lancashire. Labov (1994) discusses this feature in the American English of Philadelphia; and Wells (1982: 148) writes that "many accents have a definitely central rather than back quality for GOOSE [...] in general, a back quality may be seen as indicative of a conservative type of accent". Areas which have so far resisted this trend include Yorkshire, southern Ireland and the Caribbean.

(5) FOOT-*unrounding*

In many forms of English around the world, the /ʊ/ vowel of the lexical set of FOOT is increasingly becoming unrounded [ɣ] in the speech of younger people. This trend can be observed (at least) in England, the USA, Canada, and New Zealand. Wells (1982: 133) writes that "a more peripheral and rounded variety is perhaps generally associated with old-fashioned or rural speech in England, Wales and Ireland, and more centralised and/or unrounded varieties with innovative or urban speech". Unrounded variants also occur in New Zealand English (Bauer 1994: 389). My own observations, however, suggest that a major exception to this trend is Australia. This is supported by Turner (1994: 289), who says that Australian FOOT is identical with RP.

Discussion

A well-known problem in the social and historical sciences has to do with the problem of diffusion versus independent development. If a phenomenon appears at place A at time X, and then subsequently appears at place B at time Y, did it spread to B from A; or did it develop in the two locations independently? We know of course that linguistic innovations do spread from one location to another, and that sometimes innovations may 'jump' from one location to another, leaving intermediate areas untouched (Trudgill 1973). Indeed, there is at least one phonological feature which is often said to have 'jumped' the Atlantic in pre-electronic media times: the loss of non-prevocalic /r/ in three separate eastern coastal districts of the USA, focussing on the port towns of Boston, New York City, Richmond, Virginia, and Charleston, South Carolina, subsequent to the loss of /r/ in London, is widely believed not to be a coincidence.

However, it would appear to be entirely unreasonable to attempt to explain the five developments described above in terms of this kind of diffusion process. For example, there is no conceivable mechanism which could account for the diffusion of the NEAR/SQUARE merger from Norwich, where it occurred earlier, to New Zealand, where it occurred later, without other areas being affected. We have to assume, rather, that many or all of the changes outlined above are examples of independent development. We can interpret them, in fact, as providing evidence supporting the legitimacy of Sapir's notion of *drift*. Sapir wrote (1921: 150) that "language moves down time in a current of its own making. It has a drift." He discusses inherent or inherited tendencies in languages and language families:

> The momentum of [...] drift is often such that languages long disconnected will pass through the same or strikingly similar phases.... The English type of plural represented by *foot: feet, mouse: mice* is strictly parallel to the German *Fuss: Füsse, Maus: Mäuse* [...] documentary evidence shows conclusively that there could have been no plurals of this type in Primitive Germanic [...] There was evidently some general tendency or group of tendencies in early Germanic, long before English and German had developed as such, that eventually drove both of these dialects along closely parallel paths. (1921: 172)

Sapir's argument was essentially that language varieties may resemble one another because, having derived from some common source, they continue to evolve linguistically in similar directions as a result of similar linguistic changes. They have not (or not just) maintained shared characteristics from some parent variety but have rather (or as well) inherited a shared *tendency* or *propensity* to the development of the same (or similar) characteristics, even after separation.

In Trudgill et al. (2000) it was argued that "drift happens", and that Sapir's insight had considerable relevance for the history of colonial Englishes. We showed, with particular reference to New Zealand English, that some similarities between different geographically separated varieties of a single language may in some cases be due not to characteristics inherited directly from some parent variety, nor to any diffusion or direct contact between them, nor to their having derived from similar dialect mixtures, but to processes of a type which we can label with this term *drift*. In some versions, the drift theory can acquire rather mystical interpretations involving the 'spirit' or the 'genius' of the language. To counteract this mysticism, it is necessary to state what the structural preconditions are which give rise to such tendencies or propensities towards the development of similar characteristics.

In the above cases, we can suppose that the structural preconditions were as follows:

(1) For the NEAR-SQUARE merger, we can point out that the functional load borne by this opposition is very low. This is particularly evident in the case of non-rhotic varieties, where /ɪə/ and /ɛə/ have phonemic status. According to Gimson (2001: 148), /ɪə/ and /ɛə/ are the two most infrequent vowels in English, apart from /ɔɪ/, forming respectively 0.54% and 0.87% of vowel tokens in RP (compare with /ɪ/, which constitutes 21.2%). There are rather few minimal pairs: monosyllabic possibilities include: *mere – mare; peer – pear/pair; tear – tear; beer – bear/bare; dear/deer – dare; cheer – chair; fear – fare/fair; sheer – share; here – hair; leer – lair; rear – rare*. As this list shows, there are even fewer pairs where confusion is likely to occur. It is not surprising, then, if such a relatively unimportant distinction has been lost more than once in different and widely separated forms of English. In the case of rhotic accents such as that of Newfoundland, it is clear that this merger is also part of a long-lasting trend in English involving vowel mergers before /r/. Most

accents of English, for example, have merged the original short vowels of *fir, fern, fur* in monosyllables. And many forms of North American English have merged the vowels of polysyllabic items such as *mirror – nearer; merry – Mary – marry; hurry – furry; hoary – horrid*. Very many English accents around the world have also merged the vowels of *poor* and *pore*, and of *hoarse* and *horse* (see Trudgill & Hannah 2002).

(2) In the case of /str/ > /ʃtr/, the structural conditions are perhaps even clearer. We can see here a simple regressive assimilation process at work. The /t/ in English /tr/ clusters is not at all identical to the allophones of /t/ that occur elsewhere; /tr/ is in fact typically realised as a postalveolar affricate. According to Jones (1963: 80): "The Southern English **tr** and **dr** seem to be intermediate between single affricates and sequences of two sounds." This is supported by Knowles (1987: 74):

> The combinations of /tr/ and /dr/ are rather special. This is because /r/ is made in the same general region as the alveolar consonants. To get from the alveolar stop position to the approximant position, the tongue necessarily passes through the close narrowing which produces turbulence. The articulation of /tr, dr/ is consequently very similar to that of affricates [...] they are sometimes classed as affricates in phonetics books.

The change in pronunciation of /s/ to [ʃ] in the environment before this cluster would thus appear to represent a partial assimilation of place of articulation to that of the following consonants. And assimilations are readily accounted for in terms of ease of articulation. Sound changes which favour ease of articulation are never surprising. The more or less simultaneous timing of this change in the different locations around the world is perhaps more problematical, but we can hazard an explanation for this by supposing that the retraction of /s/ could not have happened before the affrication of /tr/; and that the affrication of /tr/ could not have happened before /r/ became a post-alveolar approximant, something which has still not happened in many north of England and Scottish accents (where an alveolar flap is usual), and which probably did not occur in southern England until the late 19th century (see Gordon et al., forthcoming: chapter 2).

(3)   In the case of th-fronting, we can point out that [θ] and [ð] are highly marked articulation types, being rather rare in the world's languages. Maddieson (1984) cites only 8 of his 317 sample languges i.e. 2.5% as having both of these articulations. These sounds are also acquired late by children; and they are well known to cause difficulties for non-native learners. Marked articulation types, as is also well known, are especially susceptible to loss. The interdental fricatives have, for example, disappeared from all the other Germanic languages apart from English and Icelandic, in spite of being present in Old Norse, Old Saxon and Old High German. It is therefore, again, no surprise that they are disappearing from a number of different varieties of English. It is of interest, however, that while the varieties we have mentioned are merging the interdentals with labio-dentals, in varieties which have characteristics deriving from language contact, such as some forms of Caribbean English, Irish English, and the English of New York City, the fricatives have been lost not through th-fronting but through merger with /t/ and /d/.

(4)   The fronting of GOOSE has many parallels elsewhere and reflects Labov's Principle III: "In chain shifts, back vowels move to the front" (Labov 1994: 116). Many examples of this could be cited, including the fact that Norwegian and Swedish fronted /uː/ to /ʉː/ in the early 16th century; Proto-Greek /uː/ fronted to Ancient Greek /yː/ before becoming /iː/ and then Modern Greek /i/; modern French /y/ derives from /u/; and so on (see Haudricourt & Juilland 1949). Martinet (1955) argued that such frontings are due to the relative lack of articulatory space for the pronunciation of back vowels as opposed to front vowels. We can thus suggest that this development in many different types of English is part of a universal tendency in linguistic change.

(5)   The FOOT case is more difficult to account for. We can, however, observe that the unrounding of FOOT is more or less

identical with the unrounding of STRUT which began in the south of England in the 16th century. In the southeast of England (Ihalainen 1994: 261), probably starting around "the end of the sixteenth century" (Brook 1958: 90) – because it is at around this time that "foreign observers commented on the new pronunciation" (Strang 1970: 112) – the beginnings of the "FOOT-STRUT split" (Wells 1982: 196) set in. This is "one of the most unaccountable things that has happened in the history of English" (Strang 1970: 112).

Certain elements of the Great Vowel Shift seem to be repeating themselves in modern English e.g. the late mediaeval diphthongisation of /i:/ to [əɪ] in PRICE which eventually gave rise to modern /aɪ/ is currently being repeated in the form of the contemporary (diphthong-shift) diphthongisation of /i:/ to [əɪ] in FLEECE. Similarly, it seems possible that STRUT unrounding and lowering might be about to repeat itself, this time in the case of those words which avoided it the first time round, such as *put*, or which are the result of later shortening of /u:/, such as *foot*. In this case I can do no better than to say that perhaps English has a tendency to promote such changes, without being able to say what the structural conditions are which lead to this tendency.

One additional phonological change in pan-world English which has attracted much attention is the development of the High Rising Terminal (Britain 1992), which is often described as "making statements using question intonation". This has been reported, especially in the speech of young women, from California, New Zealand, Australia, and, more recently, England. There has been much argument as to where it started, and how it can have diffused from one area to another. The above discussion suggests that maybe this argument is misguided and that this feature, too, may have begun in several different places independently.

In any case, we can assert with some confidence that, even as native varieties of English are diverging from one another phonologically, *drift* phenomena still continue to occur in modern English. The same changes may from time to time take place in a number of different varieties independently and thus appear in different parts of the world without any diffusion having taken place. As always, we are of course entirely unable to say why the changes involved have taken place in the locations where they have taken place and not (or not yet) in other locations.

References

Batterham, M. (2000). 'The apparent merger of the front centring diphthongs'. In: A. Bell & K. Kuiper (eds.). *New Zealand English*. Amsterdam: Benjamins. 111-145.

Bauer, L. (1994). 'English in New Zealand'. In: R. Burchfield (ed.) 382-429.

Britain, D. (1992). 'Linguistic change in intonation: the use of high rising terminals in New Zealand English'. *Language Variation and Change* (4) 77-104.

Burchfield, R. (ed.) (1994). *The Cambridge history of the English language, vol. 5: English in Britain and overseas – origins and development.* Cambridge: Cambridge University Press.

Campbell, E. & E. Gordon (1996). 'What do you fink? Is New Zealand English losing its 'th'? '. *New Zealand English Journal* (10) 40-46.

Foulkes, P. & G. Docherty (eds.) (1999). *Urban voices: accent studies in the British Isles*. London: Edward Arnold.

Gimson, A.C. (2001). *An introduction to the pronunciation of English*. 6th ed. [*Gimson's pronunciation of English,* revised by A. Cruttenden]. London: Edward Arnold.

Gordon, E., L. Campbell, G. Lewis, M. Maclagan, & P. Trudgill (forthcoming). *The origins and evolution of New Zealand English*. Cambridge: Cambridge University Press.

Gordon, E. & M. Maclagan (1985). 'A study of the /iə-eə/ contrast in New Zealand English'. *The New Zealand Speech-Language Therapists Journal* (40) 16-26.

Gordon, E. & M. Maclagan (1989). '*Beer* and *bear, cheer* and *chair*: a longitudinal study of the *ear/air* contrast in New Zealand English'. *Australian Journal of Linguistics* (9) 203-220.

Gordon, E. & M. Maclagan (2000). ''Hear our voices': changes in spoken New Zealand English'. *The TESOLANZ Journal* (8) 1-13.

Gordon, E. & M. Maclagan (2001). 'Capturing a sound change: a real time study over 15 years of the NEAR/SQUARE merger in New Zealand English'. *Australian Journal of Linguistics* (21) 215-238.

Haudricout, A. & A. Juilland (1949). *Essai pour une histoire structurale du phonétisme français*. Paris: Klincksieck.

Ihalainen, O. (1994). 'The dialects of England since 1776'. In: R. Burchfield (ed.) 197-274.

Janda, R., B. Joseph & N. Jacobs (1994). 'Systematic hyper-foreignisms as maximally external evidence for linguistic rules'. In: S. Lima, R. Corrigan & G. Iverson (eds.), *The reality of linguistic rules*. Amsterdam: Benjamins. 67-92.

Janda, R. & B. Joseph (forthcoming). 'Reconsidering the canons of sound-change: towards a big-bang theory'.

Jones, D. (1963). *The pronunciation of English*. 4th ed. Cambridge: Cambridge University Press.

Kirwin, W. (2001). 'Newfoundland English'. In: J. Algeo (ed.), *The Cambridge history of the English language, vol. 6: English in North America*. Cambridge: Cambridge University Press. 441-455.

Knowles, G. (1987). *Patterns of spoken English*. London: Longman.

Labov, W. (1984). 'Field methods of the project on language change and variation'. In: J. Baugh & J. Sherzer (eds.), *Language in use: readings in sociolinguistics*. Englewood Cliffs: Prentice-Hall. 28-53.

Labov, W. (1994). *Principles of linguistic change: internal factors*. Oxford: Blackwell.

Lawrence, W. (2000). '/str/ > /ʃtr/: assimilation at a distance?' *American Speech* (75) 82-87.

Maclagan, M. & E. Gordon (1996). 'Out of the AIR and into the EAR: another view of the New Zealand diphthong merger'. *Language Variation and Change* (8) 125-147.

Maclagan, M. & E. Gordon (2000). 'The NEAR/SQUARE merger in New Zealand English'. *Asia-Pacific Journal of Speech, Language and Hearing* (5) 201-207.

Maddieson, I. (1984). *Patterns of sounds*. Cambridge: Cambridge University Press.

Martinet, A. (1955). *Economie des changements phonétiques*. Bern: Francke.

Sapir, E. (1921). *Language*. New York: Harcourt Brace.

Shapiro, M. (1995). 'A case of distant assimilation: /str/ > /ʃtr/'. *American Speech* (70) 101-107.

Strang, B. (1970). *A history of English*. London: Methuen.

Stuart-Smith, J. (1999). 'Glasgow: accent and voice quality'. In: Foulkes and Docherty (eds.).

Turner, G. (1994). 'English in Australia'. In: R. Burchfield (ed.) 277-327.

Trudgill, P. (1973). 'Linguistic change and diffusion: description and explanation in sociolinguistic dialect geography'. *Language in Society* (3) 215-46.

Trudgill, P. (1974). *The social differentiation of English in Norwich.* Cambridge: Cambridge University Press.

Trudgill, P. (1986). *Dialects in contact.* Oxford: Blackwell.

Trudgill, P. (1988). 'Norwich revisited: recent changes in an English urban dialect'. *English World Wide* (9) 33-49.

Trudgill, P. (1998). 'World English: convergence or divergence?' In: H. Lindqvist, S. Klintborg, M. Levin & M. Estling (eds.), *The major varieties of English.* Växjö University: Acta Wexionensis. 29-36.

Trudgill, P. (1999). *The dialects of England.* 2nd ed. Oxford: Blackwell.

Trudgill, P., E. Gordon, G. Lewis & M. Maclagan (2000). 'The role of drift in the formation of Southern Hemisphere Englishes: some New Zealand evidence'. *Diachronica* (17.1) 111-138.

Trudgill, P. & J. Hannah (2002). *International English.* 4th edition. London: Edward Arnold.

Wells, J. C. (1982). *Accents of English.* Cambridge: Cambridge University Press.

RICHARD MATTHEWS

English vowel phonology and the quest for the 'fourth dimension'

In an ideal linguistic world, the pursuit of language study would include and integrate everything that is relevant to language. The latter half of the last century, however, was marked by the increasing fragmentation and specialization of the subject, and this was particularly evident in the development of the phonetic aspect of language study. Phonetics was increasingly pushed out or fell out of linguistics departments and, even worse, out of the linguistics curriculum. Phonetics and phonology became two distinct disciplines, whose respective practitioners often took little cognizance of each others' work. The fact that Ladefoged felt it necessary to use, if indeed he did not coin, the term 'linguistic phonetics' as long ago as 1967[1] can only be interpreted in the light of this development. The dedicatee of this volume is someone who has always believed in the essential integrity of phonetics and linguistics.

This paper will look at the history of one aspect of the description and analysis of English vowels that was a victim of this estrangement of phonetics and phonology. By 'fourth dimension' I mean a fourth dimension (or fourth parameter) in the description and classification of vowels, beyond the three dimensions generally accepted: height, advancement, and rounding. And by 'vowels' I mean those approximants and resonants that form the peak, with or without on- and off-glides, of a syllable; (near) steady state and dynamic syllable peaks, in other words.

---

1   In the preliminary version of his *Preliminaries to Linguistic Phonetics* (1971).

The reason for using the term 'fourth dimension' is that there is something elusive and controversial about it that is reminiscent of the fourth dimension in physics.

Vowel descriptions and classification

Standardly, we generally make use of three dimensions or articulatory parameters: relative height; degree of advancement (or backness); degree of rounding, in that order. Height, first, because languages with simple linear distinctive vowel systems are organized vertically rather than horizontally: e.g.

Kabardian:　　　ɨ ↑　　　　　　　　　cf. Choi (1991)
　　　　　　　　ə
　　　　　　　　ɐ ↓

Cf. non-occurring: *e　　ə　　　o
　　　　　　　　　←―――――――→

Second, advancement (or backness):

Greenland　　　i ←――――→ u　　　cf. O'Connor
Eskimo:　　　　　　↕　　　　　　　　(1973: 216)
　　　　　　　　　　a

Third, rounding:

Turkish:　　　　　　　　　　　　　　　cf. O'Connor
　　　　　　　　　　　　　　　　　　　(1973: 219)

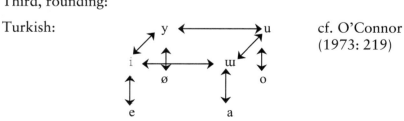

If a language were to maximize all three parameters, and the parameters were calibrated with three degrees for height, two degrees of advancement, two degrees of rounding, we could have maximally twelve vowel distinctions accounted for:

	front		back	
	unround	round	unround	round
high	i	y	ɯ	u
mid	e	ø	ɤ	o
low	æ	œ	a	ɔ

Table 1: Maximal 3 × 2 × 2 system

This configuration looks surprisingly like that of Chomsky & Halle (1968) without the putative fourth dimension of 'tense vs. lax'. In their symbolization, this looks like:

	front		back	
	unround	round	unround	round
high	i	ü	ɨ	u
mid	e	ö	ʌ	o
low	æ	œ	a	ɔ

Table 2: Chomsky & Halle's (1968) vowel system

Increase the number of degrees of height and advancement by one each, and we get 24 distinctions:

	front		central		back	
	unround	round	unround	round	unround	round
close	i	y	ɨ	ʉ	ɯ	u
close-mid	e	ø	ə	ɵ	ɤ	o
open-mid	ɛ	œ	ɜ	ɞ	ʌ	ɔ
open	æ	Œ	ä	ö	ɑ	ɒ

Table 3: Maximal 4 × 4 × 2 system

This is a system for which the IPA alphabet barely has enough symbols.[2] But languages do not maximize such potential distinctions. Though English has fewer than 24 full tonic vowel distinctions, it can maximally be analyzed with 3 contrastive heights; the extended advancement parameter is only partially exploited (central /ɜː/ and /ʌ/); and the roundedness one hardly at all (default values of back vowels). This means that we need another parameter. If so, what are its phonetic bases? Traditionally and popularly, length, a phonatory factor, has been invoked. But length only poorly includes diphthongs, of which English has several; it is also only part of the story.

Though the durational difference between /ɪ/ and /iː/ in the same environment, for example, 'pit' and 'peat' is of the order of 1 : 1·5, that is arguably 'short vs. half-long' in IPA terms; before a voiced final, it is more like 1 : 2, i.e. 'short vs. long'.[3] Even if we can explain the objective, but not distinctive length difference between /ɪ/ and /æ/ in the same environment, for example, 'pit' and 'pat', something of the order of 1 : 1·6 as a consequence of

2   I have used here the vowel symbols of the 1996 correction of the 1993 chart, except that /æ/ has been placed as fully open, and /ä/ has been used for a fully open central vowel.

3   The ratios cited here are extrapolated from the figures reported in Gimson (1980: 98).

greater aperture, there is still the qualitative distinction between /ɪ/ and /i/ to be explained. Chomsky & Halle in *The Sound Pattern of English* took the qualitative distinction to be more significant than the quantitative,[4] and availed themselves of the parameter of 'tension' for this purpose from the 19th century tradition of phonological analysis of standard German.

The fourth dimension and beyond

Sweet, Sievers and others in the latter half of the 19th century modified a dimension proposed by Alexander Bell of 'primary' vs. 'wide'. Bell's distinction was poorly defined, but Sweet refined the articulatory description, renamed it 'narrow' vs. 'wide', and suggested it for the observed qualitative distinction between long and short pairs of vowels in German, Northern English and other Germanic languages, but not, notably, southern forms of British English. Sweet's vowel classification would look like Table 4,[5] given a reversal of the front-back dimension (Sweet placed back vowels on the left, and front vowels on the right). Sweet observed:

> [...] in forming narrow sounds, there is a feeling of tenseness in that part of the tongue where the sound is formed, the surface of the tongue being made more convex than its natural "wide" shape, in which it is relaxed

---

4   Kenyon & Knott (1953), Kurath (1964) and Jones (1960) among others all assumed or claimed that quantity was not primarily distinctive in American English. Abercrombie (1967, and elsewhere) developed a transcription that dispensed with the length mark for RP, but it is clear from his work on rhythm that he did not disregard phonetic length.
5   I will not go into the partially related problem of how or even whether vowel articulations should be arranged to iconize the articulatory configurations in the oral tract, be it a quadrilateral like Bell and Sweet's, a trapezium like Passy and the IPA's, or a triangle like Viëtor's.

and flattened. This convexity of the tongue naturally narrows the passage – whence the name. (Sweet 1877)

This important distinction applies to all vowels: every vowel, whatever its position in the scale, must be either narrow (tense) or wide (lax) [...] French i in *fini* and English i in *finny* are both high-front vowels but the former is narrow [i], the latter wide [ɩ]. In passing from [i] to [ɩ] the passage between the front of the tongue and the palate is further narrowed, not by raising the whole body of the tongue, but by altering its shape: in a narrow vowel the tongue is bunched or made convex; in a wide vowel the tongue is relaxed and comparatively flattened. (Sweet 1910: 27-28)

	narrow			wide			
	front	mixed	back	front	mixed	back	
high	i	ï	ʌ	*i*	*ï*	*ʌ*	un-round
mid	e	ë	a	*e*	*ë*	*a*	
low	æ	ä	ɐ	*æ*	*ä*	*ɒ*	
high	y	ü	u	*y*	*ü*	*u*	round
mid	ə	ö	o	*ə*	*ö*	*o*	
low	œ	ö̇	ɔ	*œ*	*ö̇*	*ɔ*	

Table 4: Sweet's 3 × 3 × 2 × 2 system

While not entirely in agreement with Sweet, Jespersen in his *Lehrbuch der Phonetik* (1904) drew a comparable distinction between 'dünn' (thin) and 'breit' (broad).[6] The alternative terms 'tense' and 'lax' were no doubt reinforced by Sievers' 'gespannt' and 'ungespannt'.

---

6   Since his argument and demonstration is relatively involved and does not add much to our overview, I have not quoted it.

Jones, however, did not adopt 'tense' vs. 'lax':

> Those who consider that vowels may be differentiated by degrees of muscular tension distinguish two classes, *tense* vowels and *lax* vowels. [...] The difference in quality between the English vowels of *seat* siːt, and *sit* sit is ascribed by some writers to a difference of tension. [...] It is not by any means certain that this mode of describing the sounds really corresponds to the facts. A description of the short i as a vowel in which the tongue is lowered and retracted from the 'close' position [...] is generally sufficiently accurate for ordinary practical work. [...] It is generally advisable to apply the terms *tense* and *lax* only to the case of close vowels. It is extremely difficult to determine in the case of the opened vowels whether the sensation of 'tenseness' is present or not, and there is in regard to some vowels considerable difference of opinion on the subject. (Jones, [9]1960: 39-40)

Though Passy, who was influential in the formative years of the Association Phonétique Internationale (API), now International Phonetic Association (IPA), was an adherent of such a distinction, it was a Jonesian three-dimensional cardinal vowel system that was ultimately adopted.

On the other hand, Heffner explicitly affirms such a distinction and notes:

> When we examine the evidence for the tongue positions of the vowels we collide with disturbing facts such as E.A. Meyer's demonstration that the elevation of the tongue for [ɪ] is often a good deal less than that for the vowel [e], or the observation of Henry Sweet, that one may produce either the series [i], [e], [æ], or the series [ɪ], [ɛ], [æ] by continuously changing the tongue elevation without producing any of the supposedly 'intervening' vowels of the other series as the tongue is raised or lowered. In short the difference between [ɪ] and [e] or between [e] and [ɛ], or between [i] and [ɪ], is not due merely to the elevation of the tongue. The inviting hypothesis that there are in the several laryngeal articulations three types for each series, front and back, and that the laryngeal articulation, let us say, for the high category is then subject to modification by the tension and position of the tongue into two subtypes [i] and [ɪ], is apparently untenable in the light of Meyer's findings as to the breath consumption or "Luftfüllung" of the various vowels. According to these studies [ɪ] and [ɛ] are produced with a wider glottis and a greater volume of air-flow than are the vowels [i] and [e]. This implies that the subglottal air pressures are less for the [ɪ] and [ɛ] type vowels than for [i] and [e]. However, these facts do permit us to apply the terms open : close or lax : tense to the two groups in

the sense that the glottal opening and air pressures are relatively open and lax for vowels like [ɪ] and [ɛ], while the glottal opening and the air pressures are relatively close and tense for vowels like [i] and [e]. We may retain the old terminology if we shift its reference from tongue elevations and tongue muscle tensions to laryngeal positions and air pressures. [...] We have then not only differences in tongue position but differences in laryngeal behavior which mark the differences in quality between [i] and [ɪ] or between [e] and [ɛ], or between [e] and [ɪ]. [...] Practical phonetics here demands a grouping for which scientific phonetics has thus far failed to produce an adequate basis. (1950: 96-97)

Heffner's extension of the denotation of 'tense' vs. 'lax' to the laryngeal positions is a highly significant one, which I will come back to.

We can differentiate three partially conflicting views on vowel classification:

1) the three-dimensional view (IPA), shown in Figure 1, with height calibrated for 4 degrees. In this, what is termed 'lax' is treated as the lowering and/or centralization of the dorsal posture.

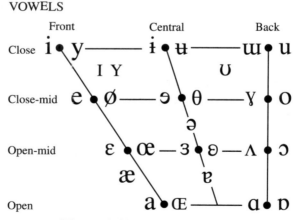

Fig. 1: The IPA's expanded 4 × 3 × 2 system of vowels

2) the three-dimensional view (SIL)[7], as in Table 5 (cf. Smalley 1963: 363), with height calibrated for six degrees. In this, what is termed 'lax' is treated as the lowering but not necessarily centralization of the dorsal posture.

	front		central		back	
	unround	round	unround	round	unround	round
high	i	ü			ɯ	u
lower high	ɪ		ɨ			ʊ
mid	e	ø			ɣ	o
lower mid	ɛ		ə			
low	æ	œ	ʌ			ɔ
lower low	a		ɑ		ɒ	

Table 5: The SIL's 6 × 3 × 2 system of vowels

3) the four-dimensional view (Preliminaries to Speech Analysis/ SPE) with height calibrated for 3 degrees, and 'tense vs. lax' as a parameter for all degrees of height.[8]

---

[7] SIL = Summer Institute of Linguistics. Smalley's chart is taken to be representative of Pike's approach to phonetics. It would also match the kind of chart to be found in Keller (1961). Bloch & Trager (1942) developed a 7 × 3 × 2 system.

[8] It is not, however, claimed that all these actually occur.

	front				back			
	unround		round		unround		round	
	tense	lax	tense	lax	tense	lax	tense	lax
high	ī	i	ǖ	ü	ɨ̄	ɨ	ū	u
mid	ē	e	ȫ	ö	Ā	ʌ	ō	o
low	ǣ	æ	œ̄	œ	ā	a	ɔ̄	ɔ

Table 6: Maximal 3 × 2 × 2 × 2 system

Let us look now at the claims made for 'tense' vs. 'lax' by Jakobson & Halle, bearing in mind that they cite Jones in arguing for 'tense vs. lax', and quote him in such a way as to falsify his intention:

> A tense vowel compared to its lax counterpart is produced with a greater deviation from the neutral position of the vocal tract, i.e. from the position that the vocal tract assumes in producing a very open [æ]; consequently a tense vowel displays a greater deviation from the neutral formant pattern. (Jakobson/Halle (1962), reprinted in Jakobson/Fant/Halle ([4]1963: 57))

> The heightened sub-glottal air pressure in the production of tense vowels is indissolubly paired with a longer duration [...] tense vowels are necessarily lengthened in comparison with the corresponding lax phonemes: Tense vowels have the duration needed for the production of the most clear-cut, optimal vowels; in comparison with them the lax vowels appear as quantitively and qualitively reduced, obscured and deflected from their tense counterpart towards the neutral formant pattern. (ibid.: 58)

> In sum, the production of lax as opposed to tense phonemes involves a lower (vs. a higher) air pressure in the cavity behind the only or main source (i.e. below the vocal cords for the vowels, and behind the point of articulation for the consonants). Furthermore, tense phonemes are produced with more deviation from the neutral, central position than the corresponding lax phonemes: the tense consonants show primarily a longer time interval spent in a position away from neutral, while the tense vowels not only persevere in such a position optimal for the effectuation of a steady, unfolded, unreduced sound but also display a greater deformation in the vocal tract. (ibid.: 60-61)

But Jakobson, Fant & Halle (³1961) say:

> Tense phonemes are articulated with greater distinctness and pressure than the corresponding lax phonemes. The muscular strain affects the tongue, the walls of the vocal tract and the glottis. The higher tension is associated with a greater deformation of the entire vocal tract from its neutral position. This is in agreement with the fact that tense phonemes have a longer duration than their lax counterparts. The acoustic effects due to the greater and less rigidity of the walls remain open to question. (Jakobson, Fant & Halle ³1961: 38)

So while an articulatory-acoustic-auditory definition is attempted by Jakobson & Halle, Jakobson, Fant & Halle equivocate about the acoustic angle. What is more, there are comments on the characterization of 'sharp vs. plain' and 'flat vs. plain' that suggest that size of pharyngeal cavity is not the same thing as the articulatory side of 'tense' and 'lax'.

> The opposition flat vs. plain as a secondary tonality feature of vowels supplements the optimal grave vs. acute opposition by an attenuated grave and/or acute: for instance /u/ and /i/ by /ɨ/ and/or /y/. In a few Caucasian, Nilotic and Hindu languages, a similar attenuation is performed by a dilation of the pharynx (sharpening) for the grave vowels and its contraction (flattening) for the acute vowels. This pharyngeal behavior generates two series of centralized vowels opposed to the back and front vowels respectively, e.g., in Dinka (Anglo-Egyptian Sudan) /ü/ – /u/, /ö/ – /o/; /ɨ/ – /i/, / ĕ/ – /e/... (ibid.: 36)

The *Preliminaries to Speech Analysis* classification of early generative phonology has, then:

1) linked quantity (long vs. short) with quality (tense vs. lax), length being conditioned by tenseness

2) linked tense vowel articulations with tense consonants (fortes), and mutatis mutandis, lax vowels with lenis consonants, by appealing to auditory criteria

3) made claims for the physiological and physical correlates of tense and lax that involve subglottal air pressure and formant dispersion respectively.

Catford (1977) argues at length against the Chomsky, Halle, Jakobson, Fant position, citing evidence that "flaccidity of the walls of the vocal organs produce no effect upon the vowel quality", as noted in Chiba & Kajiyama (1958), demonstrating that "greater deviation from the neutral position", which they take to be [ɛ], for tense vowels is meaningless, though it might work if [ə] were taken as the neutral position, and that putatively lax English [ɪ] can be considerably lengthened under certain prosodic conditions.

He could have cited numerous languages where vowels that would otherwise qualify as lax take part in short-long oppositions: Icelandic: <i> and <u> (cf. <í> and <ú>): /ɪ/ vs. /iː/ and /ʏ/ vs. /ʏː/;[9] High Alemannic, Bärndütsch: <i> vs.<ii> (cf. <y, yy>), <ü> and <u>: /ɪ/ vs./iː/, /ʏ/ vs. /ʏː/, /ʊ/ vs. /uː/; Low Alemannic, Alsatian: <i> vs. <ee> (cf. <y̆, y>), <u> vs. <oo> (cf. <ü, üü> - there is no close back /u/): /ɪ/ vs. /iː/ and /ʊ/ vs. /uː/; and Kaiserstuhl both long and short <í> and <i> e.g. *Díschli* vs. *Schdíil*: /ɪ/ vs. /iː/, cf. *wid* vs. *Schii*: /i/ vs. /iː/.[10] His conclusion:

> It emerges that with respect to vowels the tense/lax parameter is extremely dubious, and that Daniel Jones was probably right to disregard it. There may be differences of tension of various muscles involved in positioning the tongue for vowels, but we are far from knowing enough about these differences to be able to utilize them as a phonetic parameter. In any case, the effective result of such differences can usually be described in terms of tongue-height and/or horizontal position. (Catford, 1977: 207-208)

Ladefoged observes:

> Differences in vowel quality can usually be described in terms of variations in the degrees of height, backness and lip rounding. But in some languages there are differences in vowel quality that cannot be described in these

---

9 In Icelandic, vowel length is in complementary distribution with consonant length, e.g. /–ɪtt/ vs. /–iːt/. In a more abstract phonology, it could be predicted by rule on the basis of syllable structure.
10 On Icelandic: see Árnason (1980), on Bärndütsch and Alsatian: Keller (1961), on Kaiserstuhl: Noth (1993), David Clement (personal communication).

> terms. For example in Twi (a West African language spoken mainly in Ghana) the two sets of vowels that operate in the vowel harmony sets differ mainly in the width of the pharynx. In the one set there are **wide** vowels in which the root of the tongue is drawn forward so that part of the vocal tract in the pharynx is considerably enlarged. In the other set there are **narrow** vowels, in which there is no advancement of the tongue root. (Ladefoged 1975: 203)

> In English there are no pairs of vowels that are distinguished simply by one being wide and the other narrow. But this aspect of vowel quality does operate to some extent in conjunction with variations in vowel height. The high vowels [i] and [u], as in "heed" and "who'd", are wider than the mid high vowels [ɪ] and [ɷ][11], as in "hid" and "hood". The terms tense and lax are sometimes used to describe wide and narrow vowels. As far as the high vowels are concerned, this usage fits in quite well with the way in which we were using these terms to describe English vowels [...] But it is less appropriate for describing the difference between other tense-lax pairs of English vowels. It is best to regard vowel width as a phonetic quality, which is definable in physiological terms. The terms tense-lax may then be retained to specify phonologically determined sets of vowels. In this way the set of vowels that can occur in open syllables may be called the tense vowels, and the set of vowels that can occur before [ŋ] may be called the lax vowels. (ibid.: 204)

It can be seen that Ladefoged tacitly reversed Sweet's terminology: what was narrow (passage) for Sweet is wide (pharynx) for Ladefoged; what was wide (passage) for Sweet becomes narrow (pharynx) for Ladefoged. What was (systematic) phonetic for Sweet, is (abstract) phonological for Ladefoged. Moreover it is clear that the sort of phenomena that Ladefoged is referring to in Twi are comparable to that cited by Jakobson, Fant & Halle for Dinka. In other words, the proposal of ±ATR (Advanced Tongue Root) is not to be taken as being a proposal for Generative Phonology's 'tense vs. lax'. Durand (1990) was, I think, somewhat overhasty in equating 'tense vs. lax' with ±ATR: even Halle & Clements (1983) do not go quite this far. They say only that there might be a link and that the two do not contrast.

---

11   [ɪ] and [ɷ] have now been supplanted by [ɪ] and [ʊ].

> advanced/unadvanced tongue root: [±ATR]. As its name implies, this feature is implemented by drawing the root of the tongue forward, enlarging the pharyngeal cavity and often raising the tongue body as well; [–ATR] sounds do not involve this gesture. ([+ATR] vowels such as [i, u, e, o] vs. [–ATR] vowels such as [ɪ, ʊ, ɛ, ʌ, a].)
>
> tense/lax: [±tense]. Tense vowels are produced with a tongue body or tongue root configuration involving a greater degree of constriction than that found in their lax counterparts; this greater degree of constriction is frequently accompanied by greater length. (Tense vowels vs. lax vowels.) We note that this feature and the last (ATR) are not known to cooccur distinctively in any language and may be variant implementations of a single feature category. (Halle & Clements 1983: 7)

Lindau (1978) argues emphatically against this, seeing her 'expanded', i.e. +ATR, as being distinct from her 'peripheral', i.e. position with respect to the periphery or centre of vowel space.

> It is probably fair to conclude that the tongue root mechanism is not used in any consistent way to distinguish between tense and lax vowels [...] As Stockwell 1973 has noted, the difference is between peripheral and non-peripheral vowels. It is worth noting here that, from an acoustic point of view, the difference between the so-called tense and lax vowels is not the same as the difference between [expanded] and [constricted] vowels. The tense-lax vowels differ on a peripheral-central axis, while the [expanded] and [constricted] vowels differ on a vertical axis of the first formant. (Lindau 1978: 558)

We should bear in mind that ±ATR was proposed to handle languages where, for example: /e/ and /o/ (+ATR) contrast with /ɪ/ and /ʊ/ (–ATR), rather than the Sweetian contrast of /i/ and /u/ (narrow) with /ɪ/ and /ʊ/ (wide), which covers what the IPA otherwise handles by centralization.

This position is underlined by the fact that in its 1989 revision of its chart and principles, the IPA accepted ATR, but by not providing a symbol for it, rejected the 'tense vs. lax' parameter:

> Vowels with contrasts in tongue root advancement (or equivalently pharynx expansion) may be indicated by marking the Advanced Tongue Root vowels with the "tiny T" diacritic rotated 90 degrees clockwise to

indicate advanced tongue root (+ATR), and/or by marking the retracted tongue root (-ATR) with the same diacritic rotated 90 degrees anti-clockwise. Thus [o̘] for a +ATR vowel and [o̙] for a -ATR vowel. [...] Several proposals concerning vowels were rejected. It was decided that: [...] No symbolization for the dimension tense-lax should be recognized. (JIPA 1989, 19:2, p.74)

How, then, has a parameter based on 'narrow vs. wide', alias 'tense vs. lax', come to exclude 'tense vs. lax'? Somewhere conceptualization has shifted significantly. Let us examine how the 'tense vs. lax' definition has evolved:

a) synonymous with narrow vs. wide constriction shape of dorsum   [tongue articulation]

b) sensation of muscular tension in tongue concomitant with 'narrow'   [muscular effort]

c) higher vs. lower sub-glottal (sub-laryngeal) pressure
    [phonation]

d) smaller vs. greater pharyngeal cavity   [root articulation]

It seems to me that the articulatory definitions of 'narrow vs. wide' and +ATR vs. –ATR are compatible, as anterior and posterior concomitants of a set of tongue shapes. This may have something to do with the perception of muscular tension, but not with sub-laryngeal pressure.[12]

We can usefully note Delattre's observations on 'tense vs. lax' from an acoustic perspective:

> Objective measurement of the degree of tension or laxness in the muscles of articulation has not yet been possible. If such a thing exists as a language characteristic, it might correlate with such factors as the proportion of steady-state vs. movement, the speed of movement, the time it

---

12 Pilch (1973) suggests a link between 'gespannt' (tense) and 'scharfem Abglitt' (abrupt off-glide) and between 'entspannt' (lax) and 'weichem Abglitt' (smooth off-glide), but these terms are a reversal of 'tense' and 'lax' as used by Chomsky, Halle, Fant, Jakobson. This may be no more than a physiological concomitant of the quantity distinction.

> takes to pass from fast change to relative steady-state, etc. which can be measured on spectrograms and tested by ear in synthesis. (Delattre 1965: 15)

This, however, relates more to the relative tenseness of articulation within a language as a whole, not as a feature in the classification of vowels.

Even if the tense-lax parameter were upholdable for German, Chomsky & Halle's use of it to distinguish sets such as:

'lax'	ɪ	e	æ		ɒ	ʊ		ʌ
'tense'	aɪ	iː	eɪ	ɑː	juː	əʊ	uː	ɔː	aʊ

involves considerable manipulation of the phonetic facts.

As long ago as the beginning of the last century, Sweet noted in connection with his own 'narrow vs. wide' distinction:

> The E. vowel in *see* varies between the two extremes, [ii] in Sc., Ir., and N.E., and [*ii̯*] in S.E. The latter is a semi-consonantal diphthong [...] It varies greatly, being sometimes almost monophthongic, and only half wide – intermediate between narrow and wide – while in vulgar pronunciation it is broadened more or less in the direction of ei and əi. The vowel in *say, name, vein* varies similarly between the Sc. [ee], the N.E. [e*i̯*], and the S.E. [e*i̯*], which in vulgar speech is broadened in the direction of əi. (Sweet 1910: 28)

He makes comparable comments about the back vowels standardly transcribed today as /uː/ and /əʊ/.

Delattre (1965), Gimson ([3]1980), inter alia, comment on the length of /æ/ compared with other so-called 'short' vowels. There is a tendency for there to be a length difference between British English and American English, but British English also has a subphonemic, syntactically-based difference between nouns and verbs or adjectives: 'lad' shorter than 'sad'. Phenomena like this were noted by Jones long ago, and have been attested for varieties other than RP (cf. Jones [9]1960: 235; Fudge 1977). In American English, 'short-o' is typically [ɑː] and in many varieties has fallen together with the putative 'tense' vowel [ɔː]. This leaves for some forms of American English only /ɪ e ʌ ʊ/ as 'lax' vowels.

Lass (1976) presents a number of arguments against 'tense vs. lax'. The conclusion of his appendix is worth quoting:

> Until there is more evidence for THE FEATURE ITSELF [i.e. tense vs. lax] than proprioceptive intuitions and circular argument from supposed effects; and until there is some genuine evidence, in each relevant case, that 'corresponding pairs' of vowels are indeed pairs, I would prefer to assume that if two vowels differ in length and/or peripherality, then position is what distinguishes them; and if two vowels differ in length, then length is what distinguishes them. And if two vowels differ in both quality and length, it is the job of a thorough phonological analysis of the language in question to decide what kind of structure they are members of. That last decision is certainly not to be left to 'universal' feature inventories. (Lass 1976: 50)

Given this, and numerous more recent statements, about both Southern English and General American, the Chomsky & Halle classification of English vowels is not upholdable. And yet it is amazingly tenacious: Giegerich (1992), for example, despite the advances in metrical and dependency phonology that he espouses, still employs 'tense', and gives the following definition:

> Tense sounds are produced with a deliberate, accurate, maximally distinct gesture that involves considerable muscular effort; nontense sounds are produced rapidly and somewhat indistinctly. Giegerich (1992: 98)

He admits not only that this definition is "somewhat vague", but also that there are problems with the applicability of the contrast to low vowels. Nevertheless, he concludes:

> Weighing up these phonetic problems of the feature [Tense] against its considerable classificatory benefits, we cannot but decide in its favour: as we have seen, the phonological classification of the English vowel system would without the use of this feature be an extremely difficult task. (ibid.: 98)

Both Catford and Ladefoged allow, in their different ways, that the terms can be used as labels for phonological categories. But is this any more defensible? It certainly is not when the inverted comma labelling of theoretical linguistics is taken at its face value and becomes the basis for standard description in language teaching. A description of English /iː/ and /ɪ/ as a close front unrounded pair, 'tense' and 'lax' respectively is not a helpful description.

An obfuscation in sound change

Not only in synchronic terms has Chomsky & Halle's application of 'tense' and 'lax' to English led to obfuscation: it is apparent too in their reconstruction of early New English, which they use to bolster up their claims about rules in the abstract phonology of current English.

Thus in reconstructing Hart's system in their terms, they assume a development from Middle English:

ī >   īy >   ēy   >   ey [13]

i.e. tense (and long) underlying i from ME gives a tense (and long) diphthong which is then shifted (lowered) and then laxed.

Only if one assumes the exclusivity, or universality, of one's system can these processes be upheld. More or less contemporary parallels, Sweet on 19th century southern British English and Wells on 20th century Estuary English, suggest something different – and simpler!

ī >   iy >   ey   [in SPE notation]
or:
iː>   ɪi >   ëi   [in IPA notation]

---

13   This appears to have motivated Roca and Johnson's quirky explanation of English Great Vowel Shift, using IPA notation: [iː → ɪi → eɪ → əɪ → aɪ] (Roca & Johnson 1999: 195, 215-218). Though it does not equate 'tense' and 'long', it does view breaking as the creation of a lax off-glide to a tense peak. This kind of breaking is what one might expect for the creation of diphthongs like: [ie̯] and [uo̯].

Chomsky & Halle state:

> In the absence of evidence either for or against, we shall assume the diphthongized vowels were not laxed at first. (Chomsky & Halle, 1968: 255, fn 8)

This is a footnote that ignores the basis of Jespersen's arguments, which depend on [ei] and [ou] as reflexes of ME [ī] and [ū] not having tense alias long peaks. Such a claim can only be made if 'tense' is indivisible from 'long' – but Hart's own evidence is that ME [ī] and [ū], which were long and may have been tense, developed into [ei] and [ou], the peaks of which were not long in his description. Moreover in Hart's description, the latter contrasts with [ōu] from ME [ou].[14]

I would maintain, therefore, that the SPE approach also created some myths about the diachronic development of English.

Discussion

'Tense vs. lax' in the *Preliminaries to Speech Analysis* approach is an attempt to link articulatory, phonatory, durational and muscular factors to an auditory label. Little apart from the durational seems to be applicable to English. Nor does the ±ATR feature seem to be immediately relevant to English, as a classificatory feature. This does not mean that tense vs. lax as descriptors of typical voice quality in particular languages, cf. Laver's use as a "quasi-permanent muscular setting" might not

---

14   Danielsson (1963) also concluded that Hart's system did not include a systematic long/tense vs. short/lax distinction, in that long [ɛː] (for Chomsky & Halle 'lax') was paired with short [ɛ]. Similarly for back vowels. Of course, Chomsky & Halle could classify long [ɛː] as [ǣ], but what would they then do with [æː] for 'long-a'?

be an appropriate parameter for some languages or groups of speakers. Nor does it mean that certain vowels might not give the physiological perception of 'tensity' or 'laxity'. 'Tense' or 'lax' may or may not be the fourth phonetic dimension that differentiates: [i e y ø u o] as phonetic reference values from [ɪ ë ʏ œ ʊ ɔ̈] in German. Here, too, the quantitative dimension needs to be accommodated in phonological analysis. In English, the sort of label we should be giving the phonological classes of English should come from phonotactics and/or metricality: 'free vs. checked' vowels is one possibility; another is 'free-syllabic vs. closed-syllabic', or even 'autosyllabic vs. non-autosyllabic' (or perhaps episyllabic) for 'tense vs. lax' respectively.

If we look at the history of such a phonotactic-metrical division of the vowels of English, it becomes clear that there have been one or two forebears – apart from those who have spoken simply of short vs. long vowels. None other than Alexander Ellis contemplated a three-way division of English vowels (Kelly 1981), which was influenced in part by Klopstock's analysis of German[15] and perhaps Latham's *Handbook of the English Language*, and was discussed in detail with Isaac Pitman. This foresaw a division between independent alias perfect alias full vowels (in: *neat, date, palm, caught, cur, bone, fool*) and dependent alias imperfect alias stopped vowels (in: *knit, debt, Sam, cot, curry, full*). Independent/perfect/full vowels could appear in both open and closed syllables. The independent/perfect/full vowels were to be subdivided into long (in stressed syllables) and short (in unstressed syllables), e.g. *August* /ˈɔːgəst/ vs. *august* /ɔˈgʌst/ or *Julie* /ˈdʒuːli/ vs. *July* /dʒuˈlaɪ/.[16]

If a phonotactic metrical division of English vowels is adopted, then a division between tonic and atonic vowels must

---

15 Klopstock's distinction was between offen (open) as in *Röhre*, gedehnt (prolonged) as in *schön*, and abgebrochen (truncated) as in *gönnte* (Kelly 1981). This was thus a differentiation between: open syllable vs. closed syllable, long vs. closed syllable, short.
16 These are not exactly Ellis's examples (or Kelly's). I have adapted them to give better (near) minimal pairs.

precede it. In tonic (primary and secondary stressed) syllables, a division has to be made between checked (= stopped/ imperfect/ dependent) syllable peaks, which are 'checked', etc. by a consonant, and free (= full/ perfect/ independent), which may occur in both open and closed syllables. In atonic syllables, the differentiation is purely phonotactic: [i], for example, in open atonic syllables, and [ɪ], for example, in closed atonic syllables. This means that phonologically, we have an initial choice between tonic and atonic vowel peaks; tonic subdivides into closed and open; closed into checked and free. Atonic divides simply into closed and open, and the audible phonetic difference is conditioned by syllable shape.

References

JIPA = Journal of the International Phonetic Association

Abercrombie, D. (1967). *Elements of General Phonetics*. Edinburgh: Edinburgh University Press.
Árnason, K. (1980). *Quantity in Historical Phonology. Icelandic and related cases*. Cambridge: Cambridge University Press.
Bell, A. M. (1867). *Visible Speech – the science of universal alphabets*. London: Simpkin Marshall.
Catford, J. C. (1977). *Fundamental Problems in Phonetics*. Edinburgh: Edinburgh University Press.
Chiba,T. & M. Kajiyama. (1958). *The Vowel: Its Nature and Structure*. Tokyo: Phonetic Society of Japan.
Choi, J. D. (1991). 'An Acoustic Study of the Kabardian Vowels'. In: *JIPA* (21:1) 4 - 12.
Chomsky, N. & M. Halle. (1968). *The Sound Pattern of English*. New York: Harper & Row.
Danielsson, B. (1955). *John Hart's Works on English Orthography and Pronunciation [1551, 1569, 1570]. Part I. Biographical and bibliographical Introductions, Texts and Index Verborum*. (Stockholm Studies in English V). Stockholm: Almqvist & Wiksell.

Danielsson, B. (1963). *John Hart's Works on English Orthography and Pronunciation [1551, 1569, 1570]. Part II. Phonology*. (Stockholm Studies in English XI). Stockholm: Almqvist & Wiksell.

Delattre, P. (1963). 'Voyelles diphthonguées et voyelles pures'. In: *The French Review* 37 (1) 64-76.

Delattre, P. (1965). *Comparing the Phonetic features of English, French, German and Spanish. An Interim Report*. London: Harrap.

Durand, J. (1990). *Generative and Non-Linear Phonology*. London: Longman.

Fischer-Jørgensen. (1990). Intrinsic F_0 in Tense and Lax Vowels with Special Reference to German. In: *Phonetica* (47) 99-140.

Fudge, E. (1997). 'Long and short [æ] in one Southern British speaker's English'. *JIPA* (7) 55-65.

Giegerich, H. J. (1992). *English Phonology. An Introduction*. Cambridge: Cambridge University Press.

Gimson, A. C. (^{3}1980). *An Introduction to the Pronunciation of English*. London: Edward Arnold.

Halle, M. & G. M. Clements (1983). *Problem Book in Phonology: a workbook for introductory courses in linguistics and modern phonology*. Cambridge, Mass.: MIT Press.

Heffner, R-M. S. (1950). *General Phonetics*. Madison: University of Wisconsin Press.

International Phonetic Association. <http://www.arts.gla.ac.uk/IPA/ipa.html>

Jakobson, R. & M. Halle. (1956). *Fundamentals of Language*. The Hague: Mouton.

Jakobson, R., C. G. M. Fant & M. Halle. (^{3}1961, ^{4}1963). *Preliminaries to Speech Analysis. The distinctive features and their correlates*. Cambridge, Mass.: MIT Press.

Jakobson, R. & M. Halle. (1962). 'Tenseness and Laxness'. In: Abercrombie et al. (eds.) *In Honour of Daniel Jones*. London: Longman. Reprinted in: Jakobson, Fant & Halle (1963) 57-61.

Jespersen, O. (1904). *Lehrbuch der Phonetik*. Leipzig: Teubner.

Jespersen, O. (1907). *John Hart's Pronunciation of English (1569 and 1570)*. Heidelberg: C. Winter.

Jones, D. (^{9}1960). *An Outline of English Phonetics*. Cambridge: Heffer.

Keller, R. E. (1961). *German Dialects. Phonology and Morphology with selected texts*. Manchester: Manchester University Press.

Kelly, J. (1981). 'The 1847 Alphabet: an Episode of Phonotypy'. In: R.E. Asher & E. J. A. Henderson (eds.) *Towards a History of Phonetics*. Edinburgh: Edinburgh University Press.

Kenyon, J.S. & T.A. Knott (1953). *A Pronouncing Dictionary of American English*. Springfield, Mass.: Merriam.

Kurath, H. (1964). *A Phonology and Prosody of Modern English*. Heidelberg: C. Winter.

Ladefoged, P. (1971). *Preliminaries to Linguistic Phonetics*. Chicago: University of Chicago Press.

Ladefoged, P. (1975). *A Course in Phonetics*. New York: Harcourt Brace Jovanovich.

Lass, R. (1975). *English Phonology and Phonological Theory*. Cambridge: Cambridge University Press.

Latham, R.G. (1851). *A Handbook of the English Language*. London.

Laver, J. (1980). *The Phonetic Description of Voice Quality*. Cambridge: Cambridge University Press.

Lindau, M. (1978). 'Vowel Features'. *Language* (54) 541-563.

Noth, H. (1993). *Alemannisches Dialektbuch vom Kaiserstuhl und seiner Umgebung*. Freiburg: Schillinger.

O'Connor, J. D. (1973). *Phonetics*. Harmondsworth: Penguin.

Pilch, H. (^{3}1974). *Phonemtheorie. 1. Teil*. Basel: Karger.

Roca, I. & W. Johnson. (1999). *A Course in Phonology*. Oxford: Blackwell.

Sievers, E. (^{5}1901). *Grundzüge der Phonetik - zur Einführung in das Studium der Lautlehre der indogermanischen Sprachen*. Leipzig: Breitkopf & Härtel.

Sweet, H. (1877). *A Handbook of Phonetics*. Oxford: Clarendon.

Sweet, H. (^{2}1910). *The Sounds of English. An Introduction to Phonetics*. Oxford: Clarendon.

Viëtor, W. (^{3}1894). *Elemente der Phonetik des Deutschen, Englischen und Französischen*. Leipzig: Reisland.

Wells, J.C. (2002). *Estuary English*.
<http://www.phon.ucl.ac.uk/home/estuary/home.htm>

ALAN CRUTTENDEN

A two-tone approach to urban North British

In the twentieth century descriptions of British English intonation were dominated by analyses couched within the nuclear tone approach. Beginning at the primary accent (or 'nucleus') in a tone-unit a number of pitch contours ('nuclear tones') were described and associated with different meanings. The descriptions were almost entirely of RP. The number of nuclear tones thus described varied from four to seven. American English, on the other hand, has been dominated by descriptions based on pitch points rather than contours, firstly in terms of four pitch levels (1-2-3-4) and later of two tones (H(igh) and L(ow)); the latter system has been codified as ToBI (Beckman & Ayers 1997). Nevertheless, even in this tradition the attachment of meanings has commonly been to sequences of pitch points (e.g. Ward & Hirschberg 1985), the most important of such sequences beginning at the last pitch accent, which is informally called the nucleus just as in the British tradition.

However there was a much older descriptive framework for English intonation, the 'two-tune' approach, first articulated in Jones (1909) and fully codified in Armstrong & Ward (1926). In these descriptions, contours were divided into two, based on the presence of a final fall or a final rise. There were variations on the two tunes based on special circumstance; in particular emphatic versions of each tune are identified.

The two dominant British and American twentieth century traditions mentioned in the first paragraph can be related (as far as meanings are concerned) to the two-tune tradition by making a basic distinction between falling nuclear tones (which includes high falls and low falls and rise-falls from the British approach, or the absence of a high boundary tone in the ToBI approach) and rising nuclear tones (which includes rises and fall-rises from the British approach, and the presence of a high boundary tone in ToBI).

In Cruttenden (1981, 1986[1997]) I tried to put this basic falling vs. rising tradition into a language universal framework by suggesting that falling tones were universally associated with 'open' meanings and rises with 'closed' meanings. Open meanings cover either or both of textual and interactional incompleteness whereas closed meanings cover the presence of both textual and interactional completeness. In one respect this is seen as a strong universal: no language has only falls for open meanings and rises for closed meanings. But in other respects it is a weak universal, for example, many languages usually have falls at the end of declarative sentences but may have a rise for 'statements with implications' (e.g. English and French) or a language (or a particular regional variety of a language) may have a complete absence of rises but make a difference comparable to fall vs. rise by the use of a rise ending mid or a rise ending high (e.g. Belfast English).

Mancunian

Bearing this background in mind I now turn to the presentation of some data on Mancunian intonation. The data were gathered from the interactions between two pairs of informants, all born in Salford in the region of Greater Manchester. The intonation could therefore be more precisely called Salford intonation, though I take East Manchester including Salford to have the most remarkable intonational variety in Manchester. The data is elaborated on further in Cruttenden (2001) where details of the informants and technical details can be found.

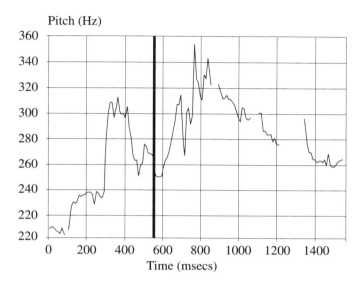

Fig. 1: Rise-slump (7 syllables):
'And he did and then he become a Christian.'

In this data 85% of the nuclear tones are accounted for by four contours: rise-slump (illustrated Fig. 1), slump (Fig. 2), rise-level (Fig. 3) and fall-level (Fig. 4). Rise-slump involves a rise followed by a slight descent to not lower than a mid pitch, slump involves the slight descent without the preceding rise while in the rise-level the slump is replaced by a high level. The fall-level involves a long fall followed by a low level; this tone is unlike the falling tones described for RP in that the level is strongly maintained with no hint of a drift downward or a diminution of loudness.

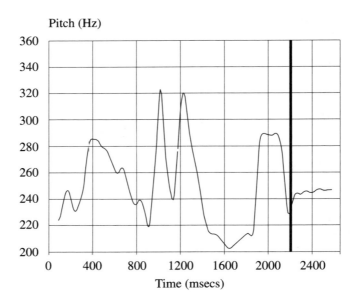

Fig. 2: Rise-level:
'But three floors were absolutely destroyed <u>anyway</u>'.

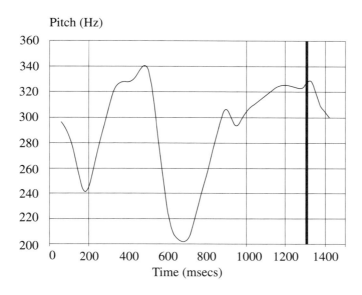

Fig. 3: Slump:
'They were here last <u>night</u>'.

Typical usage divides these tones into two groups. Rise-slump, slump and rise-level (Group A) are variations used for 'closed meanings' e.g. unmarked declaratives, *wh*-interrogatives and imperatives, and aggressive *yes/no*-interrogatives. Fall-level (Group B) is used for 'open' meanings, e.g. unmarked *yes/no*-interrogatives, declaratives with implications, softened *wh*-interrogatives and imperatives (i.e. requests). It is apparent that Mancunian Group A equates in its meanings with RP fall and Mancunian Group B with RP rise. The basic paradox to be explained is how does a rise-plateau (a major variant of Group A) equate with a fall; and fall-plateau (the only variant in Group B) with a rise? The next section attempts to set and answer this question within the more general background of tonal perception.

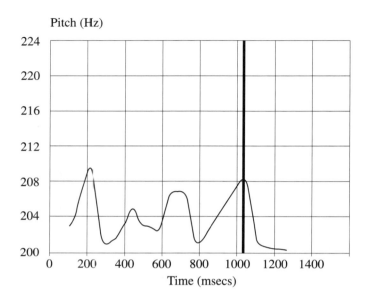

Fig. 4: Fall-level:
'*She's so caught up in other <u>things</u>*'.

Tonal Perception

There has been much discussion of how pitch height is perceived, e.g. linearly (and acoustically) in Hz, logarithmically (and musically) in semitones, or psychoacoustically in scales like Mels, Barks, or ERB rate but almost no experimentation about the perception of falls, rises and levels, particularly where these occur in sequence. What one would like to know about in the present context is how levels are perceived following rises and falls.

Alan Cruttenden 99

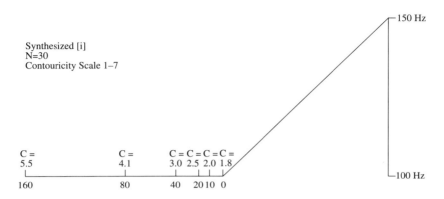

Fig. 5: Contouricity judgements (C) for 90 msec rising contour following variable durations, where 1 = Level and 7 = 'really steep'. (Adapted from Greenberg & Zee 1979)

A perceptual experiment was carried out by Greenberg & Zee (1979) on the perception of a rising F0 following a level F0 ('contouricity judgements'). Subjects were asked to say how steep (on a 7-pt scale) they judged a rise to be following different durations of level F0. The results are shown in Fig. 5 (taken from Greenberg & Zee). It is clear that the perception of a rise varies according to what precedes; at the extremes the rise is judged as having a steepness of 5.5 following a level tone of 160 msecs while judged to have a steepness of only 2.0 following 10 msecs. This is only very indirectly relevant to the (potential) judgement or interpretation of the reverse, i.e. a level on 'fist' following a rise. But it at least shows that our judgements about contours may depend on what surrounds them.

A somewhat more direct piece of evidence concerns the realisation of an intonational-phrase final fall-rise in English. Figs 6-10 show F0 traces of myself reading the sentences 'I saw the **wheel**', 'I saw his **will**', 'I've had my **fill**', 'That was a very big **feast**', 'You've got a very big **fist**', with a final fall-rise on the final word. The tracings show the rising part of the fall-rise becoming less and less and on 'fist' almost flat; yet all were read with the same 'tune'. Evidently a fall-level in this case has equal status to a fall-rise.

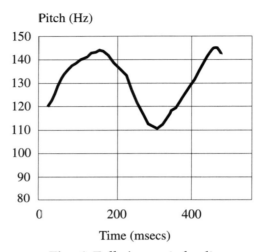

Fig. 6: Fall-rise on 'wheel'

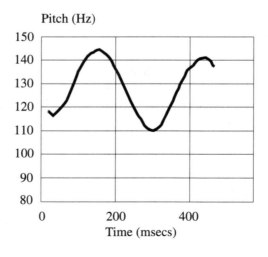

Fig. 7: Fall-rise on 'will'

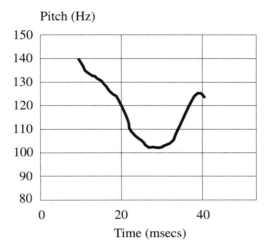

Fig. 8: Fall-rise on 'fill'

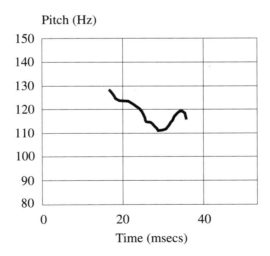

Fig. 9: Fall-rise on 'feast'

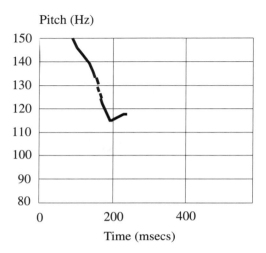

Fig. 10: Fall-rise on 'fist'

A third piece of evidence concerns the so-called 'calling contour'. The calling contour involves a sequence of a high level followed by mid level (often the distance between the two musically around an interval of a minor third). I use a raised equals symbol to represent this contour, e.g. ⁼. Ladd (1978) termed it a 'stylized' intonation, 'stylized' because it was taken to be a stylized version of a simple falling tone. But semantically the contour is closer to the falling-rising tone. So calling someone (who is either some distance away or, if nearby, is not paying attention to you) is more likely to have a fall-rise than a fall, e.g. √Anne rather than) Anne and hence related to ⁼Anne; similarly a warning or a tease with the stylized tone, e.g. *Be ⁼careful, You've got a hole in your ⁼trousers*, seem more related in meaning to the fall-rise rather than the fall. Despite the fact that intonational meaning on its own provides only tenuous evidence for formal similarity or for intonational representation, together with the previous evidence it does suggest that a high pitch followed by a a lower level pitch is, at a higher semantico-perceptual level, more closely related to the fall-rise.

So the general suggestion about tonal perception is that a fall followed by a level (as in Mancunian) is a variant of fall-rise and hence corresponds to the rising group of tones in RP. Similarly the rise followed by level can be interpreted as a variant of rise-fall.

Cross-Dialectal Base Forms: Mancunian and RP

The base cross-dialectal closed tone can now be set up as a rise-fall. RP regularly deletes the rising part of this rise-fall. Mancunian, on the other hand, either truncates the falling part or replaces the falling part by a level (high) plateau. The base cross-dialectal open tone is set up as fall-rise; RP optionally deletes the falling part. Mancunian, on the other hand, replaces the rising part by a low level pitch. Within each dialect there are less frequent variations; in particular Mancunian may combine the plateau and the slump to produce a rise-plateau-slump.

Among other urban north British dialects, the broad dialect of Liverpool, 'Scouse', is reported as having similar tones to Mancunian. Knowles (1975, 1978) reports two common tones, the 'step', which is similar to the Mancunian rise-level, used for 'completeness' (i.e. the closed tone) and the 'drop', similar to the fall-level, used for incompleteness (i.e. the open tone). Northern Ireland, as represented by Belfast and Derry (Jarman & Cruttenden 1976, McElholm 1986), commonly deletes the falling part from the cross-dialectal base rise-fall, leaving a simple rise as the closed tone; and also deletes the falling part from the cross-dialectal base fall-rise, leaving a simple rise for the open tone also. The difference between the closed and open tones is left to be conveyed by the universal pitch range characteristic whereby open tones have a higher pitch than closed tones. So the distinction between closed and open in Northern Ireland is conveyed by the difference between a low rise and a high rise.

Data from Northern Ireland are also presented in Nolan & Grabe (1997), and in their cross-dialectal comparison with RP they suggest that an 'unmarked' (=closed) rise-plateau and 'marked' rise-plateau-fall (=open) contrast in Northern Ireland. However the only use they detail for the rise-plateau-fall is for confirmation-seeking questions, a usage which for other dialects seems to fall into the 'closed' category. So I am not convinced that the distinction between rise-plateau and rise-plateau-fall is really the basic distinction in Northern Ireland rather than a distinction within the 'closed' category.

Intonational Variation and a Constraint

Thus a fruitful way of viewing inter-dialectal variation in intonation is in terms of two basic tones – similar to the analysis proposed by Jones nearly a hundred years ago (Jones 1909). The proposed framework of 'base' tones plus deleted falling and rising parts at first glance smacks of armchair game-playing. But there is one constraint which limits the complete arbitrariness of such procedures and shows that intonational variation is not as semantically arbitrary as that in segmental phonology. The various variational possibilities plus the constraint are represented in Table 1.

The inter-dialectal base is shown on line 1 and urban north British variants (in Manchester, Liverpool, Northern Ireland and Edinburgh) on lines 2 to 5. RP deletes the first part for both closed and open tones (leaving F vs R), Mancunian levels the second part in each case (leaving RL vs FL), Northern Ireland English deletes the second part from the RF and the first part from the FR (leaving rises for both closed and open tones), Edinburgh (Brown, Currie & Kenworthy 1980) deletes the first part from the RF and the second part from FR (leaving falls for both closed and open tones). What makes this not entirely a game is the constraint on line 6 which would involve deleting the first part from RF and the second part from FR producing rises for closed tones and falls for open tones.

	Closed	Open	Dialectal rule
Base	RF	FR	
RP	F	R	Delete first element
Mancunian	RL	FL	Level second element
NIE	R(F)	(F)R	Delete rising element
Edinburgh	(R)F	F(R)	Delete falling element
Non-occurring	R(F)	F(R)	(Delete second element)

Table 1: Base Forms and dialectal rules

References

Armstrong, L. E. & I. Ward (1926). *Handbook of English intonation.* Leipzig and Berlin: Teubner. Second edition. (1931). Cambridge: Heffer.

Beckman, M. E. & G. M. Ayers (1997). 'Guidelines for ToBI labelling'. <http://ling.ohio-state.edu/phonetics/E_ToBI>.

Brown, G., K. Currie & J. Kenworthy (1980). *Questions of intonation.* London: Croom Helm.

Cruttenden, A. (1981). 'Falls and rises: meanings and universals.' *Journal of Linguistics*, 17, 77-91.

Cruttenden, A. (1986). *Intonation.* Cambridge: Cambridge University Press Second edition (1997).

Cruttenden, A. (2001). 'Mancunian intonation and intonational representation'. *Phonetica*, 58, 53-80.

Greenberg S. & E. Zee (1979). 'On the perception of contour tones'. *UCLA. Working Papers in Phonetics,* 45, 150-7.

Jarman E. & A. Cruttenden (1976). 'Belfast intonation and the myth of the fall'. *Journal of the International Phonetic Association*, 6, 4-12.

Jones, D. (1909). *The pronunciation of English.* Fourth edition (1956). Cambridge: Cambridge University Press.

Knowles, G. (1975). 'Scouse: the urban dialect of Liverpool'. Unpublished Ph.D. thesis, University of Leeds.

Knowles, G. (1978). 'The nature of phonological variables in Scouse'. In: P. Trudgill (ed.), *Sociolinguistic patterns in British English.* London: Edward Arnold.

Ladd, D. R. (1978). 'Stylized intonation'. *Language, 54,* 517-39.

Ladd, D. R. (1996). *Intonational phonology.* Cambridge: Cambridge University Press.

McElholm, D. D. (1986). 'Intonation in Derry English'. In: Kirkwood, H. (ed.), *Studies in Intonation.* Occasional Papers in Linguistics and Language Learning, 11, University of Ulster.

Nolan, F. & Grabe, E. (1997). 'Can 'ToBI' transcribe intonational variation in Britsh English?' In Botinis, A., G. Kouroupetroglou,' & G. Carayiannis (eds.) *Intonation: theory, models and applications. Proceedings of an ESCA Workshop, Athens, September, 1997.* European Speech Science Association.

Ward, G. & J. Hirschberg (1985). 'Implicating uncertainty: the pragmatics of fall-rise intonation'. *Language, 61,* 747-76.

SARAH EBNER

A dynamical systems approach to speech and language

While it cannot (yet) be said that dynamical systems theory is firmly and widely established in mainstream linguistics, neither can it be said to be marginal or negligible. In certain areas of research (especially in speech motor control and articulatory phonology) the theory has led to new insights and new questions to the extent that a so-called paradigm shift, comparable to the rise of generative linguistics in the 1960s, becomes a definite possibility. For this to happen, however, the theory must become far more accessible than it is at present.

The following brief account of dynamical systems is necessarily inadequate, but will hopefully enable the reader to appreciate some of the applications to speech and language that will then be described. The examples are not necessarily representative of the state of the art, but are intended to give some idea of the possibilities both for empirical research and for the development of a dynamical systems theory for speech and language. In some cases earlier research has been re-interpreted from a dynamical systems perspective. In other cases 'dynamically' inspired experiments have tackled old questions in a new way. It is a sign of the growing maturity of the approach that such experiments are backed by a considerable body of theoretical literature.

Although few if any researchers would claim that a dynamical systems approach is appropriate for *all* linguistic questions, nonetheless the holistic nature of the approach is attractive. As further applications are tried it will become clearer where its limits lie.

Dynamical systems

A system consists of components that are related to each other in such a way that they can be viewed collectively as a single entity (Norton 1995). In this sense the concept is commonly applied to both speech and language. The single entity 'language system' can be said to consist of the related components morphology, syntax, semantics and phonology, which can be viewed as (sub-)systems, which themselves consist of (sub-)systems. For example, the phonological system of a language includes a vowel system and a consonant system. The physical speech production system also involves sub-systems, namely the respiratory system, the phonatory system and the articulatory system. A *dynamical* (or *dynamic*) *system* is a system that changes in time. A system that seems fixed or static may well change on a larger time scale. A vowel system, viewed synchronically, may appear static, whereas a diachronic study reveals changes over the centuries. The mathematical theory of dynamical systems can be applied to both perspectives.

The first dynamical systems to be studied were physical systems, ranging from the solar system to mass-spring systems and pendula, all of which can be modelled by differential equations. Most real systems display nonlinearity, and in many cases the appropriate nonlinear equation can be formulated but not solved exactly (Norton 1995). However, even if no exact *quantitative* solution can be found (i.e. no accurate prediction can be made of the position of a variable x at a precise moment of time), *qualitative* techniques of analysis will predict whether x will reach a discrete point or maybe oscillate between two positions (Saltzman 1995). In the former case x is said to be in the *basin of attraction* of a *limit point attractor*. In the latter case x is in the basin of attraction of a *limit cycle (periodic) attractor*. Point attractor dynamics are appropriate, for example, for modelling the lip closure for [b] or [m] whereas the rhythmic babbling of an infant can be modelled by limit cycle attractor dynamics. In each case the lower lip or, alternatively, the lower jaw, can be represented by *x*, whose position and velocity at each point of time can be plotted on a *state space* of appropriate dimension (in this case a plane), forming a timed path (Kelso et al. 1985).[1]

The number of variables involved in the production of a single syllable such as [ba] is vast (Kelso 1995). Nonetheless, thanks to the *self-organization* that is characteristic of dynamical systems, these so-called *degrees of freedom* can be reduced considerably, as muscles combine in *synergies*, which can be seen as functional collectives appropriate for such tasks as bilabial closure.

As the *control parameters* of a system change, new attractors can appear, old attractors can disappear or the comparative strength of competing attractors can alter, in a process of *pattern formation*. These changes are reflected in the observable behaviour of the system, often described in terms of *collective variables* (or *order parameters)*. When the change is abrupt, this is called a *phase transition* (term used in physics) or *bifurcation* (term used in mathematics). For example, when the syllable [ip] is repeated faster and faster (i.e. when speech rate is manipulated as the control parameter), at a certain rate the syllable is heard to switch to [pi]. This coincides with a shift in the collective variable, the relative phase of glottal opening to lip closure (Tuller & Kelso 1990). In pattern formation, the recent history of the system interacts with the changing values of the control parameter to determine behaviour. When the direction of change of the control parameter is reversed, the current behaviour may persist beyond the value that triggered off the original switch. The system is said to display *hysteresis*. "This is another way of saying that several behavioral states may actually *coexist* for the same parameter value; which state you see depends on the *direction* of the parameter change."(Kelso 1995: 21)

---

[1] Limit points and limit cycles are not the only possible attractors. Some dynamical systems display so-called *chaotic* behaviour in which trajectories of the system converge on one of a variety of *chaotic* attractors. Chaos theory is a branch of dynamical systems theory that is developing rapidly and can be applied to speech and language studies where appropriate.

Speech is produced by physical systems, but mathematical dynamical theory is equally capable of modelling the systems that comprise the more abstract language system, as will be seen below. It is therefore important to distinguish between physical systems and mathematical systems.

Modelling speech production

Dynamical systems are an important concept in studies of motor behaviour and control, including the motor control of speech. At the periphery, the set of speech articulators used in producing speech sounds works as a (bio-)physical dynamical system. In so-called 'task dynamics', each speech *gesture*[2] results from the bi-directional coupling of central (predominantly cortical) dynamics and peripheral dynamics. The articulatory synthesizer developed at Haskins Laboratories from the 1980s on (e.g. Kelso et al. 1985, Saltzman 1995) was originally restricted to the simulation of isolated individual gestures, modelled as point attractors at the abstract level of *tract variable* coordinates. Tract variables normally come in pairs, one specifying constriction location, the other specifying constriction degree. For bilabial constrictions such as [b], [p], and [m] the tract variable lip protusion (LP) defines the location while lip aperture (LA) defines the degree of constriction. Each tract variable is associated with a set of model articulators (for LA these are the upper and lower lips and the jaw) that are controlled by the transformation of the tract variable dynamical system into the corresponding articulator

---

2   Following Saltzman & Munhall, the term 'gesture' can be said "to denote a member of a family of functionally equivalent articulatory movement patterns that are actively controlled with reference to a given speech-relevant goal (e.g. a bilabial closure). Thus, in our usage, gesture and movement have different meanings." (1989: 334)

coordinates. The ensuing dynamical system at the articulatory level displays the flexible self-organization described above and can replicate, for example, the immediate compensatory behaviour shown in muscle synergies when one member of the synergy (or *coordinative structure*) is perturbed (Saltzman 1995).

Until recently the modelling of successive, simultaneous and overlapping speech gestures, (i.e. normal speech) could only be achieved by implementing a specially constructed *gestural score*, based on the phonological primitives proposed by articulatory phonology. Using gestural activation coordinates to represent the current strength of each gesture, the gesture is either 'switched on' (maximal influence) or 'switched off' (no influence). In spite of its limitations (no intrinsic dynamics at the intergestural level, simplified on/off activation coordinates), this model successfully simulated the effect of different flanking vowels ([i] vs. [æ]) on the place (but not the degree) of constriction of an intervening alveolar consonant. The recent adoption of Jordan's (1990) recurrent, sequential network architecture will however permit the intrinsic shaping of activation trajectories, with each output node representing a gestural activation coordinate and the value of each node ranging continuously from zero to one, "allowing each gesture's influence over the vocal tract to wax and wane in a smoothly graded fashion." (Saltzman 1995: 167)

Articulatory phonology and phonetics

In dynamical systems theory, self-organization at different levels harnesses large numbers of variables (degrees of freedom) into structures with considerably fewer degrees of freedom. Geometrically, degrees of freedom can be represented by different coordinates on a state space whose dimensions correspond to the number of variables. Hence self-organization reduces a high-dimensional system to a lower-dimensional system. This is a general principle that sets no single level of organization above another (in importance), but nonetheless ensures that a low-dimensional coordinative structure at one level can itself function as one of a set of variables at another level, which set may then self-organize into a coordinative structure at yet another level. In articulatory phonology it is this principle that links phonetics to phonology in a bi-directional fashion, so that "these apparently different domains are, in fact, the low- and high-dimensional descriptions of a single (complex) system" (Browman & Goldstein 1995: 177). The physical possibilities of articulation constrain the phonology (of any language) and the phonology (of a particular language) constrains the phonetic output of its speakers. The gestures described above are the primitives of articulatory phonology.

The origins of phonological systems

Using computer simulations involving interactions between the agents of a population, de Boer (2000, 2001) has demonstrated how a phonological system may arise through self-organization. Universal characteristics of such systems have a functional explanation, summarized by de Boer (2000: 178) as "articulatory ease, acoustic distinctiveness and minimum effort of learning". Nonetheless, optimization is not an individual discovery of the language learner but "must be an emergent property of the interactions in the population" which can be considered to be a complex dynamical system.

In the simulations, populations of agents, equipped with human-like abilities to produce, perceive and learn speech sounds, "learn to imitate each other as successfully as possible with an open system of vowel sounds." (de Boer 2001: 40) Starting with empty sound systems, the agents have a pre-programmed need to imitate. (New sounds have to be added every now and then to get imitation started.) All vowels consist of a prototypical acoustic signal and a prototypical articulatory position. The incoming acoustic signal is compared with the stored acoustic signals (the prototypical sounds), the agent assigning each perceived sound to the nearest prototype (phoneme), which may not be very similar at all initially. Each imitation (using an articulatory synthesizer for greater realism) generates a new acoustic signal, to which noise is added. Through imitation and feedback the agents learn about each other's repertoires of sounds. The more agents who share a system, the more successfully it is imitated. In the course of these imitation games, self-organization ensures that near optimal vowel systems are the ones most commonly produced. "Optimal systems could be considered *attractors* of the dynamic system that is formed by the agents (their perception and their production) and the interactions between the agents." (2001: 43) Although the term attractor cannot be used in its strict mathematical sense here (because vowel systems can and do change) this weaker use of the term is generally accepted (Kelso 1995).

The vowel systems that emerge can be shown in (two-dimensional) acoustic or (three-dimensional) articulatory space. In either case, vowels form clusters, and it is clear that any initial (random) configuration will evolve towards the strongest of a limited set of attractors (de Boer 2001: 127). Random fluctuations (or, presumably, a parameter change) can push the system towards a different attractor (i.e. the phonological system can change).

Simulations involving the appearance and disappearance of agents (representing birth and death) and even incorporating the effects of aging in the population enhance the realism of the simulation. Both in reality and in simulations the vowel systems that result from self-organization in populations of speakers depend not only on the most efficient distribution of vowels in acoustic space but also on the need for an individual speaker/agent to be able to imitate the vowel-prototypes of the majority of the other members of the population, who may have settled on a sub-optimal but good enough system regarding articulation and perception. Such modelling of the origin of phonological systems using the theory of dynamical systems is of interest for the light it casts both on phonology (synchronic and diachronic) and on the dynamics of language as a whole.

Prosody, perception and meaning: disambiguating sentences as a form of categorical perception

It is a well known fact that prosodic cues can disambiguate sentences such as the following example from Raczaszek et al. (1999: 374-5):

Pat or Kate and Bob will come.

Acting on the assumption that the sentence can be seen as consisting of four feet:

1) "Pat or," 2) "Kate and," 3) "Bob will," 4) "come."

the authors took the relative duration of the first two feet as a control parameter in a putative dynamical system. Systematic manipulation of this durational ratio (both vowel and pause length were manipulated) led to the emergence of alternative meanings of the sentence, seen as "stable regions of the dynamics of a perceptual system", (1999: 372) in other words, as competing attractors, leading to a type of categorical perception. The meaning of the sentence is thus seen as a global pattern rather than as a function of "on-line processing of particular local cues" (1999: 389). It is the collective variable (order parameter), whose evolution can be modelled as an equation, "reflecting stability of the percept as a function of the control parameter" (1999: 381). Similar work in perception studies involving visual ambiguities (Kelso et al. 1995) suggests that the categorical perception of [Pat or Kate] vs. [Kate and Bob] may well reflect the underlying dynamics of a general cognitive system rather than a purely linguistic system.

As the control parameter was systematically manipulated in the experiments, the other possible prosodic cues remained in their original state, allowing the authors to ascertain to what extent the order parameter (i.e. the meaning induced by the temporal control parameter) influences the other components of the dynamical system. As predicted by the theory, once a particular meaning has been established, even prosodic cues that would normally bias interpretation in the other direction, can be incorporated in the contrary pattern.

Seeking to justify their claim that the perception of sentence meaning can be treated "in dynamical terms of a pattern formation process" (Raczaszek et al. 1999: 372), the experimenters looked for evidence of multistability (bistability), i.e. for values of the control parameter at which either meaning could be perceived, depending on the context (the recent history of the system). Since four out of the nine subjects showed less clear identification functions (possibly because conflicting cues from the unmanipulated prosodic parameters affected some individuals more than others, reflecting different strategies of perception), only the results of the five other subjects were considered. As predicted, in almost all cases there was a region in which the direction of change in the control parameter determined which meaning prevailed. In most cases this involved hysteresis,[3] as explained above. The effect of context was of course seen most strongly in sequential presentations of the stimuli. However, for those subjects who showed hysteresis, random presentation of stimuli also showed the effect of previous responses. The probability that a certain meaning will be perceived tended to be

---

3   Hysteresis can be seen as the tendency of a system to persist in its present state for as long as possible. The opposite phenomenon, i.e. a tendency of the system to change states as *soon* as possible, was also observed by Raczaszek et al. (1999). Known as *enhanced contrast*, this phenomenon, like hysteresis, reveals the presence of bistability, while hysteresis shows how important recent history (previous judgements) can be. In the experiments carried out by Raczaszek et al. hysteresis was generally more common, with some indications that the readiness to switch shown in enhanced contrast may reflect a more flexible cognitive style in some persons.

greater if the same meaning was perceived in the previous example.

A second experiment, using a similar procedure, recorded the time it took to make each identification. According to the theory, switching from one interpretation to another can be seen as the transition from one stable pattern to another. Before the transition occurs, the first pattern (or attractor) becomes less stable. The attractor and its basin can be visualized as a well that becomes shallower as the attractor loses strength. The theory predicts that the system will take longer to settle in a shallow well, displaying so called *critical slowing down*. As predicted, subjects took longer to respond to examples close to transition points, than to those further away.

Altogether the authors make a strong case for the application of dynamical systems to the perception of meaning in ambiguous sentences. It can be seen that dynamical concepts suggest what the researcher should look for (control parameters, collective variables, attractors, phase transitions, hysteresis, etc.) In order to prove (or at least support) a dynamical hypothesis, the appropriate data has to be collected, processed and interpreted, as was done in this case.

Syntax and semantics

Sentences like the one discussed above are disambiguated when prosodic cues guide the hearer to a particular syntactic bracketing. The hearer's ability to interpret these cues was seen to be of a general cognitive nature. Cognitive science and dynamical systems theory also meet in the work of Petitot, who combines the ideas of cognitive grammar with *morphodynamics*, a dynamical interpretation of syntactic structures based on work by the mathematician, René Thom. Cognitive grammar maintains that syntax and semantics must be understood at the level of the cognitive processes that are involved in the production and understanding of sentences (Petitot 1995, Port & van Gelder 1995). Morphodynamics refers to the dynamic theories of 'morphologies', a morphology being "a system of qualitative discontinuities in a substrate" (Petitot 1995: 231). For example, the attractor landscape of 'sentence meaning', as described above, can be seen as a morphology. The underlying discontinuities (phase transitions or bifurcations) are the meaning switches caused when the control parameter reaches a certain value. Petitot (1995) gives as an example the categorical perception of phonemes.

In a dynamical model of constituent structure, semantic roles are not seen as arbitrarily assigned labels, but can be defined in a configurational way. They appear as attractors in a landscape and the "syntactic relations expressing events of interaction [verbal actions] between them" (Petitot 1995: 231) correspond to bifurcations of the attractors. As stated by Port & van Gelder (1995: 230): "An Agent is an Agent because of the particular place of the corresponding attractor within a specific catastrophic^4 transformation of attractor arrangements or configurations." The set of possible transformations represents the set of (universal) cognitive archetypes of relations between semantic roles, and each "basic elementary and nuclear sentence of natural language [...] is syntactically structured by one of these cognitive archetypes." (1995: 229) The positions attractors take with respect to each other correspond to what Petitot calls 'actants' or 'actantial roles', which can be considered equivalent to case roles such as agent and patient. Thus Petitot's approach accounts for the set of universal types from which natural languages draw their cases.

---

4   A *catastrophe* is a bifurcation that involves the disappearance of an attractor (Abraham & Shaw 1988: 71).

Speech and language acquisition

Motor aspects of speech acquisition have received considerable attention using a dynamical systems approach. Thelen (e.g. 1991) has been especially influential in this area, applying the principles of pattern formation in complex systems to the motor behaviour of speech at a particular (real) time and to the changes that occur in ontogenetic time.

Within a particular set of boundary conditions, certain speech articulations or "movement configurations" (1991: 342) can be viewed as attractors (using the concept in a non-mathematical sense). The stability of these articulations can be explained in terms of energetic efficiency and/or the effects of learning. The changing anatomy of the child's vocal apparatus, as well as practice (vocalizing) and experience (e.g. perception of the ambient language) can and does change the 'geometry' of these attractors. That is, when the value of the control parameter(s) reaches a critical point, a phase transition (phase shift, in Thelen's terminology) takes place.

Following Thelen (1991), the attractor states of a newborn infant are determined almost entirely by the intrinsic dynamics of its neuromuscular and physiological systems, although some pre-natal influence from the environment must be assumed. These attractor states remain stable until environmental demands of a social and physical nature, interacting with the (changing) intrinsic dynamics, cause changes in the attractor landscape. Each stage-like change in pre-linguistic vocal behaviour[5] can be seen as a phase shift. Changes in anatomy and in the control of movement lead to spontaneous organization and reorganization of oral structures, especially at the expansion stage, so that one can talk of 'multistability'. The more linguistic dynamics of babbling

---

5   Neo-natal 'comfort sounds' are followed by 'gooing', expansion of sound repertoire, canonical (non-variegated) babbling and variegated babbling.

emerge as the intrinsic dynamics of the system interact with the linguistic environment.

The development of categorical perception can be expressed in terms of the development of stable phonological attractors. Of all the syllabic categories that babies have experienced, [ma], [ba] and [da] are the simplest to articulate, so that the rhythmic repetition of such syllables can be seen as "the energetically least costly attractor state" (Thelen 1991: 355) for the child's speech production system. Thelen suggests that the organization of babbling resembles the underlying organization of adult speech, which she takes to be a cyclic (periodic) attractor.

Moving to the [more abstract] field of language acquisition, van Geert (1993, 1995) has studied the growth of the lexicon and the early stages of the growth of syntax using various forms of a dynamical equation, the so-called 'logistic growth' equation. Linguistic growth cannot take place without resources. These resources are reminiscent of the boundary conditions given by Thelen for the emergence of speech sound attractors. The internal resources of the child include the mental capacity to remember, seen as an "internal spatial resource" (1995: 314) and the necessary time for learning (seen as an internal temporal resource). Other internal resources are of an informational nature, e.g. "knowledge of conceptual categories and event structure" (1995: 314), and resources of motivation and energy. The child must also have a normal sensory capacity. The environmental resources of the learner can also be divided into spatial and temporal resources (how much space and time is given to the child), informational resources, (e.g. the lexicon to which the child is exposed) and motivational resources (such as encouragement and reinforcement). General material resources complete the set.

These resources are on the one hand limited and on the other hand linked as a dynamical system. If one resource is lacking, it can be compensated for by another. At the same time, the sum of the available resources determines the *carrying capacity* of a particular component of the cognitive system. Carrying capacity can be seen as an attractor. This might be the maximum possible number of words in the lexicon at a certain stage of development.

Any growth level below carrying capacity is unstable and leads to further growth towards equilibrium (more words are acquired). A growth level above carrying capacity leads to oscillations around the equilibrium level. For example, boredom with the task of learning words may lead the child to devote his/her attention to another task, such as the acquisition of syntax. Once syntax has lost its attraction, the pendulum may swing back to lexical acquisition.

For forms of language growth such as the acquisition of inflections or syntax, use of the logistic growth equation has shown "characteristic chaotic fluctuation over a trend of overall increase" (van Geert 1995: 320) in individual children. However, (phase) transitions, such as the sudden acquisition of verbs or the use of function words, are not captured by the standard logistic growth equation. In a *transition* model, van Geert adds the assumption that "the growth rate r itself is a function of the growth level" (1995: 326). In the terminology used above, the growth level (or better, the effort by the child or the carer that leads to the achievement of the necessary growth level) acts as a control parameter. When it reaches a critical value, i.e when the "seed" of the necessary information or knowledge has been acquired,[6] new linguistic behaviour (a new attractor?) suddenly appears. The transition model can be extended to deal with random occurrences, for example encounters with situations that further learning.

---

6   As van Geert (1995: 314) says: "It is trivial that there must be something that can grow (e.g. a cauliflower seed, or at least a minimal lexicon) in order for growth to occur."

Further applications

Dynamical systems theory could be applied and has been applied to many other areas, e.g. the origins and evolution of language, pidginisation and creolisation, syntactic parsing, and of course many aspects of speech production. Although this approach is considered to be incompatible with traditional, symbol processing computational linguistics, the artificial neural networks used in connectionist computation are themselves "typically continuous nonlinear dynamical systems" (van Gelder & Port 1995: 32), and are frequently used for dynamical modelling. This has implications for computational linguistics.

On a more speculative note, one rather wide area that seems suitable for a dynamical systems approach is stress shift, seen as a synchronic and a diachronic phenomenon that may be of a linguistic nature, a phonetic (production-oriented) nature or a perceptual nature. The full-vowelled syllables that compete for lexical stress in a word like *thirteen* can be seen as the attractors in a bistable system. Finding the appropriate control parameter(s) and collective variable(s) will no doubt depend on the nature of the system.

Conclusion

What can a dynamical systems approach achieve in speech and language studies? In the first place, it appears to offer a new basis for observation. Some of the dynamical properties that can be observed were described above, e.g. oscillations, chaotic behaviour, resistance to perturbation, hysteresis. With or without a precise data series, the behaviour of the observed system can be compared to a known mathematical system with similar qualitative behaviour. In so far as the two systems match each other, insight can be gained into the nature of the system under study, i.e. qualitative predictions can be made and tested. Even if there is no appropriate mathematical model available, adopting a dynamical perspective can guide research methods in a fruitful manner (Port & van Gelder 1995). For speech and language studies this means laying more emphasis on performance factors. So-called noise is necessary and desirable! Random fluctuations in the parameters are a source of change in a self-organizing system. The concept of self-organization, as seen for example in de Boer's work, is also a tremendous tool for testing claims of *innateness* for specific language universals. Structures that can emerge from self-organizing interactions in a population are presumably not innate.

Dynamical systems theory has a comparatively long history, starting in the 17th century, and a tremendous range of application in contemporary science, including physics, chemistry, biology, ecology, sociology, economics, psychology and child development. This means that fairly recent developments, including dynamical theories of speech and language, can call upon a wealth of past and present experience in other fields, leading to a rapid increase in knowledge of how linguistic systems function in time. Recognizing similar processes and structures at different levels leads to a global perspective that can 'home in' on any component of (almost) any size, without losing sight of the whole. This, anyway, is the ideal case. At the same time it furthers a view of linguistics as part of a larger whole and should thus favour interdisciplinary research. This requires more than the superficial adoption of a new vocabulary, although adopting a common vocabulary can certainly help mutual understanding.

The range and depth of linguistic research from a dynamical systems perspective could only be hinted at in these pages, but even the few examples described above show that it is worth the effort to acquire some knowledge of this difficult theory. Only then can one begin to judge the contribution of dynamical systems theory to speech and language studies.

References

Browman, C. P. & L. Goldstein (1995). 'Dynamics and articulatory phonology'. In: Port & van Gelder (eds.), 175-193.

de Boer, B. (2000). 'Emergence of sound systems through self-organisation'. In: Knight et al. (eds.), 177-198.

de Boer, B. (2001). *The origins of vowel systems*. Oxford: Oxford University Press.

Jeannerod, M. (ed.) (1990). *Attention and performance XIII: motor representation and control*. Hillsdale, NJ: Lawrence Erlbaum.

Jordan, M. I. (1990). 'Motor learning and the degrees of freedom problem'. In: M. Jeannerod (ed.), 796-836.

Kelso, J. A. S. (1995). *Dynamic patterns: the self-organization of brain and behavior*. Cambridge, Massachusetts and London, England: A Bradford Book, The MIT Press.

Kelso, J. A. S., P. Case, T. Holroyd, E. Horvath, J. Raczaszek, B. Tuller & M. Ding (1995). 'Multistability and metastability in perceptual and brain dynamics'. In: Kruse & Stadler (eds.), 159-184.

Kelso, J. A. S., E. Vatikiotis-Bateson, E. L. Saltzman & B. Kay (1985). 'A qualitative dynamic analysis of reiterant speech production: phase portraits, kinematics, and dynamic modeling'. *Journal of the Acoustical Society of America* (77) 266-280.

Knight, C., M. Studdert-Kennedy & J. R. Hurford (eds.) (2000). *The evolutionary emergence of language: social function and the origins of linguistic form*. Cambridge: Cambridge University Press.

Krasnegor, N. A., D. M. Rumbaugh, R. L. Schiefelbusch & M. Studdert-Kennedy, (eds.) (1991). *Biological and behavioral determinants of language development*. Hillsdale, NJ: Lawrence Erlbaum.

Kruse, P. & M. Stadler (eds.) (1995). *Ambiguity in mind and nature: multistable cognitive phenomena*. Berlin: Springer.

Norton, A. (1995). 'Dynamics: an introduction'. In: Port & van Gelder (eds.), 45-68.

Petitot, J. (1995). 'Morphodynamics and attractor syntax: constituency in visual perception and cognitive grammar'. In: Port & van Gelder (eds), 227-281.

Port, R. F. & T. van Gelder (eds.) (1995). *Mind as motion: explorations in the dynamics of cognition*. Cambridge (Mass): The MIT Press.

Raczaszek, J., B. Tuller, L. P. Shapiro, P. Case & S. Kelso (1999). 'Categorization of ambiguous sentences as a function of a changing prosodic parameter: a dynamical approach'. *Journal of Psycholinguistic Research*, 28 (4), 367-393.

Saltzman, E. L. (1995). 'Dynamics and coordinate systems in skilled sensorimotor activity'. In: Port & van Gelder (eds.), 149-173.

Saltzman, E. L. & K. G. Munhall (1989). 'A dynamical approach to gestural patterning in speech production'. *Ecological Psychology*, 1 (4), 333-382.

Smith, L. B. & E. Thelen (eds.) (1993). *A dynamic systems approach to development: applications.* Cambridge (Mass): MIT Press.

Thelen, E. (1991). 'Motor aspects of emergent speech: a dynamic approach'. In: Krasnegor et al. (eds.), 339-362.

Tuller, B. & J.A. S. Kelso (1990). 'Phase transitions in speech production and their perceptual consequences'. In: Jeannerod (ed.), 429-452.

van Geert, P. (1993). 'A dynamic systems model of cognitive growth: competition and support under limited resource conditions'. In: Smith & Thelen (eds.), 265-331.

van Geert, P. (1995). 'Growth dynamics in development'. In: Port & van Gelder (eds.), 313-337.

van Gelder, T. & R. F. Port (1995). 'It's about time: an overview of the dynamical approach to cognition'. In: Port & van Gelder (eds.), 1-43.

MARTIN DURRELL

From regularity to irregularity in morphology: *Ablaut* in the West Germanic Languages[1]

Proto-Germanic had two major inflectional classes of the verb, which are still apparent in the modern Germanic languages. The 'strong' verbs mark tense through vocalic alternations going back to Indo-European *Ablaut* (English *sing - sang - sung*; German *singen - sang - gesungen*), whereas the 'weak' verbs show by a suffix including a dental consonant (English *open - opened*; German *öffnen - öffnete*). The development of *Ablaut* from Proto-Germanic to the modern West Germanic languages is of interest because it provides an example of what we might call 'deregularization' – the development from a (relatively) regular set of morphological alternations to the characteristic irregularity found in the modern languages. This development shows different patterns in the various West Germanic languages and dialects which provides important evidence about the nature and function of morphological irregularity. In recent years these data have moved into the forefront of linguistic theory, not least through the account of some aspects of the development in English in Pinker (1999), and my aim here is to consider this and other recent approaches in the light of data from a wider range of West Germanic languages and dialects, following on from the account

---

1   An earlier version of this contribution was read to the Classics Faculty, University of Cambridge, in February 2000. I must acknowledge my gratitude to Geoff Horrocks for the invitation to Cambridge, and to him and those present for their helpful suggestions. I am also grateful to Jim Blevins and Harald Clahsen for their comments. It is offered with thanks to David Allerton, who first introduced me to historical and comparative linguistics.

in Durrell (2001), and sketching some of the possible implications for competing theories of irregularity in inflectional morphology.

Competing theoretical approaches

Approaches to morphological irregularity can be summarised initially in terms of the competing extremes outlined by Pinker (1999: 96-100) or Sánchez Miret et al. (1997: 149-150). In one view, morphological alternation is primarily rule-governed and assumes that we can formulate write rules to account for inflection except for a small (and by implication insignificant) residue. This assumption underlies most accounts within the phonological component of a generative model, exemplified, for instance, by Halle & Mohanan's (1985) account of the strong verbs in modern English or Wurzel's (1970) analysis of German. Alternatively, all inflectional word-forms, irregular or not, are seen as stored independently in the lexicon. Such an assumption, whereby all inflection, regular and irregular, is treated as reflecting the same mechanism, has become widespread in recent years within so-called 'connectionist' models; independent forms may be linked in networks which exhibit recurring patterns, but any regularities are ultimately derived. Examples of this are Rumelhart & McClelland's (1987) account of English verbs, and further instances are reviewed in Sánchez Miret et al. (1997). A synthesis of these approaches is provided by the so-called 'dual-mechanism' model, propounded in particular by Pinker (1999) on the basis of earlier work since the late 1980s. This distinguishes between 'regular' inflections, with forms derived by the operation of rules (the English or German 'weak' verbs) and 'irregular' inflection, which may utilise connectionist strategies between independently stored word-forms.

Modern English and German

The situation in modern English and German seems to be fatal for any assumption that vocalic alternations are purely rule-governed. There have been numerous attempts to analyse English and German strong verbs in such terms, and all of them have serious drawbacks. Within the class of strong verbs the vowel alternations do not reflect natural phonological processes, and any link between them and the phonological environment is ultimately arbitrary, as shown in Durrell (2001: 6-8). To take an example from German, verbs with [a(ː)] in the present may have [i(ː)] or [uː] in the past, e.g.:

Present	Past	Past Participle	
fangen	fing	gefangen	*catch*
halten	hielt	gehalten	*hold*
schlafen	schlief	geschlafen	*sleep*
fahren	fuhr	gefahren	*go*
wachsen	wuchs	gewachsen	*grow*

Table 1: Modern German strong verbs in -*a*-

It is possible, as Barbour (1982: 339) does, to specify whether the past tense vowel will be [i(ː)] or [uː] in terms of features of the following consonant, but this solution is *ad hoc*, since no phonological feature of the consonants involved can be associated in any significant way with the selection of vowel in the past tense. The possible exception is the selection of short [ɪ] before the velar nasal, as that does reflect a phonological regularity of German. However, this rule only captures a single verb, i.e. *fangen*. The vowel alternations in modern German or English strong verbs are not phonologically motivated, but arbitrary, occurring solely as exponents of the morphosyntactic property

{PAST}, and it is inappropriate to state them in phonological terms at all.

A possible alternative approach could entail accepting that, for example, English *sing* has the stem forms *sing – sang – sung* which are located in the lexicon. But how that can be achieved is controversial. Lieber (1981) proposed that strong verb forms should be represented in the lexicon as whole word-forms rather than being derived by the operation of phonological rules on an invariant base form. Wiese (1996: 132) takes a similar view, and proposes the following lexical entry for the typical German strong verb *trinken* 'drink':

(a) /trɪnk/$_{[V]}$ (b) /trank/$_{[V, +past]}$ (c) /trʊnk/$_{[V, +part]}$

This implies that the various stem-forms are stored and learnt separately and that, essentially, the stem forms are suppletive. However, we might, following Bittner (1988), see these alternations as rather different to 'classic' suppletion, as in English *go – went*, where parts of the paradigm are formed from wholly unrelated roots. In a typical strong verb like English *sing – sang – sung*, the distinction between present and past is located precisely in the alternation of the vowels, and these alternations typically recur in a number of verbs. As Pinker (1999) shows, this situation is in no way incompatible with a connectionist view or the 'dual mechanism', reflecting the fact that these forms might be learned and stored as distinct units.

Against a lexis-based account, though, there is evidence that speakers do not just store independent forms, but that they have access to the recurrent vowel changes as whole sets. This points to a rather different solution which is possibly not compatible with connectionist models, i.e. to see the stem allomorphs with their vowels as operating within sets of paradigms organised into inflectional classes, and that the relevant verbs are stored in the lexicon with an indication of their inflectional class, which is constituted specifically by the relevant sets of vocalic alternations. It would seem at least desirable to explore the possibility of capturing all available generalisations by identifying, for instance, German *bleiben* 'stay', *greifen* 'grasp' or *steigen* 'ascend' as members of the same set, so that we only need to state the set of vowel alternations [aɪ – i(ː) – i(ː)] in the three stem forms (present, past tense and past participle) once rather than separately for each of the forty verbs which manifest this alternation. Typical lexical entries would look like the following:

bleiben	[aɪ – i(ː) – i(ː)]	*remain, stay*
greifen	[aɪ – i(ː) – i(ː)]	*grip, grasp*

There is considerable evidence from the diachronic development of *Ablaut* in a number of West Germanic languages which provides evidence for this view, as will be outlined in the following sections.

Gothic

Gothic is, of course, not even a remote ancestor of any West Germanic language, but it exhibits archaic forms and largely reflects the Proto-Germanic patterns of *Ablaut* alternation. The Gothic strong verbs are conventionally divided into seven classes, see Table 2.

These classes reflect the phonological environment of the alternating vowels. For example, Classes I to III continue Indo-European *e*-grade *Ablaut* in the present, *o*-grade in the past singular and zero grade in the past plural and past participle. The differences between them reflect the fact that the alternating vowels were followed in each case by different Indo-European non-obstruents which are vocalised in zero grade: in class I this was a *j*, in class II a *w*, and in class III a nasal or liquid followed by another consonant. The alternations in the other classes are similarly largely predictable from the form of the root syllable (although the Gothic Class VII has reduplication in the past stem, in some verbs accompanied by lengthened grade *Ablaut*), and, as Motsch (1967) showed, the Gothic alternations exhibit a degree of phonological regularity which can be summarised in a small number of coherent phonologial rules. It is thus not implausible that *Ablaut*, as systematised as an exponence of the relevant morpho-syntactic categories, was, at least in Proto-Germanic and earlier individual dialects such as Gothic, simply a matter of phonological rule. Strong verbs could be identified in the infinitive by their characteristic suffix – which differed from that of the of weak verb classes – and the structure of the stressed syllable determined the vowel of the non-present stem-forms.

	Present	Past sg.	Past pl.	Past part.	
I	steigan	staig	stigum	stigans	*ascend*
II	biudan	bauþ	budum	budans	*offer*
III	bindan wairþan	band warþ	bundum waurþum	bundans wairþans	*bind* *become*
IV	niman	nam	nēmum	numans	*take*
V	giban	gaf	gēbum	gibans	*give*
VI	graban	grōf	grōbum	grabans	*dig*
VII	haitan lētan	haihait lailōt	haihaitum lailōtum	haitans lētans	*call* *let*

Table 2: Strong verbs in Gothic

West Germanic

Evidence that speakers have access to vocalic alternations as sets of paradigmatic alternations in specifiable inflectional classes comes from analogical historical developments within the West Germanic languages. Such analogies fall into various types, and all of them throw light in some way on *Ablaut* as a morphological phenomenon. Early West Germanic dialects show similar patterns to Gothic, and it might be maintained that we are still dealing with rule-governed alternations. Old Saxon may serve as a typical example:

	Present	Past sg.	Past pl.	Past subj.	Past part	
I	grīpan	grēp	gripun	gripi	gigripan	*grasp*
II	biodan	bōd	budun	budi	gibodan	*offer*
III	bindan	band	bundun	bundi	gibundan	*bind*
	helpan	halp	hulpun	hulpi	giholpan	*help*
IV	beran	bar	bārun	bāri	giboran	*bear*
V	sehan	sah	sāhun	sāhi	gisehan	*see*
VI	faran	fōr	fōrun	fōri	gifaran	*go*
VII	haldan	hield	hieldun	hieldi	gihaldan	*hold*
	hlōpan	hliop	hliopun	hliopi	gihlōpan	*run*

Table 3: **Strong verbs in Old Saxon**

A common Northwest Germanic innovation is that the class VII verbs no longer have reduplication but a new *Ablaut* in long ē (if the present stem has a front vowels in the) or *eu* (if the present stem has a back vowel), see Vennemann (1994). In West Germanic, these verbs have a variety of vowels in the present stem and the past participle, but ē or *eu* in the past. This development suggests, in principle, that the process has been morphologised within the inflectional classes, i.e. that speakers extended a general rule which was morphological rather than phonological in nature. The selection of vowel does not reflect a general phonological regularity – the important factor was that there should be a vowel in the past stem which contrasted clearly with that of the non-past stems.

In later languages, these relatively regular patterns were much disrupted by the operation of phonological change, and these irregularities were subjected to analogical processes which re-established a degree of paradigmatic regularity. The most far-reaching of these took place in the middle or early modern period of most of the languages, when the exponence of number through alternation in the vowel of the past tense was eliminated. At the end of this process the past tense had a uniform vowel in most of the languages. These levellings could involve the generalisation of the vowel of the past singular into the past plural stem *or* that of the past plural into the past singular stem. The past participle was also often drawn into the levelling process, and its vowel could spread into the past stem (or vice-versa). Even more interestingly, in those classes where the past subjunctive had an umlauted vowel (i.e. in classes like II and III, where the past stem had a back vowel which could be subjected to the process of umlaut), this umlauted vowel spread in many Low German dialects first into the past plural stem, and subsequently into the past singular stem. An explanation of this development is given in Durrell (1999), and Table 4 exemplifies it for Class III verbs in Middle Low German, before the levelling between the singular and plural stems of the past tense:

Present	Past sg.	Past pl.	Past part.	
binden	bant	bünden/bunden	(ge)bunden	*bind*
helpen	halp	hülpen/hulpen	(ge)hulpen	*help*

Table 4: Class III strong verbs in Middle Low German

The levelling between the singular and plural stems of the past tense took place across nearly all West Germanic, with the exception of the Westphalian dialects of Low German, which, uniquely in West Germanic, retain this number distinction (though often with the characteristic umlaut from the subjunctive in the past plural). A significant feature of this failure of analogical levelling of number in the past tense, together with the complex phonological changes which are characteristic of Westphalian, is that the strong verbs in these dialects are nowadays all effectively isolates in the vowel alternations they manifest, as shown in Durrell (1990). Very few verbs share the same pattern of vocalic alternation in their stem-forms, and it would seem plausible that speakers store the individual forms independently.

Present	Past sg.	Past pl.	Past part.	
kriëgen	kreeg	kriëgen	kriëgen	*get*
flaigen	flaug	flüegen	fluogen	*fly*
finnen	fant	fünnen	funnen	*find*
helpen	halp	hölpen	holpen	*help*
stiärwen	starf	stüörwen	stuorwen	*die*
stiälen	stall	stailen	stuolen	*steal*
giëwen	gaff	gäffen	giëwen	*give*
saien	saog	säögen	saien	*see*
wassen	woss	wössen	wassen	*wash*
slaopen	slaip	slaipen	slaopen	*sleep*

Table 5: Selected strong verbs in Westphalian (dialect of Münster)

The levelling of the number distinction in the past tense affected all other West Germanic languages, but the result of this process is significantly different in all of them. One of the least known and in many ways one of the most interesting is Lëtzebuergesch, where the vowel *-ou-* [oʊ] has been generalised in the past indicative of strong verbs and *-éi-* [eɪ] in the past subjunctive, see Werner (1990) and below, Table 6.

Unlike in any other West Germanic language or dialect, the individual vowels in Lëtzebuergesch appear to have been re-interpreted as having significance in isolation and generalised across a number of verbs. Nevertheless, this analogical regularisation is limited and, as Werner (1990) points out, the regularisation failed to form a stable morphological class. Luxembourg lies very close to a notable morphosyntactic isogloss in the German dialects, south of which the inherited past indicative has been lost. In practice only twelve past indicative forms and eighteen past subjunctive forms are in current use (Bruch 1955: 81). The remaining verbs all have a high token frequency, where irregularity is to be expected, and we might be justified in adducing separate lexical entries for each form. Furthermore, the levelling did not extend to the past participle in Lëtzebuergesch, where the vowels are wholly unpredictable, and there are many more strong verbs which exhibit *Ablaut* in the past participle which have lost their simple past indicative or subjunctive forms, as Keller (1961: 275-76) shows. Nevertheless, we have in the Lëtzebuergesch past tense a unique instance in Germanic of alternating vowels appearing to function as isolated exponents of grammatical meaning.

Present	Past	Past subj.	Past part.	
bleiwen	blouf	bléif	bliwwen	*stay*
gesinn	gesouch	geséich	gesinn	*see*
goën	goung	géing	gaang	*go*
halen	houl	héil	gehal(en)	*hold*
kommen	koum	kéim	komm	*come*

Table 6: Strong verbs in Lëtzebuergesch

High German

It is sometimes assumed that only the weak verbs have formed a productive class in High German in historical times. However, Hempen (1988) and Kühne (1999) show that a number of verbs joined the strong class in the Old and Middle High German periods (i.e. up to 1350). These are typically either wholly new verbs, derivatives, loans or former weak verbs, and Hempen (1988: 194-200) and Kühne (1999) list nearly 50 such verbs.

Most of them were adopted into the most frequent patterns of vocalic alternation: 26 are in Class I (e.g. *pfîfen* 'whistle', *swîgen* 'be silent') and another 15 in Class III (e.g. *glimmen* 'glow', *verderben* 'spoil'). These verbs were probably attracted analogically into strong classes on the basis of the phonological form of their infinitives, and, in the case of the large Class I, this obviously operated on the basis of their root vowel, i.e. Middle High German -*î*- [iː]. As Wurzel (1984: 168-9) pointed out, of the 65 Middle High German verbs with present stems in -CîC-, 50 are strong and only 15 are weak. The phonological shape of the root seems to have provided a basis for the analogical development underlying inflectional class assignment and that, although this has clearly by no means been automatic, we would appear to be dealing here with an inflectional class which has developed a certain degree of 'stability' in Wurzel's terms rather than simply with alternations of a kind akin to suppletion. It would seem that speakers were able to access the sets of ablauting vowels and assigned class membership on the basis of them, working on the relative regularity that 80% of verbs with -*î*- in the present stem belong to the strong class, with the -*î*- of the present stem alternating with -*ei*- in the past singular and -*i*- in the past plural and past participle, as in the examples in Table 7.

	Present	Past sg.	Past pl.	Past part.	
MHG	stîgen	steig	stigen	gestigen	*ascend*
	grîfen	greif	griffen	gegriffen	*grasp*
NHG	steigen	stieg(en)		gestiegen	*ascend*
	greifen	griff(en)		gegriffen	*grasp*

Table 7: Class I strong verbs in Middle and New High German

This analogical extension of *Ablaut* may have occurred at a stage when the strong verbs formed a more coherent set than in modern German, but this is explicitly denied by Hempen (1988: 189). Nevertheless, this extension has been widely ignored, and, indeed, the strong verb classes have not been fully closed even after the restructuring of *Ablaut* in Early New High German, especially, as the material in Theobald (1992) indicates, in substandard or dialectal varieties. Two developments are interesting in this context. First, classes with large numbers of relatively frequent verbs attract new members with an appropriate phonological structure, i.e. one which permits analogy with existing members of the relevant strong verb class. Bittner (1996) lists seven verbs with a present stem in /aɪ/ which join Class I between the fifteenth and the eighteenth centuries, e.g. *schweigen* 'be silent' and *weisen* 'show'. A few other verbs occasionally adopt strong forms, often *either* in the preterite *or* the past participle. For example, the originally weak verb *fragen* 'ask' has a strong past form *frug*, in regional varieties or older forms of standard German, see Dammers et al. (1988: 423-24) and Theobald (1992: 227-30). Since the number of verbs with the *Ablaut* pattern /aː/ - /uː/ (i.e. Class VI) is quite small, the most plausible explanation for this is as a unique lexically based analogy based on the similarity of the root, probably involving the frequent strong verb *tragen* 'carry', rather than, as in the case of *schweigen* and *weisen*, analogy with a large, stable class.

Dutch

Developments in Dutch provide an interesting comparison to High German, because more strong verbs have been retained there and more verbs have become strong since the medieval period than in any other West Germanic language (Ponten 1976). However, there has been considerable reorganisation of the inherited patterns. In modern Dutch, five patterns of vowel alternation account for nearly three-quarters of the 200 strong verbs (Hempen 1988: 284):

	Present	Past	Past part.		
(a)	blijven	bleef	gebleven	*stay*	(48 verbs)
(b)	binden	bond	gebonden	*bind*	(25 verbs)
(c)	duiken	dook	gedoken	*dive*	(20 verbs)
(d)	trekken	trok	getrokken	*pull*	(17 verbs)
(e)	gieten	goot	gegoten	*pour*	(14 verbs)

Table 8: Strong verb classes in Modern Dutch

The simplification of the paradigms through levelling, which here notably involves the past participle as well as the past tense stems, appears simultaneously to have helped to stabilise them, and this may have facilitated further analogical levelling towards these classes. Furthermore, the simplification in the preterite and the past participle of four of these five groups to -o- (whether long [oː] or short [ɔ]) seems to have produced an identifiable pattern which subsequently attracted verbs from other classes and new formations, as would be typical of a regular productive class. This development seems to approach the type exemplified by Lëtzebuergesch, in that a particular set of vowel alternations in the preterite and the past participle may have been identified as marker of non-present categories in isolation.

A further relevant development in Dutch concerns some Middle Dutch Class III verbs with the vowel -e- in the present stem which, following certain phonological changes, also had -e- in the past stem, e.g. Middle Dutch *werpen* 'throw' with the past stem *werp* (Hempen 1988: 241-44, 289-90). This resulted in the tense distinction being no longer clearly marked, and this deficiency was subsequently rectified in a number of ways. The expectation could be that the verbs would simply be attracted into the major productive inflectional class of the weak verbs, but, in practice, of the 37 verbs of this type, only 8 became weak. The remainder were retained as strong verbs, with the largest number (15) adopting the productive $o - o$ alternation (e.g. *bergen – borg – geborgen* 'store'). A further seven, like *werpen*, *helpen* 'help' and *sterven* 'die', took the vowel [i] in the past stem, apparently by analogy with Class VII verbs like *roepen* 'call' (past stem: *riep*). These developments emphasise the non-phonological nature of *Ablaut* alternations in later Germanic. With these verbs, the inherited vowel of the past stem was no longer able to fulfil its morphological function because of phonological changes, and it was simply substituted by another vowel by interparadigmatic analogy from another class. In fact, early modern Dutch shows much uncertainty with these verbs, and all the vowels *e*, *a*, *ie*, *o* and *u* are attested in their past stems at some point before the final selection was made. It is clear that we are not dealing here with a phonological process of any kind; the choice of individual vowel is quite arbitrary, and the only relevant criterion is the establishment of a paradigmatic contrast between the vowel of the past stem with the vowel of the present stem.

English

Aside from Westphalian Low German, the modern English strong verbs are the most difficult of any West Germanic language to classify systematically. As a consequence in particular of the number of conditioned phonological developments in English and the levelling of the past tense and past participle stems the uniformity of the inherited strong verb classes has been disrupted more than in any of the other West Germanic languages. As a consequence, even the originally large Class I, which is still clearly identifiable in Dutch and High German, now only counts six remaining members, e.g. *drive* (Quirk et al. 1985: 110). Furthermore, the identity of the strong verbs as a coherent inflectional class was significantly destabilised by the fact that a large number of originally weak verbs like *read*, *cut* and *meet* have become irregular through phonological changes such as consonant assimilations and vowel shortening (Bammesberger

1984: 78-79). In effect, it is scarcely appropriate in modern English, as it still is in German or Dutch, to adduce two inflectional classes of 'weak' and 'strong' verbs; rather we are dealing with, on the one hand, the great bulk of 'regular' verbs, and on the other a relatively small set of 'irregular' verbs with very few patterns of alternation being found with more than a handful of verbs, as in Westphalian Low German. There has been significant lexical attrition, and a high proportion of originally strong verbs have joined the regular class, so that modern English has notably fewer strong and irregular verbs than German or Dutch, and those which remain are almost exclusively verbs with relatively high token frequencies (Bybee 1985: 120).

Nevertheless, it is not unknown for weak or regular verbs to have become strong in English, too, along similar lines to those we have seen in the other West Germanic languages. Bybee & Moder (1983: 253) show how the *sting* – *stung* class has attracted new members since Old English, and Pinker (1999: 92-96) shows how native speakers of English are able to generalise irregular patterns to novel verbs under experimental conditions. One of the best known of these recent developments is in American English, where the past form *snuck* for *sneak* has entered general usage over the past fifty years or so. Unlike the examples we have seen so far, there is no direct analogy for this development, since no other English verb in [i] has a past in [ʌ]. Neither is an explanation possible for it in terms of Bybee & Moder's (1983) notion of a 'prototypical class member', i.e. a common verb which can serve as the basis for analogy, as we saw with High German *fragen*. Hogg (1988) has seen the deregularisation of *sneak* as explicable through a phonaesthetic process. The vowel [ʌ] of the new past stem has parallels in other verbs with past stem in [ʌ], and a few of these, too, such as *strike - struck* and *stick - stuck* have emerged since early modern times. Indeed, it seems that [ʌ] has spread as a marker of the past and past participle stems, rather like the -o- of Dutch, see Bybee & Moder (1983: 263). According to Hogg (1988), the phonological structure of the root could have facilitated an analogy with *slunk*, *stuck* and similar words to produce what was in origin the facetious form of a colloquial word. Occasional imaginative coinages of this kind with vocalic alternations do occur in speech, and they underlie the results of the experiments reported by Pinker (1999: 92-96, 112-114), and the process described by Hogg has much in common with the notion of connectionist networks. What this development shows is that the principle of signalling tense by vowel change is still potentially productive, as it must have been in the development of the new *Ablaut* in Proto-Germanic Class VI and West Germanic Class VII. The phonology of the vowel selected as an alternant in stem forms is, as we have seen from cases in other languages, ultimately immaterial. However, if the development of such a form can involve phonaesthetic links across the lexicon, including nouns and adjectives as well as verbs, it could be concluded that such past tense stems are stored separately as lexical entries which can be recalled independently of the verb of which they are an inflectional form.

Conclusion

We have seen how the modern West Germanic languages all exhibit various developments of inherited *Ablaut* patterns, and a variety of conclusions may be drawn from these. First, there is counter-evidence to the view that it is appropriate to deal with *Ablaut* as a phonological phenomenon, at least not since the stage exemplified by Gothic. The vowel alternations are arbitrary – what appears to matter above all is that there is simply a different vowel in the present and past stems – and no valid phonological generalisations can be made between the vowels in the various stem forms.

We also saw that, with one exception, we cannot attribute any grammatical meaning to the individual alternating vowels in isolation; the vocalic alternants are as much part of the lexical stem of the verb as they are as exponents of any morphosyntactic property. The exception is Lëtzebuergesch, where certain frequent vowels appear to have been reinterpreted as having such significance and generalised to other verbs. However, this development was fragmentary and appears to have been halted by other developments, notably the loss of the past tense in all but the most frequent verbs. It is possible that the generalisation of -*o*- in the past tense and past participle of Dutch points exemplifies the beginning of a similar development, but questions must be raised about this, since the generalisation was partial and could be due rather to intraparadigmatic analogical processes.

The most important conclusion is perhaps the indication from these analogical developments that speakers treat the forms in different ways. Some may be suppletive and may have been learned in isolation, and, in such cases, it is plausible to suppose that each form may be stored separately in the lexicon. This appears most plausible for Westphalian Low German and English, where individual stem forms could be considered as independent lexical entries, not least because they seem available for plays on words and phonaesthetic developments, as may have happened with English *snuck*. But there is evidence from other analogical developments that speakers have access to more abstract patterns. We can perhaps distinguish two extreme types within the verbs in these languages. On the one hand, there are relatively large and stable classes, particularly in Dutch. In these cases, evidence from analogical processes suggests that speakers classify lexical items in terms of the vowel patterns, and high token frequency is not a necessary condition for membership of these non-regular classes. This conclusion is not incompatible with a connectionist view, or with the 'dual mechanism hypothesis'. On the other hand, we find classes with very few members, like the German verbs in [a(:)], which are now close to being suppletive, and high token frequency is a precondition for their remaining strong. The only instances of weak verbs joining these groups have involved very frequent verbs on the basis of unique lexical analogies, as in the case of German *fragen* 'ask'. Here, again, we may be dealing with separately stored forms.

What we have found in the development of *Ablaut* in West Germanic appears to support the view of a cline of irregularity correlating with token-frequency, though it is unlikely that this is as mechanical or automatic as that proposed by Bittner (1988) but rather a "continuum of regularity from completely predictable to completely arbitrary" such as that proposed by Pinker (1999: 117), since, as Pinker (1999: 92) says "irregular verbs are shot through with patterns". We have, first, wholly regular forms, where the processes through which morphosyntactic properties find exponence are fully predictable, as in the weak verb forms in all the later West Germanic languages, with tense being marked by a regular affixation. The residual strong verbs in Lëtzebuergesch may have been tending towards such regularity, but the process was halted. Secondly, there are more stable groupings, such as German Class I verbs like *steigen* 'ascend' or *greifen* 'grab' or the large Dutch groups. With these, low token-frequency is less liable to lead to attrition, and the frequency of subsequent analogical formations suggest that speakers have access to paradigmatic alternations in terms of vocalic alternants within whole word-forms. These constitute identifiable and relatively stable inflectional classes. Thirdly, there are partially lexicalised alternations, as in English, Westphalian, and the smaller German and Dutch groups. These are unstable in the sense of Wurzel (1984) and subject to levelling if the verbs are infrequent. They are stored separately, but the forms may be available for developments through connectionist networks as seems to have occurred with German *fragen – frug* or English *snuck*. Finally, there is 'classic' suppletion with stems from distinct roots. This is restricted to frequent items which are diachronically stable, and we may assume that the alternants are stored separately.

Returning to the questions posed at the outset, it would appear that we may need to refine our approach to morphological irregularity. These diachronic developments suggest that something more fine-grained even than a 'dual mechanism' is required to account for them. The process of the deregularisation of the Germanic ablauting verbs has produced, on the one hand, instances of suppletive-like behaviour with stem forms which may be stored as independent lexical items. These are distinct from the small, but viable, inflectional classes seen in Dutch and, to a lesser extent, in German. Here the speakers have access to the vocalic alternations as coherent sets of patterns of exponence and they show evidence of productivity. These could be the product of the kind of strategies proposed in connectionist theory, whereby phonological forms associated with certain types of exponence have become superimposed within the memory system and thereby foster generalisation by analogy. These are again distinct from the forms exemplified by the descendents of the inherited weak verb classes, which can be dealt with as derivations by means of rules. Diachronic evidence in the area of inflectional morphology would suggest that a single mechanism is insufficient for full explanation.

References

Bammesberger, A. (1984). *A Sketch of Diachronic English Morphology*. Regensburg: Pustet.

Barbour, J. S. (1982). 'Productive and non-productive morphology. The case of the German strong verbs'. *Journal of Linguistics* (18) 331-54.

Bittner, A. (1988). 'Reguläre Irregularitäten. Zur Suppletion im Konzept der natürlichen Morphologie'. *Zeitschrift für Phonetik, Sprachwissenschaft und Kommunikationsforschung* (41) 416-25.

Bittner, A. (1996). *Starke „schwache" Verben – schwache „starke" Verben. Deutsche Verbflexion und Natürlichkeit*, Studien zur deutschen Grammatik 51. Tübingen: Stauffenburg.

Bruch, R. (1955). *Précis populaire de grammaire luxembourgeois/Luxemburger Grammatik in volkstümlichem Abriß*. Bulletin linguistique et ethnologique de Luxembourg 5-7. Luxembourg: Linden.

Bybee, J. L. (1985). *Morphology. A Study of the Relation between Meaning and Form*, Typological Studies in Language 9. Amsterdam & Philadelphia: Benjamins.

Bybee, J. L. & C. L. Moder (1983). 'Morphological classes as natural categories'. *Language* (59) 251-70.

Dammers, U., W. Hoffmann & H.-J. Solms (1988). *Flexion der starken und schwachen Verben.* Vol. 4 of H. Moser, H. Stopp & W. Besch (eds.), *Grammatik des Frühneuhochdeutschen. Beiträge zur Laut- und Formenlehre.* Heidelberg: Winter.

Durrell, M. (1990). 'Westphalian and Eastphalian'. In C. V. J. Russ (ed.) *The Dialects of Modern German: A Linguistic Survey.* London: Routledge. 59-90.

Durrell, M. (1999). 'Zum Ausgleich der Ablautalternanzen im Niederdeutschen'. In P. Wagener (ed.) *Sprachformen. Deutsch und Niederdeutsch in europäischen Bezügen. Festschrift für Dieter Stellmacher zum 60. Geburtstag,* Zeitschrift für Dialektologie und Linguistik, Beihefte, Neue Folge, Stuttgart: Steiner. 25-40.

Durrell, M. (2001). 'Strong verb Ablaut in the West Germanic languages'. *Zur Verbmorphologie germanischer Sprachen,* Linguistische Arbeiten 446, S. Watts, J. West & H.-J. Solms (eds.). Tübingen: Niemeyer. 5-18.

Halle, M. & K. P. Mohanan, (1985). 'Segmental phonology of modern English'. *Linguistic Inquiry* (16) 57-116.

Hempen, U. (1988). *Die starken Verben im Deutschen und Niederländischen. Diachrone Morphologie,* Linguistische Arbeiten 214. Tübingen: Niemeyer.

Hogg, R. M. (1988). '*Snuck*: The development of irregular preterite forms'. In G. Nixon & J. Honey (eds.) *An Historic Tongue. Studies in English Linguistics in Memory of Barbara Strang).* London and New York: Routledge. 31-40.

Keller, R. E. (1961). *German Dialects.* Manchester: Manchester University Press.

Kühne, A. (1999). *Zur historischen Lexikostatistik der starken Verben im Deutschen. Textband mit CD-ROM,* Studien zur Geschichte der deutschen Sprache. Heidelberg: Winter.

Lieber, R. (1981). *On the Organization of the Lexicon.* Bloomington: IULC.

Motsch, W. (1967). 'Zum Ablaut der Verben in der Frühperiode germanischer Sprachen'. *Phonologische Studien,* Studia Grammatica 6. Berlin: Akademie-Verlag. 119-144.

Pinker, S. (1999). *Words and Rules. The Ingredients of Language.* London: Phoenix.

Ponten, J. P. (1976). 'Das Konjugationssystem im Niederländischen und Deutschen. Ein Versuch zur Typologisierung'. *Akten des V. Internationalen Germanisten-Kongresses Cambridge 1975. Jahrbuch für internationale Germanistik* (Reihe A, 2,2), 43-52.

Quirk, R, S. Greenbaum, G. Leech and J. Svartvik (1985). *A Comprehensive Grammar of the English Language.* London and New York: Longman.

Rumelhart, D. E. & J. L. McClelland (1986). 'On learning the past tense of English verbs'. In: D. E. Rumelhart & J. L. McClelland (eds.). *Parallel Distributed Processing. Explorations in the Microstructure of Cognition.*

Vol. 2: *Psychological and Biological models.* Cambridge (Mass): Bradford Books/MIT Press. 216-271.

Sánchez Miret, F., A. Koliadis & W. U. Dressler (1997). 'Connectionism vs. rules in diachronic morphology'. *Folia Linguistica Historica* (18) 149-182.

Theobald, E. (1992). *Sprachwandel bei deutschen Verben. Flexionsklassenschwankungen starker und schwacher Verben.* Tübingen: Narr.

Vennemann, T. (1994). 'Zur Entwicklung der reduplizierenden Verben im Germanischen'. *Beiträge zur Geschichte der deutschen Sprache und Literatur* (116) 167-221.

Werner, O. (1989). 'Sprachökonomie und Natürlichkeit im Bereich der Morphologie'. *Zeitschrift für Phonetik, Sprachwissenschaft und Kommunikationsforschung* (42) 34-47.

Werner, O. (1990). 'Die starken Präterita im Luxemburgischen: ideale Analogie oder vergeblicher Rettungsversuch?'. *German Life and Letters* (43) 182-90.

Wiese, R. (1996). 'Phonological and morphological rules: on German Umlaut and Ablaut'. *Journal of Linguistics* (32) 113-35.

Wurzel, W. U. (1970). *Studien zur deutschen Lautstruktur*, Studia Grammatica, 8. Berlin: Akademie Verlag.

Wurzel, W. U. (1984). *Flexionsmorphologie und Natürlichkeit. Ein Beitrag zur morphologischen Theoriebildung*, Studia Grammatica, 21. Berlin: Akademie Verlag.

Wurzel, W. U. (1990). 'The mechanism of inflection: lexicon representations, rules and irregularities'. In W. U. Dressler, H. C, Luschützky, O. E. Pfeiffer & J. R. Rennison (eds.). *Contemporary Morphology*, Trends in Linguistics, Studies and Monographs, 49. Berlin: Mouton-de Gruyter. 203-16.

CLIVE GREY

Well I'll be verbed: "walksorted" and conversion as a lexical process in contemporary British English

The back of envelopes can be quite interesting sources of data relating to linguistic change, like food wrappers and shop signs. The other day a letter arrived from BT (British Telecom), my telephone service provider. On the reverse of the envelope a message read:

(1) This mail has been walksorted.

If one can live with the word *mail* as a general substitute for *post* these days one is doing well, but what then is *walksorting*? Why is it such an odd, almost disturbing word? Needless to say it does not appear in any large dictionary yet, nor does it appear in either the online version of the OED or in databases such as Collins COBUILD collection of words and phrases; it never appears in any other context of life, in speech or in writing. I return to this word shortly. Lexical innovation is nothing new. While the direction of phonetic change is fairly predictable, so that for example it is likely that some features of so-called Estuary English will continue to spread northwards towards Birmingham and Nottingham and beyond over the next decade, any attempt to predict the course of lexical change in English is more difficult. We cannot predict which words will arise in the future in response to technological and social change, or even which types of word formation will be favoured. It is unlikely that future words will be formed by affixation of less productive suffixes such as *-dom* or *-ery*, while new forms in *-aholic* (or is it

-*oholic?*) keep appearing *workaholic, chocoholic, shopoholic, bake-aholic, food-aholic* and just recently *shoe-aholic*[1] and *challenge-aholic*[2]. The form *Lord-Of-The-Flies-athon*[3] following the pattern of *talkathon* and *sellathon* seems to stretch the pattern somewhat. The use of *well* as an intensifier, as in phrases such as *well chuffed, well bladdered* ('very drunk') is now widespread amongst younger speakers. New words appear every day and as many probably disappear from everyday speech just as often. The -*jack* affix (*hijack, carjack*) has now converted to a verb meaning 'steal a mobile phone':

(2) Over the past year I've had two phones stolen, or "jacked" and I've been threatened with a knife countless times. Someone tries to jack me probably every week.[4]

Recent lexical innovations like *pubtel* (a building, part public house, part hotel) might just survive, or they might not, depending on public attitudes to the word. Not so long ago the adjective *mega* meaning 'extra large' found its way on to the sides of loaves: *mega sliced bread* lined shelves in shops belonging to a major chain of bakers in 1995. The bare adjective hardly occurs at all these days even in speech. Many words that enjoyed general currency amongst teenagers only three years ago e.g. *bril* are now in virtual disuse in the northwest, and *pants* ('terrible') seems to have lost considerable ground in the last twelve months, unlike *totally* and *massive*. I asked students whether they liked the word *moby* ('mobile phone') as in the recently heard *Where's my moby?* Most said not, saying it sounded childish, distinctly

1 "No danger of excess baggage here, unless you're a toiletries junkie or a shoe-aholic", Heath Brown. The Times, 15 June 2002, p.62.
2 "McClellan describes himself as a challenge-aholic", Carolyne Ellis. The Times, 7 July 2002, p.8.
3 "Which male or female will be left standing at the end of ITV's Lord-Of-The-Flies-athon, Survivor?" Mike Rowbottom. The Independent, 16 June 2001, p.23.
4 "Be prepared – and be polite. How to survive phonejacking", P. Matthews (age 14). The Guardian, 27 February 2002, p.9.

uncool. They prefer the word *mobile.* Popular attitudes to new words remain fickle. The BBC Radio programme devoted to language use, *Word of Mouth,* recently identified for interest the new American words *perpwalk* ('to parade an alleged perpetrator of a crime in front of TV cameras outside a building in handcuffs on their way to a police car after arrest'), and *to Enron,* involving behaving like a corporation in its last days. Such new words inevitably invite attention when first encountered, if not overt comment. An interviewee on the BBC's *Today* programme seemed genuinely surprised that he had to explain what *24/7* meant, thinking it was in such widespread general use outside on the streets that it was odd that it should invite comment at all.[5]

Some linguistic innovations however slip silently past the unobservant, e.g. the verb *investigate,* for some speakers at least now requires the preposition 'into' before a noun, on the pattern of *investigation: We'll investigate into this.* Perhaps there is resistance to such linguistic change amongst those people who think about language use too much, people enmeshed in a world of debates about so-called standards, and indeed, falling standards and the responsibilities of English language teachers towards 'protecting' the language.

Conversion

One area of lexical change that inevitably invites less attention than new vocabulary or new use of words is that of grammatical change and processes such as noun-to-verb conversion in contemporary British English, the subject of attention here. The process has of course been recognised for decades and identified by linguists and others as 'conversion' (the term in traditional treat-

---

5 "Hell is other people talking webspeak on mobile phones", J. Humphries. The Sunday Times, 27 August 2000, p.10.

ments of English lexical change), or as 'functional shift' (some structuralists in America), or as 'derivation by zero morpheme' (other American structuralists and some British linguists, e.g. Strang), and as 'internal derivation' by lexicologists like Malkiel.

While linguists tend to view conversion as a process that is productive and interesting in the way that it allows the creation of new words without the recourse to (overt) suffixes, ordinary users of the language often take a different, more negative, view. Michael Bradley was moved to write to the *Sunday Times* letters page:

> Richard Woods should be thankful he doesn't live in America. A lack of good reading habits, combined with poor standards of literacy in printed and broadcast media, leave most Americans with an inadequate vocabulary and poor grammatical models. The worst sin is the conversion of nouns to verbs. I was recently invited to *memorialize* a dead friend, to *accessorize* my car, to *transition* to another room, to have my loan application *decisioned* and to *modem* information about colleagues.[6]

Conversion, to stay with the traditional term, as a process of word formation is not a process that could be labelled as distinctively American however. Shakespeare was well-known for using it as a stylistic device as are many later writers:

(3) How many things by season season'd are [...][7]

(4) Grace me no grace, nor uncle me no uncle.[8]

Fiction and journalism are well known as sources for similar lexical derivation. The stylistic context suggests that conversion is likely to occur in writing across a range of genres, e.g. news reporting and poetry, perhaps the most famous exponent being G. M. Hopkins:

---

6   "Losing the war of words". M. Bradley, Letters. *The Sunday Times*. Focus Section, 20 May, 2001, p.8.
7   *Merchant of Venice*, V.i.107.
8   *Richard the Second*, II.3.86.

(5) Let him easter in us, be a dayspring to the dimness of us, be a crimson-cresseted east.[9]

Hopkins extends the process quite liberally in premodifying nouns:

(6) [...] feel-of-primrose hands [10]

Computer-related literature provides a great deal of conversion data, but evidence suggests that the direction noun-to-verb conversion is unusual, though we have e.g. to *paragraph* a text and *click* as a transitive verb (and indeed *rightclick*: *you need to rightclick it just there*. The direction verb-to-noun far more frequent: e.g. the use of the words *send* and *hit* as nouns with inevitable specialisation of meaning:

(7) Photowallet is network-enabled and has multiple-image send.[11]

Similarly *the site had several thousand hits last week*. Typically conversion involves change of word class, but not always. For structuralists the issue also arose of whether to assign a zero element to a converted form, so that just as *sheep* (plural) could be analysed as two morphemes, the second being represented by a zero allomorph, so *fruits* (verb) as in *this tree fruits in spring* could also be analysed not as two but as three morphemes, the second, following Bloomfield (1935: 239), being by the zero allomorph, with *fruit* (verb) classed as a 'secondary root-word'. Strang (1970: 42) even prefers to talk of "derivation by zero morpheme" rather than conversion, while Malkiel (1978: 132) prefers the term 'internal derivation', citing *to butcher* and *to waitress* as examples. He cites similar, though less widespread, processes occurring in French: *le sérieux de la situation, le ridicule de sa conduite* over **sériosité*, and **ridiculité*.

---

9 *The Wreck of the Deutschland*, line 197.
10 *The Habit of Perfection*, cited by Ullmann (1962: 53)
11 *Personal Computer World*, June 1997, p.32.

Some linguistic characteristics of noun-to-verb conversions

McArthur (1992: 263) remarks that it is often said that there is no noun in English that can't be "verbed". It is difficult to go along with this assertion completely, since there are thousands of words one can think of which do not occur, e.g. the verb *dream* but not *nightmare*: there are no obvious clues as to why conversions occur or not, only suggestions as to what hinders the process. McArthur suggests at least three factors that seem to impede what would otherwise be a very productive process: (a) morphology: verbs terminating in a recognizable verb suffix are unlikely to form nouns in that suffix, e.g. *–ize:* thus the impossibility of **let's have an organize*; (b) inertia: where there are pairs like *believe – belief* there is no likelihood of the pair being subverted: **this is one of my believes*; and (c) utility: some words do not need to change class: **I've juried several times* (the reason said to be that in this instance legal language does not require the use of such expressions, which seems rather a weak argument). The somewhat negative definitions are not that helpful in attempting to explain the situation however. Crystal (1995: 129) claims that not all the senses of the original form are transferred to the converted form, a point that is obvious when looking at any example in any detail, thus *paper*: the verb can only be used in the sense of covering a surface, not giving an academic presentation: **I papered twice at the conference last week* is impossible. Semantic considerations are taken up by Leech (1974: 214) who provides examples such as the following:

(8) He pocketed the change.

(9) He netted the ball.

(10) ?She basketed the shopping.

(11) *They carred all their belongings.

Lexical rules, he says, are hallmarked by their partial productivity: the first and second sentences above are entirely acceptable and recorded in dictionaries, the third only "dubiously acceptable" while the fourth is "definitely outside the range of normal usage, although it is not inconceivable." Clearly there are cases of potential converted forms around, but they remain currently unacceptable:

(12) *Cherie babied / childed again last year. ('gave birth')

One wonders why there is no such verb, given the frequency of the occasion generally, so the absence of one suggests that frequency has nothing to do with the need for new words at all. We do have the verb *laboured*, which could be used to mean 'give birth', but unlike the noun (*went into labour*) the verb *labour* seems to have become generalised to any form of hard work:

(13) Cherie laboured with the vacuum cleaner for six hours.

It is not impossible that *birth* might at some stage fill the gap:

(14) *Cherie birthed again last year.

Recursiveness is also said to be a feature of conversion rules, hence the pattern N -> V -> N illustrated by *bag* ('a catch that is caught or bagged') and recursiveness is also a feature of some examples of semantic transfer. Leech identifies the problem of which is the base form and which is the derived (Leech 1974: 225): *cover* (verb) appears to give us the noun *cover*, but evidence from parallel cases, he claims, shows that the base form is in fact the noun, and it is the verb that is derived: *knife -> knife someone*; *pin -> pin something*; *whip -> whip someone*; *glue -> glue something*. The basic pattern suggests the verb comes from the noun. The process of conversion can be viewed, Leech argues, as bi-directional, where etymology may only partly explain why new words arise from each other. Lexical rules, Leech claims, of which conversion rules are just one type, are extremely powerful, and underline the gap of unused 'capacity' between the theoretically enormous generative power of lexical rules and the comparatively limited use that is made of them in practice. One of few detailed attempts at classification of types of conversion appears in the appendix to Quirk et al. (1972, paras. I.31-I.39, reproduced in part in paras. I.24-I.32 of Quirk & Greenbaum, 1973), where the following categories are suggested for noun-to-verb conversion:

[A] to put in/on N
 bottle, corner, catalogue, floor, garage, position

[B] to give N, to provide with N
 coat (of paint), *mask* ('hide something'), *commission, grease, muzzle, plaster*

[C] to deprive of N
 peel, skin, gut, top-and-tail

[D] to ... with N as instrument
 brake, knife, elbow, fiddle, finger, glue

[E] to be/act as N with respect to
 nurse, referee, father, chaperon, parrot, pilot

[F] to make/change ... into N
 cash, cripple, group

[G] to send by N
 mail, ship, telegraph, and, in 2002, *fax, email, text*

[H] to go by N
 bicycle/bike, motor, boat, canoe

We might add to these examples verbs such as *tape, gun (down)* – but, interestingly, *gun on its own does not occur – *microwave, leg, hand,* while Hughes offers: *boost, splurge, mothball, bulldoze, broker* and *boom* (Hughes 2000: 320). The verb *splurge* is making good ground even in the quality newspapers, witness:

> It is a sign of the cheapskate channel's gradual assimilation of older broadcasters' ways that [Channel 5] has not only splurged on a mini-series but placed it mid-evening, dumping the usual movie.[12]

---

12 No author cited. *Sunday Times* 8 September 2002, Culture supplement, p.75.

Clearly the verbs take on the grammatical features of 'regular' verbs – they do not, e.g. undergo vowel change in the past tense or invert with a subject when negative, thus the impossibility of *Steve skan the rabbit* (skinned) and **We canoed not down the river*, and they are almost always transitive in type, except group H, though *train, bus* and *bike* seem to be increasingly common as a transitive: *we trained it down to London* and *they bussed the children every day; we biked it down to Oxford*. The transitive verb *taxi* seems not to occur, unless referring to aircraft movement: ?*we taxied it down to London* ('used a taxi') but *the pilot taxied the plane very slowly*.

Noun-to-verb conversions tend to be almost always transitive, which may explain the impossibility of **Cherie babied last year*, but even if we construct a possible transitive sentence it may still be impossible. It seems the action involved here cannot be construed as a transitive action at present: **Cherie babied it last year*.

Compound verbs present special difficulties in a discussion of conversion: while we can say *I ached all morning* it would be unusual to say **I headached all morning*, despite its excellent conciseness. As is well known, compound words are notoriously unpredictable in terms of their meaning. They become specialized in unpredictable ways, either in terms of narrowed meaning or grammatical defectiveness. Some of the conversions develop such a specialized meaning that their original meaning is almost obscure. Take the verb *frogmarch*, the situation where four policeman carry a prisoner face down each holding a limb, so that the prisoner appears like a frog, except his limbs never normally touch the ground, unlike a frog, and where the resemblance to 'marching' seems even less close. We will not deal with *spreadeagle*. Many compound nouns do not allow conversion at all to a verb: we have *bee-sting*, but we cannot say **I was bee-stung*. We have *earthquake*, but not **We were earthquaked*. Compounds basically seem to resist noun-to-verb conversion, though we do have *sunbathe, sleepwalk, skateboard* and apparently now *perpwalk*. The sentence *we went out boatriding* seems at best marginal for some speakers. Apart from compounds some noun-to-verb conversions verbs formed by prefixing affixes like *de-* behave rather oddly also. We have *defrost* but not *defreeze*. You can *freeze* things, but you *defrost* them, not *defreeze* them later; what you can *frost* seems limited to windows in winter and cakes. Even so attempts at modification bring awkward results: *we quick-defrosted the chicken* seems unlikely. Other examples of converted compounds are *AFN was headquartered in Frankfurt after 1945*, and one heard recently: *should I clingfilm this?* said by one waitress to another in a student café. Then there is the case of *feedforward*:

(15) Perhaps you could feedforward this information to your colleagues.

One time we had *feedback*, the noun, itself derived from the verb *feed* plus adverb, then it was *feedback* the verb. In some circles this then generated the idea of transmission of information to other people, of distributing information, so we have the new verb *feedforward*, which gives the noun: *I liked your feedforward the other day*. My colleagues use the word with a grin on their faces as they say it, clearly aware of the resonance generated by the mere use of the word – 'marketspeak' is everywhere these days. Strang (1970: 42), following Marchand (1969), provides other more established examples such as *contact* (1929), *audition*, *date* (1928) and *pressure*, and claims that although English has a long tradition of making de-adjectival, de-adverbial and de-interjectional verbs, e.g. to *idle*, to *thwart*, to *hail* ('greet') these types of formations had become rare by the middle of the twentieth century.

Some conversions start off as group jargon and spread into wider use: *police have been trialling new protective helmets*, while some verbs once considered obsolescent can make a sudden return: *he pleasured me four times* reportedly said by Monica Lewinski in September 1998, but first recorded in 1538 (OED). Dictionaries of recent lexical innovation, e.g. Tulloch (1991) provide further examples: *source, resource, microwave, niche* (*we need to niche this more carefully*), *network* (of people, but also of computers), even *mousse*: *people will try to mousse everything,* first appearing in 1984. Dictionaries of contemporary slang, e.g. Ayto (1998) provide examples such as the American term *dude up* from 1899, *pig out* from a century later, *grass* 'inform' and *slum it,* nearly all of which are now British usage also, like *chill out* and *veg out*: *we vegged out on the sofa.* To these we could add *glass, doorstep, fax, email, e* as in *I e'd you a message yesterday.* With the verb *text* we have the problem of the past tense. Usage seems particularly unclear here: is it *I text you a message yesterday* or *I texted you a message yesterday*? Most speakers seem uncomfortable with both sentences, preferring *I sent you a text.* Returning to the general direction of conversion, noun-to-verb or verb-to-noun, this seems to depend on the register and genre. In everyday speech the general direction seems to be noun-to-verb, with associated metaphoric usage: *needle, root for, pencil, winkle, swipe, deck* ('knock someone to the floor'), *staff* (of buildings, desks or helplines). Tony Banks, the former Labour government sports minister, commenting on the sacking of Jo Moore, a Labour party advisor, was heard to say:

(16) Jo Moore has been, as they say in the trade, monstered by the press.[13]

Some passives can often sound awkward: while the verb *leak* is now uncontroversially used of information, not just liquids, the passive still sounds clumsy:

(17) We were leaked that the DSS computer had broken down.[14]

In the next case the passive *Volvo'd* is used to add humour to a phrase for an 'aware' audience:

(18) Injured? Volvo'd? Bike Damaged?[15]

---

13   BBC Radio 5 "Drive" programme, 28 November, 2001.
14   Simon Hughes, Liberal Democrat MP, Radio 5 "Drive" programme, 10 September 1998.
15   Advertisement for motorcycle insurance in *Bike* magazine, December 1996, where motorcyclists are reminded of the danger from Volvo drivers.

Other recent verbs are *action* (a real manager's word if there was one); *statement* as in *she's been statemented* (part of the process of identifying a language disability in an educational context), *corner, net*, and *flesh out*. Wolfram & Schilling-Estes (1998: 58) provide examples from American English such as *they treed a cat* and *everything around the island is breakwatered* as well as *boot up* (from computer disk) dating from 1989. Notice also that we have both verbs *trash* and *rubbish* in British English these days, but *trash* suggests physical damage, while *rubbish* suggests only verbal assault: *she rubbished my presentation,* but *they trashed the flat*. For the verbal assault Americans, and perhaps British black speakers also, reserve the word *badmouth* (Bryson 1990: 243). The verb *rubbish* may even be extending into formal registers now, since a reader of the 6pm Irish national radio news, noted for its careful, sedate style, read out the following just recently:

(19) Mr. Nolan rubbished talks of a cutback in government spending.[16]

where one might have expected *dismissed*. Other new conversions like *torch* ('set fire to') have acquired criminal associations: *they torched the car*. One cannot however *torch* food (e.g. toast) or paper, say letters.

Proper nouns seem unusual as sources of conversion: certain trade names are well known. The verb *hoover* continues in general use unlike *dyson*, (**I've been dysoning all morning*), and names of aircraft are unusual as sources:

(20) Chris Evans is the first big name [in radio] to reject a long-term television deal. 'I was offered $11m by ABC television in Los Angeles to present "Don't Forget Your Toothbrush",' he said this weekend. 'They were even prepared to move the

---

16 RTE Radio 1 News 8 September 2002.

show to New York so that I could *Concorde* it every Thursday.' [17]

Back to the envelopes: *moist* or *moisten*?

New verbs do not always retain their expected morphology either, as the next case demonstrates. Every year, Wirral Borough Council in northwest England sends letters out to every one of its 100,000 or so households asking for the names of all those who should appear on the next electoral roll. After filling in the names the council's prepaid form (which did not require an envelope) has to be folded in three and sent back in the post. At the bottom of the form would-be electors were invited to stick the bottom of the envelope to the middle section thus:

(21) Remoist here.

Remoist presupposes the existence of a verb *moist*, a new instance of conversion from adjective to verb. Why not *remoisten*? That *moist* is historically an adjective, and the verb *moisten* comes about by the straightforward addition of a once fairly productive Old English suffix *-en* (*damp -> dampen*) seemed not to the taste of the local council any longer. The other curious feature was that the form was never moist in the first place. The form was posted as an envelope which you opened up. Some sort of gum held the thing together in the post until it was opened up, but it was never moist at any stage, *sticky* perhaps but never *moist*. Clearly much thought had gone on in council committee rooms over which word to put on the return form: *restick? stick it down again? re-wet? re-seal?* (*Tongue it* was presumably resisted!). So electors ended up with *remoist*. The

---

17   "ITV throws a spoke into star's wheel of fortune." Nicholas Hellen. The Times, 20 March 1996. Media section, p.1.

council's experimental word lasted just one year, for the following year *moisten here* returned on the edge of the form.

Are you walksorted?

Back to *walksorted*. Personal research indicated that the word *walksort* started out as the name of a computer program, like *mailsort*, used by BT as part of a process to improve upon delivery times.

> 'Walksort' is another discount service designed for businesses posting high volume mailings within localised regions. 'Walksort' is an extension of the 'mailsort' range of products, offering customers discounts in return for finer sortation.[18]

The programme was then sold to other companies, and the need for a verb to describe the process then came about. At present the noun is far greater in frequency than the verb, but slowly the parts of the verb paradigm are appearing, first the *-ing*-form as in the following text from Cumbria Mailing Services:

> Substantially greater discounts are available if a large quantity of mail is destined for one geographical area through the use of Walksort discounts. *Walksorting* involves a higher level of sortation which further reduces the workload of Royal Mail, and offers discounts of up to 60% off your mailing costs.[19]

The verb (or any form of it) does not actually appear in any BT website text, but it is clearly taking off among private companies. That it ends up as the passive verb *walksorted* on BT envelopes to customers is a very recent development in the last year and

18 <http://www.datadirectltd.co.uk/services.htm>
19 <http://www.cumbriamailing.co.uk/html/mailsort.html>

shows how as a verb it is developing a full complement of grammatical features.

Walksorted is, of course, a compound verb, unusually consisting of two verb elements, rather like *freeze-dried* or *strip-searched*. The latter two cases are rather different however in that the second element is a conversion from an adjective. *Walksorted* is an endocentric, coordinative compound verb, (following Allerton 1979: 229), quite unusual, while freeze-drying is a kind of drying and strip-searching a kind of institutionalised searching procedure and therefore examples of the subordinative type. *Walksorted* is not just unusual because it is formed from two elements where neither element has been derived by conversion, but because *walk* only ever appears (and even then rarely) in a compound as a second element, never as the first element: *sleepwalk*, *perpwalk*, *skywalk*? (as in *Skywalker*). The verb *sort* seems not to appear in any position in compounds at all regularly. The conjunction of the two verbs is thus quite anomalous. The sentence appears in fairly large letters on the envelope, and is clearly something that BT thought customers all over Britain needed to know. That postmen try to sort, accompany and deliver letters to destination addresses, usually correct ones, has been known for some time and should come as no surprise. So why do we need a word *walksorting,* and what does *walksorting* actually mean? The word is unusual on several fronts, it is not a word that first appeared in speech, it is not slang or in vogue, and is not a lexical borrowing. It is not argot, or dialect or socially confined to one group, outside postal services, and is apparently not class- or age-related in its use. Nobody in the general population outside BT's employees is using the word, neither in speech nor in writing, but everyone has now probably seen it, as it appears on the back of telephone account correspondence in many areas. It is a word which BT management has invented with a meaning defined specifically to refer to a contractual business arrangement with customers using specific software.

Compound verb conversions are quite common these days, in business and educational institutions which think of themselves as businesses. The following was recently heard at a committee meeting: *We need to benchmark against other institutions.* This came up in a discussion of the problem of access for disabled students in a college bar. Disabled students had commented that they could not get close enough to be served as it was too high to pass over the glasses, so they were forced to come round behind the back of the bar to collect them. The committee Chair thought the college should look at what happens in similar colleges, a process of comparison now referred to quite generally as *benchmarking* in public service institutions in Britain. There are no actual physical benchmarks in existence for the height of college bars. The word *benchmark* seems to operate as a substitute for *compare*. Terms like *benchmark* owe their currency to the fashionable but fatuous adoption of marketspeak by so-called human resources managers, particularly in the public services, who want to give a veneer of credibility, respectability and quasi-professionalism to their activities, particularly in committee meetings.

It was once said of a former American president that he could not walk and chew gum at the same time. Perhaps then it is now possible to deliver letters while sorting them at the same time. If one starts to think about what *walksorting* must mean, we might assume that something other than, or in addition to, delivering letters to the right address was going on, something new, otherwise there would be no need for a new verb like this at all. Perhaps the mail arrives at the sorting office unsorted and is then given to people, quite randomly, to go about the streets sorting the letters according to address as they go along in some sort of random fashion, whereas before, the whole sorting was done in some central location and people put letters into boxes with road names on and people knew where exactly to go with them when they started out on the streets. Clearly the word has something linked with the other *sorted* – the colloquial erstwhile slang usage deriving apparently from Northern English drug slang, meaning 'task completed' thus *Have you done that? Yeah. Sorted.* In that sense my letter was thus delivered correctly, so it was *sorted* if anyone were to ask.

Leaving aside the rights of people, and indeed national corporations, to invent new words, let alone new **uses** of words as verbs like this, and the whole issue of how these words come to exist, and then only in writing, (or perhaps in speech as well but presumably amongst BT marketing staff only) we encounter one of the amazing features of English – its remarkable flexibility. The fact that verbs can be created with little effort and be presented to people for their understanding and interpretation with little training on either what they probably mean or how they might be used is one of the wonders of the language. Nobody riots, and there is little hostility over such new forms. Perhaps this is because people are not that concerned with language use in the end, or because people understand that nobody, not even private companies, can really control usage and meanings. The issue of whether the word is needed is quite a separate one.

What we can say about conversion is that where a converted verb arises by design it is not at all clear that the intended meaning will be accepted by the speakers at large, despite attempts to promote it on the backs of envelopes in mass mailings. Since it is ultimately the name of a computer program the word is unlikely to appear in everyday speech or writing, except among BT employees. Neither a brand name, nor a term to describe a new invention or a new social policy or device it is unlikely to take off in the general population, despite exposure to it. Unless people can see a reason for the word, and what it actually means, it is unlikely to survive. A committee of people may invent a new compound word with a predetermined meaning, but how people use the word, indeed whether people want to use the word, is up to users in the end. Mere exposure to the word even in writing does not guarantee survival. On the other hand, the two elements are common enough in everyday speech. People know what *walk* and *sort* mean. It is the combination which is unfamiliar. It is perhaps precisely *because* the meanings of the familiar bits are all too clear that makes the combination so odd. What *walksorted* reveals is an attempt to create a highly determined artificial, technical definition for a word composed out of two everyday words.

Noun-to-verb conversions remain one of the more unpredictable areas of English lexical change. If *walksort* does survive as a verb at all, it will be because people see it often enough on envelopes and identify it as linking with some sort of improvement in service. Also, words tend to behave like other words. If the structure of the new word is anomalous it will not stay long in the public consciousness unless there is strong reason to retain it. In the case of *walksort* there are no parallel words with *walk* as the first element. At a social level it is not a word that signals either personal, social or technological advance when used in the company of others, and it is not a word you need to know in order to survive. At a linguistic level it actually subverts speakers' awareness of the rules governing word formation in general and compounding in particular. In creating new words we can stretch social and linguistic demands so far but at some point the results often become outlandish.

Bibliography

Allerton, D. J. (1979). *Essentials of Grammatical Theory*. London: Routledge & Kegan Paul.
Ayto, J. (1998). *The Oxford Dictionary of Slang*. Oxford: Oxford University Press.
Bloomfield, L. (1935). *Language*. London: George Allen & Unwin. (First published 1933 in New York: Henry Holt).
Bryson, B. (1990). *Mother Tongue*. Harmondsworth: Penguin.
Crystal, D. (1988). *The English Language*. Harmondsworth: Penguin.
Crystal, D. (1995). *The Cambridge Encyclopaedia of the English Language*. Cambridge: Cambridge University Press.
Crystal, D. (2001). *Language and the Internet*. Cambridge: Cambridge University Press.
Hughes, G. (2000). *A History of English Words*. Oxford: Blackwell.
Malkiel, Y. (1978). 'Derivational Categories'. In: J. H. Greenberg (ed.) *Universals of Human Language*. Vol. 3. *Word Structure*. Stanford: Stanford University Press, 125-149.

Marchand, H. (1969). *Categories and Types of Present-Day English Word-Formation*. Munich: C.H. Beck. Rev. second edition.

McArthur, T. (ed.) (1992). *The Oxford Companion to the English Language*. Oxford: Oxford University Press.

Sapir, E. (1978). *Language*. London: Granada. (First published 1921 in New York: Harcourt Brace).

Strang, B. M. H. (1970). *A History of English*. London: Methuen.

Tulloch, S. (ed.) (1991). *The Oxford Dictionary of New Words: A Popular Guide to Words in the News*. Oxford: Oxford University Press.

Wolfram, W & N. Schilling-Estes (1998). *American English: Dialects and Variation*. Oxford: Blackwell.

Dorota A. Smyk

On unintentionality in morphological productivity

Productivity, the ability to form and understand novel forms, is an essential feature of human language. The fundamental observations about morphological productivity and its role in extending the lexicon are relatively easy to make. Several proposed definitions of productivity highlight the factors essential for a process to be considered productive, and specify the variables responsible for its constraints.

This paper discusses one of the variables ascribed to productive formations, namely *unintentionality*. Unintentionality, as presented in the literature on the topic, is held responsible for distinguishing productively created new words that are created in a productive way, i.e., that are the result of spontaneous, regular coining, from those that require conscious effort and are therefore excluded from the scope of productivity. In this paper I will argue against unintentionality as a crucial prerequisite of productivity.

The paper is divided into four sections. First, as a background for the discussion, a general overview of morphological productivity is given. Next, unintentionality, as one of the factors determining productivity is discussed. Having established the working definition of unintentionality, a number of examples are examined. On the basis of the analysis of these examples it is argued that unintentionality as such, although intuitively relevant, is too vague and imprecise a notion to be included in the scope of productivity studies.

Productivity as means of extending the lexicon

No natural language has a finite vocabulary. The lexicon of a language is in continuous development. New words can usually be ascribed to one of the three main mechanisms responsible for their creation: semantic change, borrowing and word formation. Whereas semantic change uses an already existing form and adds a new meaning, and borrowing takes existing words from other languages, lexeme formation[1] is a process responsible for the emergence of new, frequently complex, words. Lexeme formation mechanisms offer an invaluable source of information and form the basis for predicting future lexical development. The study of productivity is therefore interesting, as it accounts for language change and development at a lexical level.

Several explanations about the nature of morphological productivity have been presented by Schultink (1961), Aronoff (1976), Van Marle (1985), Baayen (1992), Plag (1999) and Bauer (2001). In most publications, productivity is seen as the ability on the part of the speaker and/or a feature of the language itself to give rise to new forms. The discussion on productivity can be placed within two main streams, qualitative and quantitative. Qualitative approaches attempt to define and describe productivity in terms of its prerequisites, distinctive features or conditions that need to be fulfilled in order for a process to be productive. Quantitative approaches, on the other hand, try to measure productivity using statistical methods. Both approaches aim indirectly at evaluating the degree of productivity of new formations.

An influential early definition on the topic is offered by Schultink (1961: 113):

---

[1] I use the term after Allerton (1989) but in a more general sense. Lexeme formation (in the sense used here) is a cover term for a number of morphological processes that enable the creation of new lexemes by means of affixation, shortenings, compounding or conversion.

> By productivity as a morphological phenomenon we understand the possibility for language users to coin, unintentionally, a number of formations which are in principle uncountable [...].[2]

Schultink's definition is much more restrictive than Hockett's (1958: 307) for whom "the productivity of any pattern – derivational, inflectional or syntactic – is the relative freedom with which speakers coin new grammatical forms by it". In the context of lexical neologisms, lexeme formation is not seen as a homogenous group, but is often subdivided into word formation and word manufacturing, where only word formation encompasses rule-governed, grammatical and therefore potentially productive processes in morphology such as derivation and compounding. Unpredictable marginal coinages, not necessarily rule-governed (creative processes, e.g. acronyms, blends, analogical formations), are ascribed to word manufacturing, where, as claimed by Marchand (1969: 452) "more or less arbitrary parts of words may be welded into an artificial new word". This division explains the prevailing attitude in the literature to investigate productivity in derivational processes, in most cases excluding compounding from the scope of the discussion as well. Later productivity studies tend to take this approach. According to Aronoff & Anshen (1998: 242), "morphological productivity may be defined informally as the extent to which a particular affix is likely to be used in the production of new words in the language". If we assume that only affixes are productive, this eliminates all procedures that do not require an affix, i.e. compounding, conversion, blending and acronym formation.

Though both Schultink and Hockett refer to productivity as an ability with which a language user produces grammatically correct coinages, Schultink is the first to explicitly name unintentionality and uncountability as prerequisites for a process to be

---

[2] Translated in van Marle (1985: 45) "Onder produktiviteit als morfologisch fenomeen verstaan we dan de voor taalgebruikers bestaande moglijkheid [...] onopzettelijk een in principe niet telbaar aantal nieuwe formatives te vormen."

considered productive. Whereas uncountability is a fairly uncontroversial notion, unintentionality, though intuitively understood, remains a rather unclear prerequisite.

Unintentionality as prerequisite for productivity

Within the regular patterns of affixation Schultink (1961) distinguishes three types of formations:

- intentional
- incidental
- non-intentional

The intentional formations can be illustrated as follows. Language users who employ such purposely-coined formations have the intention to distinguish themselves by means of the words used. An intentional coining might aim at achieving comical or satirical effect. The lexeme produced in this way might follow a regular morphological pattern but, according to Schultink, should still be distinguished from other formations, because of its purpose. As an illustration of an intentional coinage, consider the following fragment from a song performed by Toni Braxton:

(1a) *Unbreak* my heart

(1b) Say you'll love me again

(1c) *Uncry* these tears

In the context of a song, it is easy to imagine that the linguistic effect was intended. Morphologically *unbreak* and *uncry* follow the pattern of *undo* or *untie*, where the meaning of *un-* is to reverse an action. The pattern is normally reserved for actions for which "the physical possibility to undo the result [...] is conceivable" (Marchand 1969: 205). It is relatively easy to imagine the action of unbreaking and uncrying – reversing the process. A formation that appears odd is more often the result of a violation of a regular morphological pattern, as in the case of *unperson* in the following quote from G. Orwell's (1949) *Nineteen Eighty-Four*.

(2) Syme was not only dead, he was abolished, an *unperson*.

The prefix *un-* usually combines with verbs or adjectives but not with nouns. In terms of intentionality both examples illustrate conscious, intentional formations.

Schultink subdivides unintentional formations into incidental derivations and truly unintentional (non-intentional) formations. By incidental formations he understands lexemes actuated by the speaker without being aware of a violation of the language system. As a result, such formations often strike us as weird or odd although the speaker did not plan to achieve any special effect. To put it differently, we talk about incidental derivations when a truly unproductive, incidentally actuated pattern is a result of a speech error. Consider the following example: "They *misunderestimated* me" said by George W. Bush of his opponents on the eve of the 2000 US presidential election.

Non-intentional formations form the last group. Only these coinages can be classified as productive since they were created in an unintentional or, to be more precise, non-incidental way. Whenever there is a trace of an intention, the formation must be considered unproductive. Schultink strongly focuses on the speaker, for whom the new forms must go unnoticed. Unintentionality, therefore, presupposes automatic formation. It introduces a subdivision in morphology for word formations that are unintentional, and therefore productive, and those that are intentional, and hence creative. In its effect this subdivision largely overlaps with the word formation and word manufacturing distinction. Unintentionality therefore becomes another distinguishing criterion between productivity (rule-governed) and creativity (non-rule-governed).

Uhlenbeck (1978) also associates the concept of productivity with the specific criteria of unaccountability and unintentionality. He claims that new, productively coined words must be "unquestionably accepted and understood without any special effort and without their novelty being even noticed" (1978: 4). Words other than that are incidental or for a specific purpose. Let me stress this point: Schultink and Uhlenbeck are concerned mainly with language use, not language structure, with productivity automatically yielding predictable, rule-governed output.

Van Marle (1985: 59) is even more restrictive, and claims, "all morphological processes that demand their base to be nonnative must be precluded from the productive coining of words". He supports his restriction by pointing to the fact that if a base is nonnative, it is consciously perceived as such by the language users, which in turn means that the users are aware of the foreignness of the particular formation. Therefore, if they use it for the production of new lexemes they do so intentionally, i.e., consciously. In this way van Marle excludes a number of perfectly regular formations from the domain of productivity studies. The importance to distinguish between native and non-native elements, both bases and affixes, is also discussed by Kastovsky (1986).

Other morphologists, particularly quantitative morphologists, have also willingly adopted Schultink's definition of productivity. For Baayen & Lieber (1991) the notion of unintentionality means that new formations based on productive word formation rules go unnoticed. This automatically implies that unproductive coinages are perceived as new, that "[t]hey should strike us as cute or funny or objectionable" (Lieber 1992: 163).

Evert & Lüdeling (2001) contribute to the understanding of unintentionality by stressing another important factor. Words that are formed productively should not be recognized or noticed as new words, either by the speaker or the listener. Only those words can be said to be the result of a truly productive formation; words formed otherwise are carefully produced and are perceived as new.

To sum up, Schultink's conception of unintentionality has attracted much attention and triggered further research. Nevertheless, there are some serious problems with its application as a criterion, which I intend to show in the next section.

Selected examples

As the basis for testing applicability and usability of the unintentionality criterion I took a selection of neologisms from *The Independent*.[3] These words were automatically generated, so I checked them against the BNC[4] to verify if they can be classified as neologisms. The BNC did not yield any results for the selected lexemes except for *clonally* which returned three matches (in three different texts) in the written-text type, all for the applied-science domain. Since this frequency was below the margin of error, I decided to use the example all the same. At this point let us look at the selected examples:

(3a) The problem in my own case is not sexism, but *alphabetism*. My partner can vote in the proposed Halifax conversion, but I cannot. My surname begins with G and hers with C. Only the first-named person in a joint mortgage is entitled to vote and to participate in any subsequent shares handout.

(3b) But there is, of course, another zone of the *motorscape*, inhabited by cars of prestigious aura and German identity.

(3c) Most airlines will 'priority *waitlist*' you, which means that as soon as a seat becomes available, you get it.

---

3   These data are the result of the APRIL (Analysis and Prediction of Innovation in the Lexicon) project at the Research and Development Unit for English Studies (RDUES), University of Liverpool. The linguistic goal in the project was to provide data for descriptions of the nature of hapax legomena (words occurring only once in a given corpus) and therefore potential neologisms, and to offer insights into the nature of productivity in the language. For more information of the project see <http://www.rdues.liv.ac.uk/april.shtml>. The examples are taken from the provided samples for 1997 and 1998.
4   The search was conducted with the help of BNCweb (http://escorp.unizh.ch), a BNC tool developed at the University of Zürich.

(3d) The picture was of a compulsive skinflint, womaniser, ligger supreme and all-purpose sponger. Worse, a *mistreater* of horses, and a ruthless jockey on the track and away from it.

(3e) By the late Sixties, what had started as a few scraps became a Collection with a capital C. I'd assembled about three or four *albumfuls*, which I thought was probably enough to make a nice little anthology.

(3f) I would be beaten continuously with slippers and even sticks. I'd be held down and beaten. At the time, I accepted that I was *bullyable*. I also accepted that I was the only person who was bullied.

(3g) Philip Gould Labour's opinion pollster, he played a part in the recent replacement of the editor of the Express with a more *Blair-friendly* version.

(3h) Before 1976 and the blunder that allowed that ship of potatoes to come to Europe we had only the single strain and it reproduced *clonally*.

(3i) Either this style was supposed to represent the tumultuous media distortion that followed the Princess of Wales's death, or it was a ploy to disorientate irate *Diana-philes* before they had the chance to throw a Royal Wedding commemorative plate at the TV set.

(3j) I don't need to bother with all that interesting stuff after 11pm, like Film 98. So I'm stuck with a bland diet of soaps, *docusoaps* and documentaries.

(3k) The design document serves as the blueprint of the site and is used as a guide by graphic artists, *HTMLers* and programmers.

The question arises whether the highlighted words can be considered to be unintentionally (productively) coined formations or not. Let us revise the criteria for unintentionality and divide them into two groups, for ease of discussion.

a) System-based criteria: The word itself cannot be a result of any other formation but regular affixation. Moreover, the base for affixation and the affixation pattern must be of native origin, that is, foreign elements must be excluded.

b) User-based criteria: Both writer and reader must be unaware of the neologism coined.

In the examples, we can distinguish six relatively uncontroversial derivations (3a), (d), (e), (f), (h), and (k), one example of conversion (c), a compound (g), a blend (j) and two formations of an unclear status, (b) and (i). The results are summarized in Table 1.

	lexeme	POS	process	native	speaker	listener
a	*alphabetism*	N	*-ism* suffixation	yes	?	?
b	*motorscape*	N	*-scape* ?	no	?	?
c	*waitlist*	V	conversion N>V	-	?	?
d	*mistreater*	N	*-er* suffixation	yes	?	?
e	*albumfuls*	N	*-ful* suffixation	yes	?	?
f	*bullyable*	Adj	*-able* suffixation	yes	?	?
g	*Blair-friendly*	Adj	compounding	-	?	?
h	*clonally*	Adv	*-ly* suffixation	yes	?	?
i	*Diana-philes*	N	*-phile* ?	no	?	?
j	*docusoaps*	N	blending	-	?	?
k	*HTMLers*	N	*-er* suffixation	yes	?	?

Table 1: Analysis of examples

By virtue of the presented definitions, examples (c), (g), and (j) must be eliminated from further discussion as they do not represent affixation-based formations. Among the remaining lexemes, formations (b) and (i) pose a problem. They do not represent regular processes in Schultink's restrictive sense. The element *-phile* is sometimes classified as part of a compound of neoclassical origin, and sometimes as an affix. The suffix *-scape* is the result of a reinterpretation of the Dutch loan 'landscape'. It is often considered a result of analogy-based operation, with *-scape* having the status of a combining form rather than an affix. All the same, since both -*scape* and -*phile* are foreign elements they must be excluded from this discussion. This leaves six examples of affixation. All these affixations seem to follow an established and transparent pattern[5]. The suffix -*ism* forms abstract nouns which signify a real or pseudo-principle, or a slogan. Such words often denote "undesirable things as appear in the form of regular system, a typical behaviour or undesirable practice" (Marchand 1969: 306f). The suffix -*er* forms mainly deverbal or denominal nouns. It "can be tacked on to almost any basis: a simple or composite substantive [...] all kinds of phrases, on the general semantic basis 'he who or that which is connected with or characterized by his or its appurtenance to –'." (Marchand 1969: 279). Derivatives based on verbs mainly denote the performer of an action. Originally a second element of a compound, the suffix -*ful* has the meaning of quantity that fills or can fill. "In Modern English the plural -*s* is appended to the last element which isolates the combination morphologically" (Marchand 1969: 292). Based on the reanalysis of Old French borrowings the suffix -*able* attaches both to native and non-native bases and coins words with predominantly passive meaning. The earliest derivatives can be traced to 14th century and "the suffix has lost nothing of its productivity" (Marchand 1969: 230). The adverb-forming suffix -*ly* is no doubt the most prolific suffix in English.

The detailed analysis of the system-based criteria in the previous paragraph helps us divide selected formations into unproductive (those that did not follow the grammatical procedure) and productive, or rather potentially productive, as I have not discussed their intentionality yet. If I apply conservative principles, I will have to exclude from the discussion of productivity not only examples (3b), (c), (g), (i) and (j) as they do not show affixation processes, but also (k) within the affixation group.

---

5   This discussion is based on the descriptions of word formation processes as presented in Marchand (1969).

HTMLer has as its base an acronym[6], which makes the formation rather suspicious. Thus I am left with the following candidates: *alphabetism, mistreater, albumfuls, bullyable, clonally*.

Now, having established regular affixation based formations and having eliminated foreign elements, I will look at the user-based criteria, the speaker/writer and the listener/reader, and their language awareness.

There are two principal problems with measuring speaker and listener awareness. First, the contextual information does not give us any hint whatsoever of whether the speaker was conscious of forming a new word. Secondly, we know nothing about the targeted audience, and therefore about the listener's reaction to the new formations. If we were, however, to take unintentionality as rigidly as it is presented in the literature discussed, we would have to dispense with all the above examples. They all come from newspaper texts, which by definition are consciously, intentionally written, carefully selected language that cannot be considered spontaneous.

As far as the reader's perception is concerned everybody has a different level of language awareness. I tested the examples with a small group of native and non-native speakers. Only people who have a linguistic background found some of the words 'interesting'. The others did not notice anything abnormal and – apart from the example of *Diana-phile* – did not find words 'cute, funny, objectionable' to use Lieber's words. This seems to point against productivity as intended by van Marle.

If I confine the study of productivity to words that are without any doubt created unintentionally (in the sense discussed so far), this rules out perfectly regular formations, and all the examples discussed. This is unsatisfactory, as processes which in my opinion are decisively productive would have to be considered unproductive. Moreover, it leads to a number of problematic conclusions about duality of productivity, which will be discussed in the next section.

---

6   HTML stands for 'HyperText Markup Language'.

Discussion

The three main problems concerning unintentionality are:
- Conservative approaches are too restrictive.
- A given process may be treated as both productive and unproductive, depending on the estimation of awareness.
- Awareness (intentionality) is difficult, if not impossible, to measure.

As discussed above, when unintentionality is applied on the formal level, certain processes are automatically eliminated, by virtue of not being affixations. Selecting affixation as the only process that is susceptible to productivity seems in itself a problematic step. One argument against the exclusiveness of affixation comes from the general findings of the APRIL project. Among the processed neologisms, the number of derivations and compounds is similar. Yet, if we apply our conservative approach, compounds should be excluded. In the context of the creation of new lexemes through derivation, there is an observable participation of nonnative elements that we have also dispensed with. Plag (1999) in his thorough, empirical analysis of derived verbs, concludes that, apart from *-ize*, *-ify*, and *–ate* suffixation, conversion is the only other productive verb-deriving process in English. Ascribing productivity to a conversion process seems to be supported by the fact that most conversions are not perceived as strange, irregular formations, and go unnoticed. Blends[7] can also be seen as productive. As shown in Bauer (2001: 95), suffixation and prefixation account only for approximately 21% of new formations.

Another difficulty with the conservative approach is that only words produced in spontaneous language can be considered to be the result of a productive word formation. That might suggest that the discussion of unintentionality should be re-

---

7   See Adams (2001) for a classification of blends.

stricted exclusively to spoken language. Such a division into spoken and therefore productive, versus written and therefore unproductive language has serious implications for the study of morphological productivity. It eliminates from the scope of research most of the corpus data used both in qualitative and quantitative research. Moreover it puts into question all results of quantitative analyses based on written corpus data. One could, of course, argue for a spontaneously written language, the written language of immediacy in note-taking, diaries, letters, etc. Spoken language, on the other hand, can also be carefully planned as in case of speeches or academic lectures.

The notion of unintentionality presupposes a complete lack of awareness. Consider the following example taken from an Internet site for pet-frog keepers:

(4) They're still idiots. However, Rana and Astra are making slow deliberate steps out of the depths of *idiothood* (*idiotness?* [...]).
(http://fluffyfrog.com/ FrogPondStoriesF.html)

It is evident that the writer is looking for an appropriate word to name a concept; therefore *idiothood* and *idiotness* are conscious, intentional formations. That would suggest (even if we ignore the fact that it is a written example) that they are of no interest when studying productivity. As has also been observed by Bauer (2001), such an assumption has serious and undesirable consequences, including one process (in this case *–hood* derivation) can be both productive and not productive, or, to put it differently, the process is productive in one coinage and unproductive in another. Supporting this approach I must also accept, contrary to my intuition, that *idiothood* was not productively coined. Yet, as argued by Marchand (1969: 293), *-hood* derivatives are fairly frequent.

I can add the following examples of -*hood* derivatives:[8]

(5a) Tom was an inept loser in high school, but he became much better at it in college. He actually had nine jobs within one year and spent most of his time performing in theater or with his rock band, Greater Mental Impact. Later on he rounded out his *loserhood* by singing in a church choir and writing his own musical play.[9]

(5b) Check out the company where Jim works, Chaco, to get a glimpse at an interesting vision for the internet and the technology and people behind it. Also check out the *webhood* while you're there.[10]

(5c) Of course, the best deal of all is to own your own company. Madeleine Paquin, 37, is CEO of Logistec Corp., a Montreal stevedoring company. Paquin's father took the company public in 1969, and she and her two sisters still control 42% of the shares. Paquin has two daughters – Jessica, 4, and Valerie, 2. She balances motherhood and *CEOhood* by having two live-in nannies.[11]

(5d) Aarti Chhabria, who is just getting used to *celebrityhood* with Awara Pagal Diwana her debut film being a hit, insists on tea with lots of milk.[12]

It seems that the decision about productivity must be made for each individual coinage. This is not an optimal or even a feasible solution. In the majority of cases, contextual information is not sufficient to measure speaker's awareness objectively. Moreover, language users have different levels of awareness and therefore different levels of intentionality. There seems to be no general rule for determining unintentionality.

---

8 The examples presented are from various internet sources (URLs as of November 2002).
9 <http://www.kevinmacdonaldband.com/index_frameset.html?tom_frameset.html>
10 <http://www.physics.miami.edu/~chris/personal.html>
11 <http://www.robmagazine.com/archive/2000ROBfebruary/html/work_mothers2.html>
12 <http://www.uppercrustindia.com/11crust/eleven/feature13.htm>

One could attempt to combine all the criteria, to verify the intentionality of the act/form (means), the awareness of the speaker (problematic), and the result it has (recognition as new by the listener). Then, this combined set of criteria could be applied to every new formation establishing its productivity. All possible combinations are presented in Table 2, where 'yes' stands for intentional, and 'no' for unintentional (to the extent we can measure it, of course).

	Form	Speaker	Listener
a	no	yes	no
b	yes	yes	no
c	no	yes	yes
d	yes	yes	yes
e	no	no	no
f	yes	no	no
g	no	no	yes
h	yes	no	yes

Table 2: Combination of unintentionality criteria

In this way, the ideal situation, and – according to the definitions discussed – the only truly productive situation is when the speaker and the listener are unaware of the novelty and the message itself is based on a fully transparent, regular and necessarily affixation-based process (e). This definition seems to be seriously flawed. Consider the following fragment (6), incidentally from a text on productivity:

(6) There can be no doubt that there is a link between these two phenomena, but it should be emphasized that morphological processes may vary greatly in terms of the *specificness* of their semantic contribution. (Koefoed & van Marle 2000: 305)

I have selected the example 'specificness' because:
- the pattern is regular;[13]
- I am not sure if the word was coined intentionally, although nothing points to this fact;
- it attracted my attention.

Does this mean that since the word does not go unnoticed (g) it was coined unproductively? It is difficult to agree.

Conclusions

Unintentionality is a problematic criterion of productivity. There is no simple, practical way of determining unintentionality explicitly, in each and every case. Restricting productivity studies only to affixation processes eliminates a number of regular and frequent patterns that are decidedly productive. Written language should not be excluded from the domain of productivity studies, even though the notion of awareness might be inherent to it. Rather than drawing a distinction between written and spoken language, we might concentrate on communicative immediacy (spontaneously used language) and communicative distance. However, if unintentionality implies that a formation is easily and effortlessly understood, speaker's awareness plays no role. Even perfectly regular affixation patterns can be used intentionally. As observed by Plag (1999) verbal *–ize* forms are frequently used to name new concepts in science, which is done purposefully and with full awareness. Yet, as long as they do not contradict the semantic and phonological specification of *–ize* derivatives, they should be considered productive. I believe that the intentionality/unintentionality division seems irrelevant as

---

13 For extensive discussion on *–ness* see Aronoff (1976).

long as the new coinage is semantically transparent and follows an established pattern.

In this paper I have outlined the problems with the approach to productivity based on unintentionality as a distinguishing factor. Although intuitively unintentionality appears to be a useful criterion, there is no practical way of implementing it in productivity studies. Unintentionality as such is too general and imprecise a concept that would, if applied, eliminate from the scope of productivity large numbers of genuinely productive formations that have gained popular acceptance and use, and now pass unnoticed.

References

Adams, V. (2001). *Complex Words in English*. London: Longman.
Allerton, D. J. (1989). 'Language as form and pattern: grammar and its categories'. Chapter 3 of Collinge, N. E. (ed.), *An Encyclopaedia of Language*. London: Routledge. 68-111.
Anshen, F. & M. Aronoff (1988). 'Producing morphologically complex words'. *Linguistics* (26) 654-655.
Aronoff, M. (1976). *Word formation in generative grammar*. Cambridge (Mass): MIT Press.
Aronoff, M. & F. Anshen (1998). 'Morphology and the Lexicon: Lexicalization and Productivity'. In: A. Spencer & A. M. Zwicky (eds.). *The handbook of morphology*. Oxford: Blackwell. 237-247.
Baayen, R. H. (1992) 'On frequency, transparency and productivity'. In G. Booij (ed.), *Yearbook of Morphology*, Dordrecht: Kluwer. 181-208.
Baayen, R. H. & R. Lieber (1991). 'Productivity and English derivation: a corpus based study'. *Linguistics* (29) 801-843.
Bauer, L. (2001). *Morphological productivity*. Cambridge: Cambridge University Press.
Evert, S. & A. Lüdeling (2001). 'Measuring morphological productivity: Is automatic preprocessing sufficient?'
   <http://www.ims.uni-stuttgart.de/projekte/corplex/paper/evert/Evert Luedeling2001.pdf>
Hockett, C. F. (1958). *A course in Modern linguistics*. New York: Macmillan.

Kastovsky, D. (1986). 'The problem of productivity in word formation'. *Linguistics* (24) 585-600.

Koefoed, G. & J. van Marle. (2000). 'Productivity'. In: Booij, G. et al. (eds.) *Morphology: an international handbook of inflection and word-formation.* Berlin: de Gruyter. 303-312.

Lieber, R. (1992). *Deconstructing Morphology.* Chicago and London: University of Chicago Press.

Marchand, H. (1969). *The categories and types of present-day English word-formation.* 2nd ed. München: Beck.

van Marle, J. (1985). *On the Paradigmatic Dimension of Morphological Creativity.* Foris.

Plag, I. (1999). *Morphological productivity: structural constraints in English derivation.* Berlin: Mouton de Gruyter.

Schultink, H. (1961). 'Produktiviteit als morfologisch fenomeen'. *Forum der Letteren* 2: 110-125.

Uhlenbeck, E. M. (1978). *Studies in Javanese Morphology.* The Hague: Martinus Nijhoff.

PIUS TEN HACKEN

Phrases in words

Ever since the emergence of Chomskyan linguistics, which directed the main focus of attention in linguistics to syntax, the relationship between syntax and morphology has been an issue of the research agenda. Borer (1998: 151) refers to the interface between the two as "a battleground, on which many important linguistic wars have been fought". Chomsky's (1970) Lexicalist Hypothesis implies that morphology, or at least word formation, is in the lexicon, independent of syntax. Even though this hypothesis was widely adopted, there have always been dissenting voices. A fairly recent example is Lieber's (1992) proposal to integrate the whole of morphology into syntax. An important set of data in this discussion concerns morphological formations which seem to involve phrasal components. In this paper, three relevant types are discussed, all of them in the domain traditionally called 'compounding'.[1] The central questions are to what extent a unified analysis of these types is possible and to what extent they are compatible with a model which places word formation in the lexicon.

---

1   In ten Hacken (1994) I argued that only determinative compounding is actually compounding. Here I will use terms such as 'synthetic compounding' and 'exocentric compounding' descriptively. Unless explicitly stated otherwise, 'compounding' is used in the sense of 'determinative compounding'. 'Determinative compounding' is only used contrastively.

Synthetic compounding

As a starting point for the exploration of the interaction of syntax and word formation, synthetic compounding is particularly appropriate. Bloomfield (1933: 231f.) introduces the term 'synthetic compounding' for expressions such as *red-bearded* and *three-master*, where the suffixes *-ed* and *-er* are added to a noun only in the presence of a modifier. He proposes to analyse such words as involving a phrase, in our examples *red beard* and *three masts*. A related class of items is what Bloomfield calls 'semi-synthetic compounds', exemplified by *meat eater*. In more recent work, the latter class of processes is often referred to as 'verbal compounding', e.g. Roeper & Siegel (1978). Because of the interest in the role of argument structure in the interpretation of verbal compounds, a much more elaborate literature exists on this phenomenon, and the term 'synthetic compounding' is often used as including or even as equivalent to verbal compounding, e.g. Fabb (1998). Here, however, we will concentrate on synthetic compounding as the phenomenon originally designated by Bloomfield.

Synthetic compounds are analysed by Bloomfield as involving an affixation process applied to a phrase. He notes that although *bearded* is an existing word (he gives the example *bearded lady*), the phrase *red beard* is "the natural starting-point" for the derivation of *red-bearded*. Among structures (1) and (2), this makes (1) the preferred one.

(1) [red beard] ed
(2) red [beard ed]

Semantically the structure in (1) can be supported by considering the parallel meaning of the affixation process in *bearded* and *red-bearded*. In both cases the suffix *-ed* corresponds to 'marked by [an] X', where X is the item it attaches to. Structure (2) is advocated by Allen (1978) and many others after her. In (2), we would have the combination of two adjectives in a compound.

Such cases exist also outside the domain of synthetic compounding, but they have a rather different meaning. In the large morphological dictionary database described in ten Hacken (2002), there are 160 A+A compounds, most of which have a participle as a second member, e.g. *little-known*. There is a small class of items such as *bitter-sweet* and *white-hot*, whose meaning is the combination of the meanings of their component parts. Neither of these types fits (2), because *beard* is not a verb and *red* and *bearded* are not both predicated of a noun modified by *red-bearded*. The only reason to propose (2) is then theory-internal: Allen (1978) rejects (1) because it would violate her level-ordering hypothesis, which states that derivation precedes compounding and syntax, so that it cannot take the result of these processes as a basis. The language data militate against (2), however, and I will assume here that (1) is the correct structure of synthetic compounds of the type illustrated by *red-bearded* and *three-master*.

The next question concerns the status of the bracketed part, *red beard* in *red-bearded* and *three mast* in *three-master*. There are two options here, analysing them as compounds or as phrases. The main disadvantage of a phrasal analysis is its apparent incompatibility with the Lexicalist Hypothesis, for which syntax follows word formation so that word formation cannot take phrases as input. An evaluation of a compound analysis depends on the way this concept is used. In a 'weak' theory of compounding, the name is given to any sequence of two or more free morphemes occurring inside a word. A 'strong' theory, by contrast, attempts to associate it with a well-described, contentful construction. In a weak theory of compounding, the claim that the bracketed constituent in (2) is a compound is vacuous. In a strong theory, it can be tested by comparing it with uncontroversial members of this class.

As I argued extensively elsewhere (ten Hacken 1994, 1999, in press), there is indeed a set of items, centred around such typical compounds as *bookshelf*, which share a number of morphosyntactic and semantic properties sufficiently important to qualify them as a class. The status of *red beard* and *three masts* can now be compared with the predictions evolving from the hypothesis that they are compounds. As described in ten Hacken (1994: 98-103), for A+N compounds with a qualitative adjective, the meaning is different from the corresponding A+N phrase. A *white paper*, interpreted as a phrase, refers to the intersection of two properties, being a paper and being white. As a compound, it means a particular type of paper. The type is indicated by the adjective, but the relationship with the meaning of the adjective may well be etymological only. In the context of the EU, for instance, a *white paper* is a document in which official policy is described. As *red beard* in *red-bearded* refers to the intersection of properties rather than to a type of beard, we must conclude that it is a phrase, unless we give up the term compound as a meaningful concept.

In conclusion, this section shows that synthetic compounding, in the original sense of Bloomfield (1933) and illustrated by *red-bearded* and *three-master*, involves a phrasal element as a base for derivation. This raises a number of new questions, two of which will be addressed here:

(3)   Are there other contexts in which morphological processes take phrases as input?

(4)   Is there a uniform analysis for this phenomenon?

In sections 2 and 3, two contexts which motivate a positive answer to (3) are discussed. In section 4 I will turn to the constraints referred to in (4) and also look into the consequences for the Lexicalist Hypothesis.

Determinative Compounding

Compounding, as I developed the concept in ten Hacken (1994, 1999, in press), is a process combining two elements, one of them the head. In English, if [X Y] is a compound, Y is the head and X the non-head. Morpho-syntactic properties are percolated from the head to the compound. The non-head is used in the interpretation of the compound, but not in determining its morpho-syntactic properties. As a consequence, the choice of the non-head is not subject to morpho-syntactic constraints, but only to semantic and pragmatic conditions of plausibility and usefulness of the compound. If this view of compounding is correct, we may expect the appearance of phrases in the non-head position in compounds, unless there are independent reasons for their exclusion. A first set of examples is given in (5-7).

(5)   American history teacher

(6)   full sentence definition

(7)   repetitive strain injury

In these examples, two structures are possible with the same basic shape as (1-2) above. In a phrasal analysis corresponding to (1), they have A+N phrases as non-heads. (5) is ambiguous between an analysis in which the entire expression is a compound, [[American history] teacher], and one in which the adjective modifies an N+N compound, [American [history teacher]]. The two analyses correspond to different interpretations with a different scope of the adjective. Therefore we have to retain both structures as possible ones. In the most straightforward interpretation of (6) and in the lexicalized meaning of (7) the adjectives modify the first noun only. In view of the options considered for (5), the examples in (6) and (7) should be analysed as having an [[A+N] N] structure only.

Having thus established that A+N is a constituent in each of the examples in (5-7), we have to address the question what the status of this constituent is. Again there is a distinction between (5) on the one hand and (6-7) on the other. Since *American* in (5) is a relational adjective (RA), Levi (1978) argues that *American history* should be considered as a compound. Although some of her arguments, rooted in a generative semantic framework, are problematic, the basic observation that RA+N combinations share essential properties with N+N compounds remains valid. If we assume that compounding is a meaningful concept, based on a common ground of morphosyntactic and semantic properties, RA+N combinations can be argued to be compounds, cf. ten Hacken (1994: 89-98).

In (6-7), the situation is rather different. Here the adjectives are not RAs, so that no RA+N compound is involved. Moreover, the meaning of the A+N expressions is fully compositional, so that no A+N compound of the type *white paper* is involved either. Therefore, there is no reason to consider *full sentence* and *repetitive strain* as compounds. They are A+N phrases.

The appearance of phrasal components in determinative compounds is not restricted to A+N phrases. The examples in (8-9) incorporate prepositions.

(8) over-the-counter stocks

(9) across-the-board rule application

In the case of (8), it is easy to establish that it involves a constituent [over-the-counter], because if this constituent were broken up, e.g. [over [the [counter stocks]]], the scope of the article *the* and of the preposition *over* would encompass not only *counter* but also *stocks*. Semantically such an analysis makes no sense. Structurally, it would require a new type of morphological combination. Therefore, (8) has the structure [[over-the-counter] stocks].

It is also clear that the constituent [over-the-counter] in (8) must be a phrase rather than a compound. Calling it a compound is only possible if 'compounding' is used as a purely superficial name without theoretical interest. Therefore, in (8) and (9) the P+Det+N combination is a PP.

Our next step is to show that the entire expression (8) is a compound. Normally, PP-modifiers follow the noun, e.g. *house with a garage*. The fact that there is a genuine difference between prenominal and postnominal PP modifiers can best be illustrated with a minimal pair where both are possible. Suppose we are looking for a translation of French *sur lie*, a qualification of unfiltered wine, bottled while it is still in its first cask, with its deposit or lees. Normally, the French expression is borrowed without translation. We could consider (10) and (11) as expressions for wine with this property.

(10) wine on lees

(11) on-lees wine

The difference between (10) and (11) is that (10) describes the situation of the wine and (11) a type of wine. This is exactly the difference in meaning we expect if (10) is a syntactic phrase and (11) a compound. Therefore we can conclude that (8) is a compound rather than a phrase, with a PP as its non-head. In (9), the only further complication is that the head of the compound is itself complex, *rule application*, as the meaning shows that the PP non-head does not modify *rule*.

In conclusion, we find phrasal elements as non-heads of determinative compounds. Possible phrase types include at least NPs consisting of A+N and PPs consisting of P+Det+N. Jespersen (1942: 155) mentions N+*and*+N phrases as non-heads. Lieber (1988: 204f.) gives a large variety of phrases, to which we will come back in section 4.

Exocentric Compounding

Bloomfield (1933: 235) introduces the distinction between endocentric and exocentric compounds as one of a series of partitionings of compounding. In the modern understanding of the term, *exocentric* implies the absence of a head. Bloomfield defines an exocentric compound as one in which the head has a different category to the entire compound. As an example, for *turnkey*, the fact that it is a noun whereas its head *turn* is a verb determines that it is an exocentric compound. In modern theoretical frameworks, these observations are somewhat hard to interpret. Despite the lack of general agreement on the notion of head, discussed for syntax by Allerton (1993), it is nowadays common to assume in morphology that the fact that *turn* is a verb and *turnkey* a noun excludes a headedness relation, because a head shares categorial features with its mother. Nevertheless, in both Bloomfield's and modern frameworks, the basic observation remains that morphological constructions can be identified as exocentric if there is no feature percolation between mother and head daughter.

A significant subclass of exocentric compounds is what Sanskrit grammarians called *bahuvrīhi*. Whitney (1879: 443-452) describes these compounds in Sanskrit as determinative compounds with a nominal head which have acquired adjectival inflection. If this were the entire description of the process, it would make them similar to relational adjectives, which have a meaning as the non-head of a compound *(urban development* is synonymous to *city development)* and are inflected as adjectives in languages such as Italian, e.g. *traffico urbano* ('urban traffic'), *viabilità urbana* ('urban road network'). However, in the process of becoming adjectives, exocentric compounds also modify their meaning. Whitney calls them "possessive compounds" because if X summarizes the meaning of the underlying determinative compound, they cannot be paraphrased as 'of, relating to X', the typical dictionary definition of a relational adjective, but rather as 'having X'. In Sanskrit the internal structure can be N+N, e.g. *agnítejas* 'having the brightness of fire', lit. 'fire-brightness', or A+N, e.g. *dīrgháçmaçru* 'long-bearded', lit. 'long-beard'.

In English, the most productive type of exocentric compounding is highly similar to Sanskrit bahuvrihi, except that the result is a noun rather than an adjective. Examples are *featherbrain* and *heavyweight*. Even though they may appear as modifiers of a noun, e.g. *heavyweight boxer*, there is no reason to consider them as adjectives. Adjectives with a possessive meaning are formed with *-ed* in English. The relevant contrast between Sanskrit and English is illustrated by the translation of the Sanskrit A+N compound *dīrgháçmaçru* as a synthetic compound *long-bearded* in English. By contrast, *heavyweight boxer* is a compound with a complex noun as its non-head. The difference is obvious in *heavyweight trainer* vs. *heavyweighted trainer*, where an unmarked interpretation of the former is a trainer responsible for heavyweights, whereas the latter expression attributes the heavy weight to the trainer.

There are several possible analyses for the English examples. Levi (1978: 64) proposes that the formation process of exocentric compounds includes a "beheading" step, eliminating the head. In its most general form, this proposal has the well known drawbacks of unrecoverable deletion processes as proposed for compounding in general by Lees (1960). There are numerous alternative underlying forms for *heavyweight*, with different heads, e.g. *boxer, person, man*, the choice among which is impossible in principle because the head is eliminated without leaving a trace. Moreover, even if we could agree on a rather general noun, e.g. *person*, the meaning of *heavyweight* is not equal to that of *heavyweight person*. In the appropriate context, e.g. "In the new board, Jack is our heavyweight person", it may well refer to someone responsible for organizing matches between heavyweights rather than to someone marked by a heavy weight.

A variant of this analysis mentioned by Levi (1978: 58) in a footnote has a single head for all exocentric compounds of this type, which she gives as *haver*, i.e. the agent noun of *have*. This is in line with her approach of 'recoverably deletable predicates' (RDPs), abstract predicates characterizing the relationship between the two members of a compound. The mechanism of RDPs was developed in order to avoid the problem of irrecoverable deep structure elements, deleted by transformations in the process of producing a surface structure. As I argued in detail in ten Hacken (1994: 44-49), this approach is fundamentally flawed because it locates the origin of the relationship between the two components of a compound in the semantics of the compounding construction, rather than in the semantics of the components themselves. As a consequence, any system of RDPs gives rise to spurious ambiguity, because different, synonymous analyses are available for one compound, as well as to excessive vagueness, because the meaning of an RDP is stretched. Thus, *language problems* can be described with the RDPs CAUSE, IN, or FROM, while the difference in meaning is hardly observable. Conversely,

Levi (1978: 283) uses FOR to account for *nose drops, cooking utensils, oil well, headache pills,* and *basketball season,* among others, although the relationship between the two components of the compounds is strikingly different.

If we now return to the proposal of a head noun *haver* as the deep head of exocentric compounds such as *heavyweight,* we find that the problem of ambiguous synonymous derivations does not arise, because there is no competing head noun. Vagueness is at least in part a desirable property, because the specification as *haver* leaves a number of features unspecified which can in fact take different values. Thus, in their lexicalized meanings, *heavyweight* is [+human], *redbreast* is [−human, +animate] (a type of bird), and *hardtop* is [−animate] (a type of car).

More problematic is the vagueness of the relationship characterized by *have*. The most typical relationship seems to be inalienable possession, i.e. the type of relation human beings and animals have to their body parts. For inanimate referents, this interpretation must be extended, which seems reasonable enough for examples such as *hardtop, hardback,* and *greenback*. If one imagines the car, the book, or the banknote in these examples as animate, the top or the back become like body parts. Less straightforward are examples such as *two-piece* (a type of suit) and *quickstep* (a type of dance). It is difficult to imagine the referents as animate. An interesting problem arises for such examples as *redcap* and *redcoat*. The referent of these nouns is a human being whose function is indicated by the red piece of clothing they wear. How felicitous is the characterization of such items in terms of inalienable possession? From the point of view of human beings, clothing is a prototypical example of alienable possession. Yet, from the point of view of the function denoted by the noun, the red cap or coat is essential.

If we extend the relationship from inalienable possession to the full meaning of the English verb *have*, we avoid problems such as these, but we are confronted with another type of problem familiar from RDPs, namely the arbitrariness of the language-specific classification implied by the predicates. Even if we restrict our attention to the transitive main verb *have*, we find a highly complex conglomerate of more or less related meanings. For a characterization of exocentric compounding by *have*, we would not only need to show that all exocentric compounds can be paraphrased with *have*, but also that all senses of *have* are used in exocentric compounding. Moreover, it is well-known that verbs with the semantic properties of English *have* are typologically marked, cf. den Dikken (1997). Given the widespread cross-linguistic occurrence of exocentric compounding, such a language-specific bias in the account of their formation would be undesirable.

The problems with the characterization of the semantics of exocentric compounding disappear as by magic as soon as we consider the process not as a type of compounding with a deleted head, but as a type of derivation. Whitney (1879: 445) translates Sanskrit *dīrghácmaçru* as 'long-bearded' although the components in Sanskrit mean simply 'long' and 'beard'.[2] The English examples of exocentric compounds are semantically quite close to the synthetic compounds in *-ed*, but the result is a noun rather than an adjective. Depending on the view of morphology adopted, *red-bearded* can be analysed as the result of the combination of a phrase and a suffix or as the result of a process applied to a phrase. In the case of *heavyweight*, we can either assume an affix without phonological realization or a process which happens not to affect the form of its argument. As discussed extensively by Jespersen (1942), conversion processes have specific semantic correlates similar to (other) derivation processes.[3]

---

2   Actually, Whitney seems quite hesitant to translate Sanskrit bahuvrihi compounds by English synthetic compounds. The large majority of his examples is translated with *of* or with *having*, even when a synthetic compound seems a straightforward option, e.g. *çukrávarṇa* 'of bright color' (1879: 445).

3   Jespersen devotes most of his sections on conversion to a semantic characterization and classification of the processes, e.g. (1942: 93-112) for the conversion of nouns and adjectives to verbs.

The only specific assumption which must be made in order to analyse exocentric compounds in terms of conversion is that the conversion process takes as input the range of combinations we find in exocentric compounding. The next question is, then, what the constraints on the input of the conversion process leading to such nouns as *heavyweight* are. From the point of view of the syntactic categories involved, there are three types: A+N (*heavyweight, redbreast, quickstep*, etc.), N+N *(featherbrain, cottontail)*, and Numeral + N *(two-piece)*. For the N+N examples, the input to conversion can be analysed as a compound. In fact, although it is not lexicalized as such, *featherbrain* can be used as a determinative compound as in (12) in addition to the more common use as an exocentric compound in (13).

(12) Because of his featherbrain, you can never rely on George.

(13) You can never rely on a featherbrain like George.

In the case of A+N input, we should rather assume a phrase than a compound. The weight of a *heavyweight* is not of a particular type, as expected for an A+N compound, but within a particular range indicated by *heavy*. In the case of Numeral + N, the compound option is unavailable altogether.

The non-occurrence of simple nouns as input for this process is probably a consequence of the pragmatic aspects of word formation. A new word is formed only in response to the need to name a concept (cf. ten Hacken & Smyk (to appear)). Given certain contextual conditions, it is useful to create terms for types of books marked by the nature of their back, *hardback* and *paperback*, but it is hard to imagine an analogous use for *back*. Moreover, the interpretation of *back* as a (type of?) book is blocked in the sense of Aronoff (1976), because it is already lexicalized as a noun with a different meaning.

In conclusion, exocentric compounds are the result of conversion of phrases. The conversion process involved resembles other conversion processes and derivational processes more generally in its semantic effects.

A unified analysis?

In the preceding sections we have seen three cases in which phrases occur as components of morphological constructions. They occur as bases for suffixation in synthetic compounding and for conversion in exocentric compounding, as well as in non-head position in determinative compounds. A natural question is then to what extent a unified analysis of phrases in these different contexts is possible. The analysis of these phenomena is of particular interest because of its implications for the interaction between syntax and morphology.

A first step towards an analysis is determining the syntactic category of the phrasal constituent. In general, there are two perspectives to determining the category of a phrase. On the one hand, we can concentrate on the internal structure of XP, the nature of its head, complements, etc. In syntax, the phrase *over the counter* is a PP, because its head *over* is a P and the DP *the counter* is a complement of this P. On the other hand, we can concentrate on the distribution of XP. There are particular positions in the tree where PPs can or cannot occur and because *over the counter* matches this distributional pattern it is a PP.

Unfortunately, neither of these perspectives can be fully used in determining the syntactic category of phrases in morphology. In (8), *over-the-counter stocks* contains a sequence of words identical to the PP *over the counter* in syntax, but in the compound this sequence does not have the usual PP properties. It is impossible to determine that *the counter* is a DP in (8) because it is not accessible to any syntactic operation. This can be explained independently, because, as argued in ten Hacken (1994: 74), a compound constitutes a "single discourse element", so that the non-head cannot be referred to by pronouns and must be interpretable on its own (either generically or as a proper noun). Similar arguments can be made for the bases of affixation and conversion. Therefore the internal structure of a phrase does not play a role in morphology. The distribution cannot be used either, for the straightforward reason that the morphological distribution is not a syntactic distribution unless we give up the distinction between morphology and syntax *a priori*. The only way to determine the category of *over-the-counter* in (8) is to consider the distribution and internal structure of the phrase with the same form in syntax.

A second question to be addressed is how the phrases end up as part of words. As mentioned in section 2, Lieber (1988: 204f.) gives an extensive list of examples illustrating the occurrence of different types of phrases in the non-head position in a compound. She concludes from this variety of phrases that word formation rules have to be part of syntax rather than of the lexicon, because otherwise the relevant rule mechanisms should be imported (i.e. duplicated) into the lexicon. In view of the preceding discussion, it is not surprising that a number of category labels in Lieber's set of examples are controversial. Thus she labels (14) and (15) as CP – N:

(14) God is dead theology

(15) connect the dots puzzle

There is no way in principle to determine whether (14) has a CP or an IP as its non-head. In (15) one might even think of a VP with a bare verb as the non-head.[4] The indeterminacy of the label does not necessarily weaken Lieber's argument, because we still have to account for the formation of these phrasal constituents, and syntactic rules are obviously able to do so. Wiese (1996), however, gives a set of different examples casting doubt on the assumption that it is syntax which is responsible for these

---

4   Another type of problem arises for her alleged AP – N examples (i) and (ii):
    (i)   pleasant to read book
    (ii) easy to sew pattern
    For reasons similar to the ones mentioned in the discussion of A+N combinations in section 1, I would argue that (i) and (ii) are syntactic combinations with an exceptional adjectival complement in prenominal position.

phrases. He uses examples of cross-linguistic and cross-modal compounds such as (16-18), translated from German.

(16) her *C'est-la-vie* attitude

(17) his [shrugging the shoulders] attitude

(18) the #-key

In (16) the non-head is a French phrase, in (17) it is a non-verbal gesture,[5] in (18) a nonalphabetic sign. If we pursue Lieber's argument, these examples demonstrate that we have to include French syntax, and non-linguistic sign systems into English syntax. Clearly this is as undesirable as duplicating the relevant syntactic rules into the lexicon. Therefore we need a different solution.

As an alternative, Wiese (1996) proposes that the phrasal non-heads of compounds are quotations, encapsulated in an X^0 category. The salience of a quotation can then account for the overrepresentation of lexicalized phrases. The scope of possible quotations encompasses any syntactic phrase, as well as foreign language and cross-modal expressions of the types illustrated in (16-18). This proposal combines very well with an account of compounding as developed in ten Hacken (1994, 1999), where the non-head of a compound has an exclusively semantic function, but its syntactic category is never referred to.

Wiese's proposal is reminiscent of Di Sciullo & Williams's (1987: 78-88) treatment of what they call "syntactic words", but it has a different scope. Di Sciullo & Williams propose the rewrite rule (19) in order to account for a range of French complex lexical items, two types of which are illustrated in (20) and (21), which violate their Right-hand Head Rule (RHR).

(19) N → XP

(20) essuie-mains   ('hand towel', lit. 'wipe-hands')

---

[5] Note the difference between the phrasal compound *shrugging-the-shoulders attitude* and the one in (17), where the non-head is replaced by a silent gesture.

(21) sans-papiers ('refugees without identity papers', lit. 'without-papers')

Both (20) and (21) are exocentric compounds. The pattern in (20) is found in English *pickpocket*, but with its marginal level of productivity, cf. Marchand (1969: 380-382), it hardly qualifies for a word formation rule in present-day English. P+N combinations as in (21) do not occur as exocentric compounds in English. Di Sciullo & Williams (1987: 88) claim that "the rule in (10) [our (19)] sums up much information about these items – they have the distribution and atomicity of words but the form of phrases." While (19) may be intuitively appealing, it is blatantly incorrect from a formal perspective, as pointed out by Anderson (1992: 316f.). On the one hand the V+N combinations exemplified by (20) are ungrammatical in French without an article, on the other many syntactically correct phrases cannot occur as X^0. Therefore (19) is definitely not the correct generalization.

If we compare Di Sciullo & Williams's (19) with Wiese's encapsulated quotation analysis, we find two main differences. The first is that (19) is less general than encapsulated quotation, because (19) relies on syntax to generate the XPs whereas quotation covers non-syntactic items as well. The second is that (19) is proposed for exocentric compounding while encapsulated quotation is meant to cover non-heads of determinative compounds. These observations show that we have two different phenomena here. The phrases in the non-head position in compounds do not constitute the same set as the phrases which can be input to affixation and conversion. This is not so surprising. Whereas compounds need their non-heads only for semantic specification, without imposing syntactic restrictions, derivational processes such as affixation and conversion regularly do impose such restrictions.

In the discussion of English synthetic and exocentric compounding, three processes emerged which may involve phrases, exemplified by *red-bearded*, *three-master*, and *heavyweight*. In derivation, each process (affix or type of conversion) can in principle determine the set of bases to which it may apply independently. It is striking, then, that these processes all accept phrasal bases of the type X+N, where X is either an adjective or a numeral. On the basis of the database described in ten Hacken (2002), we can conclude that, as far as there are exceptions to this generalization, they can be accounted for by non-morphological processes.[6] The high level of productivity of the three processes involved in synthetic and exocentric compounding calls for a morphological account of the formation of their bases. The tight constraints on their distribution and internal structure suggest that English has a morphological, non-syntactic category, which I propose to call morphological phrase (MP). MPs are formed in the lexicon by a morphological rule combining an adjective or numeral with a noun. They do not have a syntactic distribution because they lack a syntactic category. They do have a morphological distribution, however, because MP is a valid morphological category. The category MP is not language-specific, but the composition rules for MPs are. Examples (20-21) suggest that French has different MP rules, but more research in this area is necessary. Finally, MPs have nothing to do with the possibility of phrases in determinative compounds, where a much larger degree of variation is possible.

In conclusion, we did not manage to come up with a unified account of phrases in synthetic, determinative, and exocentric compounding, because the behaviour of phrases as non-heads of determinative compounds diverges quite substantially from what can be observed in synthetic and exocentric compounding. For determinative compounding, Wiese's (1996) account seems to be

---

[6] The most common track for such items seems to be through the non-head position of a compound. An example is *read-only*. The Collins Cobuild corpus, <http://titanic.cobuild.collins.co.uk>, only gives the collocation *read-only memory*. The *Webopedia*, <http://www.webopedia.com>, gives a definition, "Capable of being displayed, but not modified or deleted", which is neutral as to its syntactic status, but allows also phrases such as "The right thing to do is to mount the floppy read-only", found at <http://www.freebsddiary.org/floppy-readonly.php>. (All web sites as of 3 January 2003.)

the best currently available. For synthetic and exocentric compounding, a unified account based on MPs was proposed. Both have in common that they are compatible with the Lexicalist Hypothesis. Word formation remains in the lexicon, even if it involves phrases.

References

Allen, M. R. (1978). *Morphological Investigations*, Ph.D. Dissertation, University of Connecticut.
Allerton, D. J. (1993). 'The need to keep one's head(s)', in *Contributions aux 4èmes rencontres régionales de linguistique, 14-15 septembre 1992*, Lüdi & Zuber (eds.). 7-17.
Allerton, D. J., N. Nesselhauf & P. Skandera (eds.) (2002). *Phraseological Units: basic concepts and their application*. Basel: Schwabe.
Anderson, S. R. (1992). *A-Morphous Morphology*, Cambridge: Cambridge University Press.
Aronoff, M. H. (1976). *Word Formation in Generative Grammar*, Cambridge (Mass.): MIT Press.
Bloomfield, L. (1933). *Language*. London: Allen & Unwin.
Borer, H. (1998). 'Morphology and Syntax'. In: Spencer & Zwicky (eds.), 151-190.
Brentari, D., G. Larson & L. MacLeod (eds.) (1988). *Papers from the 24th Annual Regional Meeting of the Chicago Linguistic Society, Part Two: Parassession on Agreement in Grammatical Theory*, Chicago: Chicago Linguistic Society.
Chomsky, N. (1970). 'Remarks on Nominalization'. In: Jacobs & Rosenbaum (eds.), 184-221.
den Dikken, M. (1997). 'The Syntax of Possession and the Verb *Have*'. *Lingua* 101: 129-150.
Di Sciullo, A. M. & E. Williams (1987). *On the Definition of Word*. Cambridge (Mass.): MIT Press.
Fabb, N. (1998). 'Compounding'. In: Spencer & Zwicky (eds.), 66-83.
ten Hacken, P. (1994). *Defining Morphology: A Principled Approach to Determining the Boundaries of Compounding, Derivation, and Inflection*. Hildesheim: Olms.

ten Hacken, P. (1999). 'Motivated Tests for Compounding'. *Acta Linguistica Hafniensia* 31: 27-58.

ten Hacken, P. (2002). 'Word Formation and the Validation of Lexical Resources'. *LREC 2002: Third International Conference on Language Resources and Evaluation - Proceedings*, ed. González Rodríguez, M. & C. Paz Suárez Araujo, 935-942.

ten Hacken, P. (in press). 'What are compounds?'. in Allerton, Nesselhauf & Skandera (eds.).

ten Hacken, P. & D. Smyk (to appear). 'Le rôle de l'analogie et des règles dans la formation de mots'. *Travaux Linguistiques de CerLiCO*.

Jacobs, R. A. & P. S. Rosenbaum (eds.) (1970). *Readings in English Transformational Grammar*. Waltham (Mass.): Ginn.

Jespersen, O. (1942). *A Modern English Grammar on Historical Principles; Part VI: Morphology*. Copenhagen: Munksgaard.

Lees, R. B. (1960). *The Grammar of English Nominalizations*. Bloomington: Indiana University Press & Den Haag: Mouton.

Levi, J. N. (1978). *The syntax and semantics of complex nominals*, New York: Academic Press.

Lieber, R. (1988). 'Phrasal Compounds in English and the Morphology-Syntax Interface'. In: Brentari et al. (eds.), 202-222.

Lieber, R. (1992). *Deconstructing Morphology: Word Formation in Syntactic Theory*. Chicago: University of Chicago Press.

Marchand, H. (1969). *The Categories and Types of Present-Day English Word-formation: A Synchronic-Diachronic Approach*. 2nd edition, München: Beck.

Roeper, T. & M. Siegel (1978). 'A Lexical Transformation for Verbal Compounds'. *Linguistic Inquiry* (9) 199-260.

Spencer, A. & A. M. Zwicky (eds.) (1998). *The Handbook of Morphology*. Oxford: Blackwell.

Whitney, W. D. (1879). *A Sanskrit Grammar, including both the classical language, and the order dialects, of Veda and Brahmana*. Leipzig: Breitkopf & Härtel.

Wiese, R. (1996). 'Phrasal Compounds and the Theory of Word Syntax', *Linguistic Inquiry* (27) 183-193.

ANTHONY COWIE

Some aspects of the treatment of phraseology in the *OED*

In the 'Rules and directions for collectors' drawn up by the Etymological Committee of the Philological Society (1859), examples were provided of the phraseological types that readers should record. Subsumed under 'phrases' were proverbs (e.g. *He that lovythe me, lovythe my hound, And my servaunt also*.) and idiomatic phrases (several being of the verb + object-noun type illustrated by *to save his bacon*). Two further categories followed: 'disused syntactical combinations' such as *such thirty* = "thirty time as many as" and 'constructions' (i.e. grammatical patterns such as *cleanse + with*), made harder to distinguish, perhaps, by the heading 'idioms' being applied to both (1859: 12-13).

'Proverb' and 'idiomatic phrase' were either already familiar as categories or could be made so by the examples, and were no doubt helpful to collectors. The other terms reflect a wider tendency, noted later by Harold Palmer (1938), to run together as 'idioms' expressions which pose problems of meaning and constructions that present difficulties of grammar.

James Murray's approach to the treatment of phraseology in the *Oxford English Dictionary*, though none the less remarkable, owed very little to the categorization I have just outlined. In the General Explanations of 1888, he provided for the inclusion of a general category of 'phrases' in *OED*, but gave no indication of how they were to be sub-classified, or where the resulting types were to be located and treated. Phrases could, it is true, be recognized as Main Words, if 'from their history, meaning, or importance [they could] claim to be treated in separate articles' (Murray 1888: xix). However, the phrases which are treated in

Main Articles in the *OED* were – and still are – relatively few: the great bulk, whether of unified meaning or not, appear as part of the microstructure of articles.[1]

This lack of editorial reference to the treatment of phraseology is all the more striking when one reflects that certain structural features of major entries in the *OED* are evidently designed to bring together phraseological items of a particular type and to give scope for a detailed grammatical sub-classification. These and other recurrent aspects of the handling of phraseology in the *OED* are clearly worthy of detailed analysis and appraisal, and will be examined here against the background of more recent advances in phraseology.

The study has five points of focus. After giving a brief account of relevant developments, over the past twenty years or so, in the field of phraseology, I shall attempt to describe certain recurrent features of the entry structure of *OED* with a view (a) to demonstrating how particular conventions of labelling and organization reflect the editorial view of what the major phraseological categories are – and how far they coincide with more recent descriptive accounts; (b) to examining how the various grammatical constructions in which idioms can occur are systematically presented; (c) to indicating in what ways, and how far, the permitted variation of idioms is conveyed; and, finally (d), to showing how far the difference between idioms and collocations is recognized, and whether the different categories are separately positioned and contrastively treated.

These features call for exploration in some depth, and though I have chosen to limit the analysis to three (quite widely separated) noun entries, *heart*, *leg* and *time*, the various aspects I wish to examine are well represented. Again, while I have limited

---

[1] In recent critical studies of coverage and definition in *OED 1* (Curzan 2000, Silva 2000), and perhaps more surprisingly in published accounts of how various aspects of its organization might, in the light of independent or in-house scholarly work, be revised for *OED 3* (e.g. Durkin 1999), there is little reference to the comparable need for a critical appraisal of the treatment of phraseology.

to two – idioms and collocations – the number of phraseological types considered, these also are treated in some detail. Little is said of the spread of 'pragmatic' categories that are found in the dictionary. Yet, overall, enough has been examined to show that investigation of the treatment of phraseology in the *OED* is a worthwhile enterprise, for linguists and lexicographers alike.

Some issues of definition and terminology

Within the past two decades, a good deal of attention has been given, within the field of English phraseology, to the definition of various key categories and their harmonization within general descriptive frameworks. Work by British phraseologists has drawn extensively on the earlier achievements of East European scholars, and most particularly on 'classical' Russian theory and description (Cowie 1998a), though the contribution of Harold Palmer and A. S. Hornby, in the early 1930s, in producing a grammatically based description of English 'collocations' should not be overlooked (Palmer 1933).

Most of the early East European schemes and their later refinements agree in recognizing a primary division between 'word-like' units, which function as elements in the simple sentence, and 'sentence-like' units which operate pragmatically as proverbs, catchphrases, slogans, and so on (Cowie 1994, Moon 1998b). Examples of the first type, which following Gläser (1998) I shall refer to as 'nominations', include *by heart* and *break one's heart*, and of the second, which I shall call 'propositions', *many hands make light work* (proverb) and *many happy returns of the day* (routine formula) (Cowie 2001).

Further divisions can be recognized within both major categories. I have already referred to nominations as essentially syntactic multi-word units. For example, *by heart* functions as an adjunct and *break one's heart* as a verb + object-noun predicate. The analysis and dictionary treatment of such examples is, however, further complicated by the fact that examples of a given structural type – say preposition + noun – may differ with regard to semantic opaqueness or structural flexibility, or indeed both. They may, in a word, differ in idiomaticity.

Idioms in the full sense are nominations whose semantic unity severely limits, or prevents altogether, the replacement of both or any of their components by other words. Compare *break/*fragment one's heart* and *speak one's mind/*brain*, where the effect of substitution is to produce nonsense or a non-idiom (Cowie 1994). Full idioms are often subject, too, to grammatical restrictions: *speak one's mind*, for instance, cannot be made passive: **my mind is spoken* (though compare the entirely acceptable *my mind is made up*).

As the last example may suggest, full idioms are not a watertight category: they are related along a continuum, or scale, to a large class of nominations which have a figurative meaning (i.e. in terms of the whole expression in each case) but which may also retain a literal interpretation. Examples of such 'figurative' idioms are *mark time* and *do a U-turn*. Scrutiny of OED suggests that many nominations (e.g. *at heart*, *by heart*) have been fully idiomatic for centuries; in other cases, a literal phrase (e.g. *run off the rails*) may establish itself – perhaps over no more than a few decades – through constant reuse, then undergo figurative extension and finally petrify (Cowie et al. 1983: xii).

A third type of nomination, and one to which increasing attention has been given in Britain since the early 1980s as one result of the development of large-scale text corpora, is the collocation (Howarth 1996, Moon 1998a). Collocations, like idioms, are defined partly by their occurrence in particular grammatical constructions. (Thus, there are adjective + noun collocations and verb + object-noun collocations.) There, however, the resemblance ends. Whereas in the case of figurative idioms the *whole* of the expression has undergone a metaphorical shift (consider again, *run off the rails*, *close ranks*), in the case of a collocation made up of two major-class words, only one word has (the adjective in *a tidy sum*, the verb in *waste time*). The well-worn figurative meaning of one word in those cases, and the literal meaning of the other, are two of three related properties of collocations that need to be highlighted. The third is that the figurative element may arbitrarily restrict the range of choice (the 'collocational range' or 'collocability') at the other element (Cowie 1994, Moon 1998b). Consider *a tidy sum/amount* and *waste time/hours*.

The verbs in certain collocations belong to a limited set whose members are systematically related. In the case of *have something in mind*, *keep something in mind*, *bring something to mind*, *come to mind*, for example, we have a number of so-called 'delexical' verbs which recur in many collocations with nouns other than *mind*. Moreover, those collocations are often related in terms of such oppositions as 'stative'/'dynamic' and 'non-causative'/'causative', as in the pair *come/bring something to somebody's attention* (Allerton 2002). Expressions within this general class, however, are still collocational by virtue of the independent sense of the nouns ("awareness", "consciousness", in the case of *mind*) and the limited and sometimes arbitrary choice of accompanying verbs (consider *bear* in *bear something in mind*).

Let us lastly return to the distinction drawn earlier between nominations and propositions. As we shall see, propositions in *OED* – not referred to by any all-embracing term – make up a clustering of expressions, often placed towards the end of an entry, that includes proverbs, 'ejaculations of surprise' and 'exclamatory invocations'. Phraseologists would have little difficulty in recognizing these as 'pragmatic' expressions: they differ from nominations both in spanning complete sentences and in having a speech-act function. *Bless my heart!* and *Bless his heart!* – which are imperative sentences as well as invocations – meet both these conditions (Cowie 2001, Gläser 1986).

Microstructure: the labelling and arrangement of phrases and propositions

It was suggested earlier that conventions of organization and labelling within the microstructure of *OED* were used to identify certain major phraseological categories. Let us now consider those conventions in some detail.

Unlike compounds, which are for the most part clustered at the end of an entry under the general heading 'Attributive uses and Combinations' (commonly abbreviated to *'attrib.* and *Comb.'*), nominations (including full and figurative idioms) and propositions (embracing ejaculations, proverbial sayings, and so on) are treated either in one or more parts of the entry dealing with the simple word, or in a major section designed to give special prominence to phraseology.

As regards labelling, it is significant – though there are many individual exceptions – that the editors in general designate as 'phrases' those multi-word units which can function as elements in the structure of sentences. Thus, as a general rule, phrases are nominations. (The terms will be used interchangeably in what follows.) We can see, for example, that *next the heart*, at (1) below, is a prepositional phrase, potentially operating as an adjunct, while *to have one's heart in* (a thing), at (2), functions as a predicate (specifically verb + object-noun + adjunct). Idioms and collocations, however, are not distinguished by special labelling in *OED*, though – as we shall see – they are identifiable in part from their boldface forms.

Returning to arrangement, and going into rather more detail, we find three recurrent approaches.[2] (a) A phrase may appear – either alone or with a few other expressions – as part of a numbered sub-entry dealing initially with a sense of the simple word,

---

2   For a broad and lucid account of the microstructure of *OED*, though with particular reference to the hierarchical treatment of senses, and their supporting examples, see Zgusta (1989).

to which the phrase is then shown to be related. Consider sub-entry **4. at heart**, where the indication is given that the noun in the sense 'the stomach' is chiefly to be found in the phrase *next the heart*, though with the further limitation that the phrase, like the sense of the simple word, is now obsolete or dialectal:

(1)   **4.** The stomach. *Obs.* or *dial.* Chiefly in phr. ***next the heart***: on an empty stomach, fasting (*obs.* or *dial.*) ...

An instance of two formally and semantically related phrases appearing in the same sub-entry can be found at **heart 11. b.**

(2)   **11. b.** The source of ardour, enthusiasm, or energy. So ***to have one's heart in, put one's h. into*** (a thing).

Various conventions of typography and abbreviation are worth noting here. One is that where phrases are presented, as here, as part of a sub-entry of the simple word, the standard choice of typeface is bold italic; another that a second (and any subsequent) mention of the headword is often (though not always) abbreviated; a third that parentheses and a shift from bold italic are sometimes used to indicate the place of a proform such as 'thing' or 'one's'.[3]

The above style of presentation, (a), may be found in the same major entry as style (b), where an entire numbered sub-entry – or the various lettered divisions within it, as at **mind, 9.a., b.**, etc. – are devoted to a block of phrases, with no reference necessarily being made to a meaning of the headword. Consider in this respect the arrangement at **leg, 2.**, shown in Figure 1:

---

3   The choice of a 'secondary' face for phrases in *OED 1* was lightface italic. To ensure greater clarity of presentation, bold italic, the typeface that replaced it in *OED 2* (1989), is preferred here. Note: the latter edition 'contains the whole text, unaltered in all essentials, of the twelve-volume first edition, which appeared in 1933' (1989: xi).

leg, *n.*

2. Phrases.   a. General references. ***all legs and wings***, said of an overgrown awkward young person; also Naut., of an overmasted vessel. ***on the leg***, (of a dog or horse) long in the leg, leggy. ***the boot is on the other leg*** (see BOOT *n.*³ 1b). ***to pull*** (or ***draw*** Sc.) ***a person's leg***, to impose upon, 'get at', befool him (colloq.). †***to fight at the leg*** (see quot. 1785). ***to give a person a leg up***, to help him to climb up or get over an obstacle, mount (a horse, etc.); *fig.*, to help over a difficulty; hence ***leg-up*** n., a help, support, boost. ***to hang a leg*** (see HANG *v.* 4c). ***to have a bone in one's leg*** (see BONE *n.* 9). ***to have a leg***: to be physically attractive, to have a fine appearance (*Obs.*). ***to have one's leg over the harrows***, to be out of control. ***to lift, lift up*** (or ***heave up***) ***the leg***: said of a dog voiding urine. ***to show a leg***: to get out of bed; to make one's appearance. ***to be tied by the leg***: to be prevented from doing something by some circumstance.

Figure 1: OED entry for leg, 2. Phrases

Here, it happens that very few of the listed phrases survive into present-day English (by contrast, consider ***to pull a person's leg***, ***to give a person a leg up*** and ***to show a leg***). The point I wish to stress, however, which concerns the grouping of these items and their meanings, is that no phrase can be defined by reference to a sense of the simple word *leg*. The explanation would seem to be that the phrases are regarded as semantically opaque.

Finally, in a number of longer entries, and especially longer entries devoted to nouns – thus, **back**[1], **heart, time** – we find style (c), a mode of presentation in which phrases, and after them propositions, are assigned to a separate major section of the entry, positioned directly after that devoted to 'the simple word' (at 'I') and immediately before one dealing with 'attributive uses and combinations' (at 'III').[4] The justification for the separate grouping of phrases in certain entries is that, in such cases, a sufficient number of idioms that can be defined as wholes, i.e. independently of the headword (*back*, *heart*, etc.) which they contain, are assumed to exist. It is no doubt to emphasize the unitary nature (i.e. idiomaticity) of the phrases thus treated that they are printed in regular bold print – like the headword itself – though, as we shall see, a number of forms regarded as dependent on, or derived from, an initial, key form are printed in bold italic (see Figure 2, below).

II. Phrases

* *With governing preposition.*

at heart. In one's inmost thoughts or feelings; ...

by heart. In the memory; from memory; by rote; ...

from one's **heart.** Out of the depth's of one's soul; with the sincerest or deepest feeling.

in ... heart. a. *in (one's) heart*: in one's inmost thoughts or feelings; ...

c. *in heart*: in good spirits. So in phr. *to put in* (or *into*) *heart*: to restore to good spirits.

near, next one's **heart.** ...

out of heart. a. In low spirits; discouraged, disheartened.

with ... heart. a. *with ... all one's heart, with one's whole heart*, ... with great sincerity, earnestness, or devotion; ...

b. *with a heart and a half*: with great pleasure, willingly: *with half a heart*: half-heartedly, with divided affection or enthusiasm.

---

4   The precise arrangement varies in individual cases. In the entry for **time**, for example, the section devoted to phrases occurs after three major semantic divisions of the simple word: 'I. = A space or extent of time', 'II. = Time when: a point of time ...', 'III. = In generalized sense'.

** *With verb and preposition.*

find in one's **heart.** To feel inclined or willing; ... now chiefly in negative and interrogative sentences.

a. have at heart. To have as an object in which one is deeply interested.

b. So, conversely, *to be at the heart of.*

lay to heart. To take into one's serious consideration, as a thing to be kept carefully in mind; ...

take to heart. To take seriously; to be much affected by; to grieve over; ...

*** *With governing verb.*

break the heart of. a. To kill, crush, or overwhelm with sorrow. **b.** To accomplish the hardest part of (a task), to 'break the back of'.

cry (*eat, fight, plague, slave, tease, tire, weary, weep,* etc.) one's **heart out:** to cry (etc.) violently or exhaustingly: see the verbs.

eat one's **heart:** to suffer or pine away from vexation or longing.

a. have ... heart. *to have the heart*: to be courageous or spirited enough, to prevail upon oneself (to do something); also (in mod. use and chiefly in negative sentences), to find it in one's heart, to be hard-hearted enough.

b. *have, put (one's) heart in, into*: [with cross-reference to earlier sub-entry]

take heart. To pluck up courage. (Also with qualifying adj.) *to take heart of grace,* etc.

**** *With another noun.*

heart and hand. (Also *with heart and hand.*) With will and execution; readily, willingly.

heart ... heart. a. *heart of hearts* (orig. more correctly, *heart of heart, heart's heart*): the heart's core; the centre or depth of one's heart; ... Usually *in one's heart of hearts*.

b. *a heart and a heart*, a Hebraism = duplicity, insincerity.

c. *heart-to-heart*: used to denote conversation, discussion, etc. of real frankness and sincerity; usually *attrib.* but also *absol.* as *n*.

heart and soul. a. The whole of one's affections and energies; one's whole being.

b. *advb.* With all one's energy and devotion.

c. *attrib.* Devoted and enthusiastic.

Figure 2: Phrases and their grammatical patterns

As regards the idiomatic status of these phrases, it seems clear that most are now opaque and invariable. There are, however, some interesting marginal cases. The phrases *from one's heart* and *in one's heart*, though listed separately, and having now lost all analogical force, appear to have originated as related locational/ directional metaphors, viz. *from/in one's heart* = "from/at the source or location of one's deepest feelings". (Consider also *in heart* = "in good spirits", *out of heart* = "in low spirits".) There is also an striking instance of collocability being an integral part of an idiom. In the case of *cry/weep one's heart out*, *one's heart out* is a petrified stem, to which the verbs, in a literal sense, are obligatorily linked. Historically, as the record shows, the collocational range was stretched to include *eat*, *fight*, *plague*, *slave*, *tease*, *tire*, *weary*.

Returning to propositions, these appear, as I have remarked, at the end of the block ('II') devoted to phrases, where in the **heart** entry they are subdivided thus: 'In ejaculations of surprise and exclamatory invocations', 'Proverbial phrases and locutions'. And yet, the range of pragmatic types in use (and actually included in the *OED*) is wider than traditional labels such as invocation or proverbial phrase would suggest, and some may have gone unrecognized by editors. Take, for example, *to have a heart*, which appears not alongside other propositions in the entry for **heart**, but alone at letter **d.**, sub-entry **10** – where it is particularly well illustrated. It is in fact a 'speech formula' – one of a class of propositions used to convey a speaker's attitude to other participants and their messages – here functioning as an indignant response to something another speaker has said, as this example from the dictionary makes clear:

(3) **1967** J. B. Priestley ... 'You haven't made any plans for him, have you?' 'How could I? ... Have a heart!'

Phrases and their grammatical patterns

There is another important structural feature associated with the third style of presentation. This is that, within the major section headed 'II. Phrases', items of a particular structural type which function in simple sentence structure – for example, prepositional phrases (e.g. *by heart, from one's heart*) and verb + object-noun predicates (e.g. *cry ... one's heart out, take heart*) – are arranged in sub-sections, each headed by a reference to the structural pattern concerned. All the boldface items listed in those sub-sections, with the sole exception of those marked *Obs.* (i.e. obsolete), are set out in Figure 2, above, under their respective sub-section headings.

It should be pointed out that none of the headings used is entirely helpful, while some are misleading. Consider *With governing preposition* and *With governing verb*. Since the lists that these headings introduce consist mainly of semantic units, one could argue that the prepositions and verbs included in them no more govern *heart* – whether semantically or grammatically – than *heart* governs them. The component words, as we have seen, are in fact fused in almost all cases. As regards *With verb and preposition* and *With another noun*, the latter pattern could perhaps be made more explicit by inserting the headword at the point where it occurs, and by showing that the relevant linking words are either *and* or a preposition, thus:

(4) **heart + and** or *preposition + noun*

The case of *With verb and preposition* is more complex. The heading makes no distinction between transitive and intransitive verbs, while the boldface forms that it introduces may seem at first sight to consist of intransitive constructions. In fact they are all transitive, as the examples make clear, and this could first be indicated in the heading, specifically by the insertion of a proform:[5]

(5) *transitive verb* + something + *preposition* + **heart**

Then, second, adjustments are perhaps needed to the forms themselves, reflecting in the case of **find in** one's **heart** that a final infinitive construction (with optional cataphoric *it*) occurs in all the cited examples from the sixteenth century onwards:

(6) **find (it) in** one's **heart to** do something
    have something **at heart**
    lay something **to** (one's) **heart**
    take something **to heart**

Returning briefly to the category headed *With governing verb*, it should be noted that in **break the heart of** and *have, put (one's) heart in, into*, but not in other members of this set, there is a final prepositional phrase, and that this might be included, parenthetically, in the heading:

(7) *transitive verb* + **the** or one's + **heart** (+ *preposition* + somebody or something)

---

5   In this and other suggested headings, part-of-speech labels are in italic, proforms in roman and actual lexical components of the idiom in bold roman. Any optional words are in parentheses.

Idioms and their variants

We now turn to consider in what ways the permitted variation of idioms is conveyed. As we can see from **have, put (one's) heart in, into**, quoted just above, and the obsolete **put** or **set to** or **on the heart**, variation at one or more points is indicated by juxtaposing the alternative words – though there is some inconsistency in the convention used to mark off the choices: commas in the first case, 'or' in the second. (Compare also: near, next one's heart and *to put in* (or *into*) *heart*.)

However, where variation involves a change of word order as well as a change of wording, the related phrases are set out separately. It is worth noting that of those phrases, the first is usually in bold while the other, or others, are in bold italic:

(8)   with ... heart. a. *with ... all one's heart, with one's whole heart,* ... with great sincerity, earnestness, or devotion; ...

The switch from one typeface to the other is significant. As we saw earlier, a phrase may appear – in a type (a) lay-out – as part of a numbered sub-entry dealing first with a meaning of the simple word, to which the phrase is then shown to be related. The dependent relationship of the phrase to the word is indicated by printing the phrase in bold italic. If we now look back at the much more complex lay-out illustrated in Figure 2, we shall find a relationship of dependence here too. Phrases whose definition does not require reference to their component words – thus, **take to heart, take heart** – appear first in bold print. By contrast, phrases which depend in some way upon such idioms appear afterwards, and in bold italic. There may, at a further level of dependency, be a relationship – more or less explicitly announced – between one form in bold italic and another. Consider, at (9), **c.** *in heart*, and what follows:

(9)   in ... heart. a. *in (one's) heart*: in one's inmost thoughts or feelings; ...

c. *in heart*: in good spirits. So in phr. ***to put in*** *(*or *into)* ***heart***: to restore to good spirits.

We should note, too, that the introductory bold form here, with its three included points, has a special function. Like **with ... heart,** at (8), above, it does not represent a canonical form, but is an abstraction from the various forms that it introduces. Alphabetically placed in the list of prepositional phrases in relation to the bold forms **from** one's **heart** and **near, next** one's **heart** – which represent actual idioms for which citation evidence is provided – **in ... heart** serves simply to facilitate reference.

Bearing in mind, then, that the relationships of form and meaning that exist between phrases may be shown as holding between forms in bold italic, what are those relationships? Three may be referred to here. First, there is the relationship of synonymy found between phrases that are partly alike in form. (See again the bold italic forms at (8), above.) Second, there is the copula–causative relationship represented by *(be) in heart*, *put* somebody *in (*or *into) heart* shown at (9), and well supported by examples. Third, reference may be made to an earlier and more correct form, and possibly also to the variant now usually heard:

(10) **heart ... heart. a.** ***heart of hearts*** (orig. more correctly, ***heart of heart, heart's heart***): the heart's core; the centre or depth of one's heart; ... Usually ***in one's heart of hearts***.

Idioms and collocations

I suggested earlier that a phrase might appear – as in the (a) type arrangement – as part of a sub-entry dealing initially with a sense of the simple word, to which the phrase was then shown to be related. Are such phrases collocations? In some cases they undoubtedly are. Collocations have no distinctive label in *OED*, but they are often treated in a distinctive way, in major entries such as those for **heart** and **time**, in the section or sections devoted to 'the simple word'. In what follows I shall attempt to identify some of these, and provide a critical account of how they are treated. I shall also try to determine whether all the phrases treated within a section devoted to the simple word are in fact collocations, or whether collocations and idioms are treated more or less side by side, and perhaps indistinguishably. First, though, let us deal with a phrase – or set of phrases – which belong to neither of these categories.

In the very first sub-entry of **time**, *n*. we find the following:

(11) **1.a.** A limited stretch or space of continued existence, as the interval between two successive events or acts, or the period through which an action, condition or state continues; ...as *a long time, a short time, some time, for a time*.

Here we find a good deal of freedom of choice. It can be shown, first, that for *time* in the first two phrases we can substitute a number of nouns of equivalent meaning, some ('stretch', 'interval', 'period') being suggested by the definition itself. So we have this: *a long/short time, a long/short stretch* (informal), *a long/short interval, a long/short period, a long/short while*. Note, too, that the first three phrases in the entry can be preceded by *for* and *after* – *after* replacing *for* in the fourth. These tests of substitution and extension, to which others could be added, suggest that here there are few limitations on the substitutability of elements, other than those imposed by the meaning of the noun. We have, in short, not collocations – where some arbitrary limitation is always to be expected – but well-established 'free combinations'.[6] Here, we are outside phraseology altogether (Cowie 1997, Howarth 1996).

---

6   In a comparison between OED and the dictionaries of Jakob Grimm, Emilé Littré and Matthias de Fries, Osselton points out that 'unlike the other dictionaries the OED does not set out lists of common *collocational patterns*' (2002: 73). Osselton probably had in mind what I have referred to as 'free combinations', since the Dutch examples he quotes (the equivalents of *ripe, full, golden ears (of corn)*) are indeed free; moreover,

That example may be contrasted with the complex expression that appears in the following sub-entry – though one should note at the same time that the style of presentation differs very little:

(12) The seat of love or affection, as in many fig. phrases:
to give, lose one's heart (to), to have, obtain, gain a person's heart.

Here, we may recognize more of the 'delexical' verbs mentioned earlier (cf. *bring something to mind, come to mind*), though the reference to figurative meaning should apply to the recurrent noun, not to the phrases as such (Cowie 1997). The complex expression is in fact made up of a number of two-word collocations, and there are systematic relations between the verbs, such that *give* and *lose one's heart to somebody* function in ditransitive constructions (where the indirect object is 'recipient'), while *have* and *obtain* and *gain a person's heart* function in simple transitive constructions (where the subject is 'beneficiary' and *a person* is 'giver') (cf. Fillmore & Atkins 1992).

We can see that, in example (12), the defining phrase 'the seat of love or affection ...' relates only to *heart*. The definition of the simple word, as used in those phrasal contexts, is a reminder of its independence within the collocation. In other entries, though, the two elements of the bold italic form (or forms), and their grammatical pattern, are matched with corresponding elements in the definition:

(13) **to bring, call to mind**: to summon to remembrance ...

Editors may actually favour one approach, then the other, within the same entry.

---

unlike collocations in the strict sense, such listed 'patterns' are relatively infrequent in *OED*. For modern French practice in this regard see Cowie (2002).

Earlier I asked whether all the phrases treated within sections devoted to the simple word were in fact collocations. For a possible answer to this question consider, in the **time** entry, and immediately under *a long time*, etc., the following phrases:

(14) *in no time, in less than no time* (colloq.) immediately, very quickly or soon.

These phrases are quite different from the collocations (and free combinations) we have analysed. They do not allow replacement of the noun, so that **in no interval*, **in no while* are nonsensical; nor could we claim that **in some time* contrasts with *in no time*, or **in more than no time* with *in less than no time*. The phrases are more or less transparent, but their rigidity, to which the unusual placement of primary stress (viz. *in 'no time, in less than 'no time*) contributes, suggests that they are now idiomatic.

The examples we have just considered suggest that, in sections devoted to meanings of the simple word, there may be a number of inconsistencies in the way instances of the same category are treated, while the contrastiveness of different categories may not always be fully brought out. The great strength of the dictionary, as far as the treatment of phraseology is concerned, lies in the assignment of idioms – in a number of major entries – to large sections, or blocks, labelled 'Phrases', in which idioms of various structural types are treated in grammatically labelled subsections.

Conclusion

This has been a limited study, both in the number of entries surveyed, and in the selectiveness with which I have had to deal with particular categories and individual phrases and propositions. Perhaps enough has been said, however, to make the case for further, more detailed, analyses of the treatment of phraseology in *OED*.

Then also, and leaving aside my references to the locational metaphors from which certain 'full' idioms may have derived, very little has been said of the various processes by which collocations and idioms develop over time. There is in *OED* an abundance of evidence, not always prominently displayed or consistently handled, of the semantic and formal evolution of phrases. It is to be hoped that this will be the focus of later investigations by phraseologists and lexicographers.

References

Allerton, D. J. (2002). *Stretched verb constructions in English*. London: Routledge.
Cowie, A. P. (1994). 'Phraseology'. In: R. E. Asher & J. M. Y. Simpson, (eds.), *The encyclopedia of language and linguistics*. Oxford: Pergamon Press. 3168-71.
Cowie, A. P. (1997). 'Phraseology in formal academic prose'. In J. Aarts, I. de Mönnink & H. Wekker (eds.), *Studies in English language and teaching*. Amsterdam & Atlanta, GA: Rodopi. 43-56.
Cowie, A. P. (1998a). 'Phraseological dictionaries – some east-west comparisons'. In: Cowie (1998b).
Cowie, A. P. (ed.) (1998b). *Phraseology: theory, analysis and applications*. Oxford: Clarendon Press.
Cowie, A. P. (2001). 'Speech formulae in English: problems of analysis and dictionary treatment'. In: G. van der Meer & A. ter Meulen, (eds.), *Making Sense: from Lexeme to Discourse*, Groninger Arbeiten zur germanistischen Linguistik, 44. Groningen: Center for Language and Cognition, University of Groningen. 1-12.
Cowie, A. P. (2002). 'Examples and collocations in the French 'dictionnaire de langue''. In: M.-H. Corréard, (ed.), *Lexicography and natural language processing. A Festschrift in honour of B. T. S. Atkins*. Grenoble: Euralex. 73-90.
Cowie, A. P., R. Mackin & I. R. McCaig (1983). *Oxford Dictionary of Current Idiomatic English, Vol. 2*, retitled *Oxford Dictionary of English Idioms* (1993). Oxford: Oxford University Press.
Curzan, A. (2000). 'The compass of the vocabulary'. In: Mugglestone (2000).

Durkin, P. N. R. (1999). 'Root and branch: revising the etymological component of the *Oxford English Dictionary*'. *Transactions of the Philological Society* (97.1) 1-49.

Fillmore C. J. & B. T. S. Atkins (1992). 'Starting where the dictionaries stop: the challenge of corpus lexicography'. In: B. T. S. Atkins & A. Zampolli, (eds.), *Computational approaches to the lexicon*. Oxford: Oxford University Press. 349-93.

Gläser, R. (1986). *Phraseologie der englischen Sprache*. Leipzig: VEB Verlag Enzyklopädie.

Gläser, R. (1998). 'The stylistic potential of phraseological units in the light of genre analysis'. In: Cowie (1998b).

Howarth, P. (1996). *Phraseology in English academic writing: some implications for language learning and dictionary making*. Tübingen: Max Niemeyer Verlag.

Moon, R. (1998a). 'Frequencies and forms of phrasal lexemes in English'. In: Cowie (1998b).

Moon, R. (1998b). *Fixed expressions and idioms in English. A corpus-based approach*. Oxford: Clarendon Press.

Mugglestone, L. (ed.) (2000). *Lexicography and the OED: Pioneers in the untrodden forest*. Oxford: Oxford University Press.

Murray, J. A. H. (1888). 'Preface to volume I'. In: *A New English Dictionary*, Volume I, A and B. Oxford: Clarendon Press. v-xxvi.

Murray, J. A. H., H. Bradley, W. A. Craigie & C. T. Onions (eds.) (1933). *A New English Dictionary on Historical Principles*, reissued as the *Oxford English Dictionary*, in twelve volumes. Oxford: Clarendon Press. OED 1

Osselton, N. E. (2000). 'Murray and his European counterparts'. In: Mugglestone (2000).

Palmer, H. E. (1933). *Second interim report on English collocations*. Tokyo: Kaitakusha.

Palmer, H. E. (1938). *A grammar of English words*. London: Longmans, Green.

[Philological Society] (1859). *Proposal for the Publication of a new English Dictionary by the Philological Society*. London: Trübner and Co.

Silva, P. (2000). 'Time and meaning: sense and definition in the *OED*'. In: Muggleston (2000).

Simpson, J. A. & E. S. C. Weiner (eds.) (2002). *Oxford English Dictionary*, 2nd edition, CD-ROM version. Oxford: Oxford University Press. OED 2

Zgusta, L. (1989). 'The Oxford English Dictionary and other dictionaries'. *International Journal of Lexicography* 2 (3) 188-230.

JUDITH WIESER

Opening and closing eyes:
a corpus-based study of a set of idioms

Phraseology has remained an attractive and popular field of linguistics for at least two reasons. First of all, the question of what an idiom is has still not been completely resolved, and a renewed interest in metaphor as both a linguistic and a cognitive phenomenon has stimulated linguistic research into figurative language. Secondly, new modes of research have become available: linguists are now able to search for multi-word units in large electronic corpora, and analyse them in the context of their use.

With the help of these modern resources, I want to investigate a small set of idioms with quite transparent meanings that are connected with seeing and have a comparable syntactic structure: *open one's eyes (to sth)*, *open sb's eyes (to sth)*, *close one's eyes (to sth)*, *shut one's eyes (to sth)* and *turn a blind eye (to sth)*. I chose a data-driven approach, using the internet-version of the British National Corpus (BNC) as my main source of samples and supplementing it with data from the Collins Cobuild English Collocations on CD-ROM (abbreviated here as CC). From these sources I extracted my own corpus of 277 non-literal samples, some of which will be presented below.[1]

I first give a short working definition of the term 'idiom' and briefly discuss the difficulty of distinguishing idioms from similar phenomena. After explaining how I chose the above expressions

---

1   The BNC samples will be identified by their code as it appears in the corpus, and the CC samples by text type (e.g. book, journalism) and variety (e.g. Brit., Am.). The corpus of samples, most of which I extracted from the BNC and CC in 1999, is too large to be presented as an appendix to this paper.

for analysis and establishing their basic syntactic structure, I will examine both their syntactic and semantic potential for variability. The semantic analysis will be interwoven with the syntactic analysis, with a special focus on the differences between literal and non-literal samples. In order to illustrate the meanings and function of the idioms in the context of their use, the subjects and complements that occur with the expressions will be classified semantically.

Defining idioms

Linguists working in the field of phraseology generally agree that idioms are instances of figurative (i.e. non-literal or metaphorical) use of language, although their terminology and definition of the term often differ considerably. It is also generally accepted that there is a continuum of idiomaticity, as Cowie and Mackin (1991: xii) point out, with transparent expressions at one end and completely opaque ones at the other end. Linguistic terminology traditionally differentiates 'pure idioms' from '(standard) metaphors', called 'figurative idioms' by Cowie & Mackin (1991: xii), although in practice this distinction is often difficult to draw. The term 'metaphor' typically denotes figurative expressions with an extended, but fairly transparent meaning that can be found by establishing a relation of similarity between the literal and the figurative meaning (cf. Bolinger's (1975) 'something-like' principle). In contrast, an 'idiom' in the narrow sense is a syntactically frozen phraseological unit with an opaque figurative meaning that is not totally predictable from the knowledge of the lexical components and syntactic structure (cf. Cowie & Mackin 1991: xii; Cruse 1997: 37). Hence 'pure idioms' are always "to some degree opaque" (Cruse 1997: 39), and the principle of compositionality cannot be applied to them. The less transparent an expression is, the more idiomatic it becomes on the scale of metaphoricity.

According to Cruse (1997: 37), an idiom has to fulfil both a syntactic and a semantic condition: it must be "a lexical complex which is semantically simplex"(37), i.e. it must consist of more than one lexical constituent and form a lexical unit that cannot be further split up. This definition applies to the expressions analysed here in so far as they are phrases that retain a certain grammatical identity (e.g. the use of inflections), but largely function as semantic units. However, since their meaning is fairly transparent, it seems best to classify them as 'dead' metaphors or 'figurative idioms' rather than 'pure idioms'.

Cruse (1997: 41ff.) argues that so-called 'dead' or 'frozen' metaphors (cf. Goatly 1997: 31ff.) should be distinguished from opaque idioms. Many 'live' metaphors that have become syntactically frozen and lexicalised through regular use have not wholly lost their connection to the original metaphor, and the literal meaning is still present to some degree. For example, the constituents of the dead metaphor *sweeten the pill* can be substituted by the paraphrase *sugar the medicine*. The metaphor remains transparent as it retains the basic meaning that something necessary, but unpleasant (i.e. 'bitter pill/medicine') is made more acceptable by adding something more pleasant (i.e. 'sweet') to it. In contrast, the literal paraphrase of an idiom rarely makes sense because the link to its literal meaning has become obscured.[2] As the syntactically least flexible expressions, opaque idioms cannot normally be subjected to re-ordering or interruption. Their syntactic frozenness can be partly explained by their semantic status: they function as set phrases in a speaker's lexicon that are learned, stored and retrieved as chunks (Lewis 1997, cf. 'prefabs' in Cowie 1998: 1), which are only slightly adapted to their grammatical context.

The term 'idiom' will be used in the broad sense to denote a figurative expression which functions as a lexical entity. After

---

2   According to Cruse (1997: 42), the substitution of the idiom *John pulled his sister's leg* by *John tugged at his sister's leg* is not possible without a change in meaning.

examining the syntactic flexibility and the degree of semantic transparency of the expressions in my corpus, I will try to differentiate between literal meanings and different degrees of metaphoricity.

Choice of samples

I restricted myself to a small subgroup of idioms containing the word *eye*. Applying both a syntactic and a semantic criterion, I chose the expressions *open one's eyes (to sth)*, *open sb's eyes (to sth)*, *close/shut one's eyes (to sth)* and *turn a blind eye (to sth)* (cf. Table 1) because they have similar syntactic structures, i.e. they consist of a verb phrase, and are semantically related to the opening or closing of eyes and the refusal or willingness to see.[3] Most of these expressions can have both a literal and a figurative meaning, so the literal ones had to be sorted out. As a simple search of the BNC only produced a small number of figurative samples for some of the expressions, I searched the Collins Cobuild English Collocations 'Bank of English' on CD-ROM (CC) for more non-literal samples. Table 1 shows the total number of figurative samples that form the corpus. The literal samples, for which only the approximate number of BNC occurrences is given, served as control samples that could be contrasted with the figurative samples.

For the expressions *open one's eyes (to sth)* and *open sb's eyes (to sth)*, only 41 samples could be classified as figurative. The literal samples consist exclusively of the first variant, *open one's eyes (to sth)*, which tends to be used literally, whereas *open sb's eyes (to sth)* is always used metaphorically. The 52 non-

---

3   The expressions keep one's eyes open/peeled/skinned, keep a weather eye open and with one's eyes open/closed were not included because their structure and meaning is different.

literal samples of *close one's eyes (to sth)* and *shut one's eyes (to sth)* are about equally distributed across both variants, yet there are more literal samples containing *close*. Thus *shut* tends to be used less often in literal contexts. Compared to the above expressions, the 184 samples of *turn a blind eye (to sth)*, which constitute the greatest part of the corpus, are all figurative.

Idiom	Literal	Figurative	BNC	CC	Total figurative	
open one's eyes	>500	7	7	0	41	277
open sb's eyes	0	34	29	5		
close one's eyes	>500	27	20	7	52	
shut one's eyes	>150	25	22	3		
turn a blind eye	0	176	145	30	184	
turn a _ eye	0	8	8	0		

Table 1: Number of literal and figurative samples

All of the chosen expressions belong to the syntactic category of clause idioms (Cowie & Mackin 1991: xi): they are verb phrases that consist of a verb and a direct object, i.e. a noun phrase (NP) containing the word *eye* in the singular or plural, and they sometimes take a prepositional object (PP) introduced by *to*. As Figure 1 illustrates, their basic syntactic structure is identical: VP = V + NP (+ PP).

In *open one's eyes (to sth)*, *open sb's eyes (to sth)*, and *close/shut one's eyes (to sth)*, the plural noun *eyes* is preceded by a possessive. The syntactic structure of *turn a blind eye (to sth)* differs in so far as the noun phrase contains an adjective, the determiner is an indefinite article instead of a possessive, and the noun *eye* is used in the singular. In *open sb's eyes (to sth)*, the nature of the possessive is different from the other expressions. In contrast to *one's*, *somebody's* does not agree with the subject of the verb *open*, for the subject opens somebody else's eyes, not his or her own. In the samples, the relation between the subject and the possessive had to be established in order to distinguish the expression *open one's eyes (to sth)* from the more frequent idiom *open sb's eyes (to sth)*.

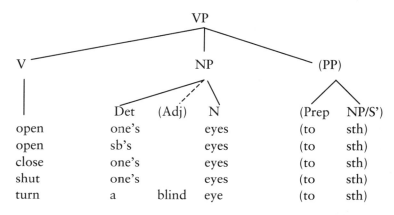

Fig. 1: Tree diagram of all expressions under examination

The two dimensions of seeing

Before the meanings of the above expressions are discussed, the general concept of seeing and the dimensions of perception it implies have to be considered. The word *eye*, which occurs in all of the idioms discussed, already has two basic meanings. According to the *Oxford Advanced Learner's Dictionary* (OALD), *eye* refers to 'the organ of sight' or the iris, yet it can also denote the 'power of seeing' or observation. This second meaning transcends the purely physical dimension of seeing and includes processes of mental perception. The word *eye* thus encompasses both the physical and the mental dimension of seeing. Correspondingly, the basic meanings of the verb *to see* can be assigned to one of these two categories of seeing (cf. OALD):

1) **physical perception**: to see = perceive with the eyes, have the power of sight, look at or watch sth or sb, meet sb, check or discover by looking, witness (cf. the noun *eyewitness*).

2) **mental perception**: to see = perceive with the mind or imagination, grasp or understand, dream or visualise, discover by thinking, experience or witness.

As the visual sense is dominant in our culture, we mainly perceive the world through our eyes, and we take what we see to be true. Therefore, it is not surprising that in our minds the concept of visual perception is closely linked to mental processes of understanding, thinking and visualisation that do not necessarily involve the physical eyes. Lakoff & Johnson (1980) identified UNDERSTANDING IS SEEING as a basic cognitive metaphor that underlies many linguistic expressions, and Goatly (1997: 48) lists 'understand/know = see' as a variant of the root analogy 'cognition = perception'. The equation of seeing and understanding has become so natural in our thinking and so established in our lexicon that people are usually not aware of using a metaphor when saying "I see" (meaning 'I understand').[4]

The expressions *open one's eyes, close one's eyes* and *shut one's eyes* are used literally if they refer to the opening or closing of the physical eyes only. In the idiomatic samples, their meaning is metaphorically extended to express more abstract concepts of seeing, i.e. mental processes of perception. The opening of the eyes is likened to the willingness or ability to perceive or discover something, whereas the closing of the eyes refers to the refusal to take notice of something. Due to the underlying cognitive metaphor firmly established in our minds, the figurative meaning is quite transparent. However, there are a few borderline cases that involve both the physical act of seeing and the mental act of perceiving something inwardly. It is sometimes difficult to decide

---

4   In the case of *see*, this leads to polysemy: the verb has a literal meaning denoting physical perception, and lexicalised extended meanings referring to mental perception or cognition.

whether an example sentence should be classified as literal or figurative, given the amount of context available. Only clearly figurative samples were included in my corpus, but such dubious cases allowed for interesting comparisons. As will be seen, the choice of preposition sometimes facilitated the decision of whether to classify a sample as figurative or literal.

In contrast, *open sb's eyes* normally has a figurative meaning that "border[s] on cliché" according to Glucksberg (2001: 14). A literal interpretation is possible, but does not make sense unless referring to a doctor examining a patient's health. The idiom *turn a blind eye* is always used figuratively and does not allow for a purely literal interpretation. The literal meaning of *blind* is extended to denote the inability or refusal to mentally perceive something. Due to the absence of the literal meaning, the expression is less transparent, but it is easily understood because of its conventionality.

In Table 2 the expressions under examination are grouped according to the dimension of seeing involved, i.e. their literal or figurative meanings (with dictionary definitions according to the OALD). Additionally, the willingness or ability to see is contrasted with the refusal or inability to see.

seeing	willingness/ability	refusal/inability
physically (literal)	*open one's eyes* = raise one's eyelids	*close/shut one's eyes* = lower one's eyelids
mentally (figurative)	*open one's eyes (to sth)* = realise sth that surprises one *open sb's eyes (to sth)* = make sb realise sth that surprises him/her	*close/shut one's eyes (to sth)* = ignore, refuse to see or take notice of *turn a blind eye (to sth)* = pretend not to notice, refuse to take notice of a situation/ state of affairs

Table 2: Categorisation according to modes of seeing

In the following sections, each expression will be analysed both syntactically and semantically. It was to be expected that these figurative expressions would be syntactically quite fixed because they are listed in dictionaries and consequently lexicalised to a high degree.

Syntactic variation and its semantic implications

The deviations from the basic structure and their semantic implications will be examined regarding verb forms, word order, the structure of the direct object (NP) and of the PP. In the figurative samples, the verbs *open, close, shut* and *turn* appear in a range of forms, with the finite forms being slightly more frequent. Despite that, the infinitive is the most commonly used form of all verbs. In approximately half of the example sentences, it is preceded by a modal auxiliary verb that expresses an obligation *(must, may, need)* or prohibition *(ought not/should not)*, an ability or inability *(can/cannot, could/could not, be able to)*, or a willingness *(want)* to either perceive or ignore something.

The basic word order V + Det + N (+ PP) is normally adhered to, yet there are a few exceptions related to verb inflection. In one instance the lexical verb *open* is used as a past participle with *have* and moved to the position after the object (have + object + past participle), expressing that the subject *(they)* is not performing, but experiencing the action:

(1) I do, of course, pray daily that they may have their eyes opened to the fact that GOD IS. (CC, book, Brit.)

The word order of *close/shut one's eyes* is inverted in one example only. In example (2), the noun phrase *(one of those huge ridiculous facts)*, which is usually contained in the PP, is moved in front of the subject, and the rest of the expression modifies it as a relative clause:

(2) It sounds ridiculous – it is ridiculous – it's one of those huge ridiculous facts that one tries to close one's eyes to, they're so absurd – [...]. (BNC, G0F 1424)

The verb *turn* is used in the passive five times, with the usual change in word order. If a gerund is used, *turning a blind eye* sometimes functions as subject or object of the sentence, replacing a noun phrase as in examples (3) and (4). Since this is not the case with the other expressions, it points to the fact that *turn a blind eye* is perceived as more of a lexical unit than the other figurative expressions.

(3) It worries me that turning a blind eye to the deliberate starvation of these patients is portrayed as contributing in some way to the high ethical standards of the nursing profession. (BNC, ANA 789)

(4) Honouring someone does not mean turning a blind eye to weakness. (BNC, CGE 1512)

Let us now turn to the syntactic variability of the NP that functions as the direct object. Its basic structure (NP = Det (+Adj) +N) is not changed, but allows for some internal variation. In *open sb's eyes*, an 's-genitive referring to a group of persons takes the place of the possessive in three cases: *people's* (BNC, ASY 537), *managers'* (BNC, EDT 1654) and *other sufferers'* (BNC, AKS 144). The possessive cannot be replaced in *open one's eyes* and *close/shut one's eyes* because it refers to the subject. Yet with *turn a blind eye*, an 's-genitive is used instead of the adjective *blind* in two instances *(turn a biologist's/father's eye on sth)*, which results in an overall change in meaning ('regard sth from the perspective of a biologist/father').

In both *close one's eyes* and *shut one's eyes*, the NP is not usually varied. In example (5), however, *shut one's eyes* approaches *turn a blind eye* in form:

(5) 'But the former River Authorities knew this and shut an eye to it.' (BNC, FA1 568)

In two examples, *close one's eyes* was used with the determiner *sb's* instead of *one's*, i.e. the subject did not agree with the possessive adjective, as in *open sb's eyes*. In example (6), the expression *close sb's eyes* seems to be the opposite of *open sb's eyes*, meaning 'cause somebody to ignore something', yet, in example (7), it signifies something like 'cause somebody to die'.

(6) You've made a fetish of arid formality, and it closes your eyes to a marvellous book like "Nations". (CC, financial journalism, Brit.)

(7) So I said Well (pause) you get very old you can't walk I said and Jesus closes your eyes and they lay you in a lovely box all lined with satin and you have a – a beautiful robe... (CC, spontaneous speech, Brit.)

The direct object in *turn a blind eye* allows for most variation. In one instance only, an adverb *(conveniently)* is inserted to modify the adjective *blind*. The most common deviations are lexical rather than syntactic in nature: both the use of an *'s*-genitive and the replacement of *blind* by a different adjective naturally leads to a considerable change in meaning. The most frequent variant is *turn a (more) critical eye on/to sth* (3 occurrences, once in the comparative). In contrast to the variant *turn a myopic eye to sth*, which also means 'to pretend not to notice', as *myopic* and *blind* are both related to the inability to see clearly, *turn a (more) critical eye* refers to the opposite process of considering something (more) closely, and is thus more related in meaning to *open one's eyes to sth*. If a typing error can be ruled out in *turn a bland eye*, the idiom is slightly changed to allude to the mildness of the people who ignore something:

(8) So the Foreign Office turned a bland eye –; nobody was exactly complaining out loud –; and we took on the whole Sims organisation as a going concern. (BNC, H86 2073)

There were two more metaphorical variants which denoted that something was regarded, i.e. mentally perceived, in the way specified by the adjective: *turn a cynical eye on sth* ('regard with cynicism'), and *turn a speculative eye on sth* ('regard speculatively, recognize as an object of speculation'). In contrast, the metaphorical variant *turn a cold eye on sb* seems to involve physical perception although *cold* is used figuratively, i.e. the subject looks at a person in an emotionally unaffectionate way:

(9)   Angelina turned a cold eye on him. (BNC, H8A 1519)

Though the adjective was not changed in the large majority of examples, some language users have creatively adapted the idiom to suit their purposes, thus creating new metaphorical (i.e. quite transparent) expressions that are based on the structure of the existing idiom, but have a new meaning, and may at some time get lexicalised themselves. These variants imply that *turn a blind eye* is not totally opaque, but can be reanalysed. The core meaning of *turn a _ eye* amounts to 'regard/perceive (sth/sb) with _-ness' or 'direct one's attention to sth/sb in a _ way'.

Choice of preposition and degrees of metaphoricity

Whereas the core of the expression is syntactically quite fixed, the complements following the direct object allow for considerable syntactic variation. Table 3 illustrates the complements of all expressions, which take the form of a prepositional phrase (PP) with *to* in the majority of examples. The choice of complement, especially of preposition, is worth examining more carefully because it is closely linked with the difference between literal and figurative samples.

Most figurative samples of both *open one's eyes* and *open sb's eyes* take a PP introduced by *to*. Only four examples take no complement, like most literal samples, and an infinitive with *to* is used instead of a PP in the remaining two examples. If used literally, *open one's eyes* is also often followed by an infinitive, typically of verbs like *see*, *look* or *glance*, that refer to physical visual perception. Yet in the two non-literal examples that contain an infinitive with *to*, the verb *see* refers to mental perception.

	open one's	open sb's	close	shut	turn a blind eye	turn a _ eye	Total
PP with *to*	5	30	21	24	113	2	**195**
PP with *on*	0	0	2	0	2	5	**9**
PP with *against*	0	0	1	0	0	0	**1**
Infinitive with *to*	1	1	0	0	0	0	**2**
No complement	1	3	3	1	61	1	**70**
Total	7	34	27	25	176	8	**277**

Table 3: Complements of the figurative samples

In both examples (10) and (11), the eyes are opened to something abstract ('Your glory' and 'a truth') that cannot be perceived by the physical eyes:

(10) Open our eyes to see Your glory, open our hearts to receive Your love, open our minds to discern Your purposes [...]. (BNC, GX0 171)

(11) He took this to be a truth 'so near and obvious to the mind, that a man need only open his eyes to see it. (BNC, ABM 1279)

Similarly, when a PP with *to* occasionally occurs in the literal samples, the eyes are opened to something concrete or something that can be physically perceived, as in examples (12) and (13), whereas something more abstract is perceived in the figurative examples (cf. semantic categorisation of PPs).

(12) I opened my eyes to the sun riding over Fair Hill. (BNC, ACK 1390)

(13) He opened his eyes to the quiet darkness, the moonlight, the breeze from the window that his helper had opened. (BNC, GWF 451)

The preposition *on* occurs with *open one's eyes* in three BNC examples which are not included in my corpus because they represent literal rather than figurative uses. Whereas example (14) might still be read metaphorically, examples (15) and (16) seem to refer entirely to physical perception. Thus the choice of *on* biases the interpretation of the whole expression towards the literal.

(14) [...] they might have time to sit back and open their eyes on the real world. (CC, journalism, Austr.)

(15) Could he not open his eyes on a better scene, a less sordid spectacle? (BNC, ADA 1913)

(16) For years, it was supposed to be crucial to bonding for baby to open its eyes on Mum and Dad in the first instants of life [...]. (BNC, ECU 494)

The prepositions *to, on* and *against* are used with *close one's eyes* and *shut one's eyes* in both literal and non-literal contexts. Whereas *to* is the favourite preposition among the non-literal samples, it is rarely used literally, as with *open one's/sb's eyes*. The prepositions *on* and *against*, on the other hand, only rarely occur in the metaphorical samples, but are frequent in literal examples, as in (17) and (18).[5] In contrast, the eyes are closed to something more abstract in the metaphorical examples (19) to (21), although the physical eyes might be involved in (21).

(17) Nora closed her eyes on tears of joy. (BNC, HP0 2869)

(18) She lifted her face to the sun, half closing her eyes against the silver dazzle that bounced across the water [...]. (BNC, CEH 3028)

(19) Now, dressed as a soldier [...], he closed his eyes on his troubles and tried to forget. (BNC, B0R 185)

---

5   Moreover, the preposition *on* can also mean 'at the moment of', especially if followed by a gerund: "Lindsey *closed her eyes* on the shocking realisation that she hadn't even given it a thought." (BNC, JXW 966)

(20) They train us to cheat on the small level so we can close our eyes on – on their big crimes [...] (CC, radio, Am.)

(21) He closed his eyes against the unbelievable horror of it all. (BNC, BPD 1106)

When the expressions *close one's eyes* and *shut one's eyes* are used literally, they are often connected with mental perception and processes of imagination, remembering and thinking. The closing of the physical eyes allows these inner processes to happen more easily, or at least this is what is expected. In the literal examples, verbs like *see* (referring to mental perception), *imagine, visualise, concentrate, focus, remember,* or *recall* often follow *close/shut one's eyes*, especially in the infinitive:

(22) She massaged the brow, standing back, closing her eyes to recall him better. (BNC, HGF 2664)

(23) breathing in a regular way, close your eyes and visualize before you an ancient [...] (CC)

(24) IF I CLOSE MY EYES, I see Lorenzo, five years old. (CC)

Thus the mental dimension of seeing can already be present to a considerable degree in the literal samples. The metaphorical meaning, however, does not point towards an increase in inner perception or understanding, but rather to the opposite: the refusal to notice something. Yet in some literal examples, the idea of escaping from an unpleasant or threatening reality is already visible. In (25) and (26), the verb *to shut out* follows *close one's eyes* when somebody wants to avoid perceiving something unpleasant:

(25) I closed my eyes to shut out the glow from the overleaf window and tried for sleep. (BNC, G02 1624)

(26) Lily closed her eyes to shut out Stephen's flushed determined face from her mind. (BNC, G0J 3601)

Especially in example (26), a double process of shutting takes place, on the physical as well as the mental level. In the figurative samples, the physical dimension of shutting normally ceases to apply, and only the mental dimension remains.

Turn a blind eye, including its lexical variants, is followed by a PP with *to* in about two thirds of the samples, yet the PP is omitted in almost all remaining examples, i.e. much more frequently than with the other expressions. Thus the potential for syntactic variation is not exploited. The use of the preposition *on* instead of *to* in two examples does not result in a difference concerning idiomaticity or meaning. In the (less idiomatic) variants, however, *on* was preferred – because it served either as a further deviation marker or as a sign of greater semantic transparency.

Syntactic and semantic categorisation of the prepositional phrases

The structure of the PP that occurs in 205 samples allows for considerable syntactic variation because the NP used as part of the PP can consist of a variety of structures. Apart from premodification by adjectives or *'s*-genitives, the noun is often followed by complex postmodifying structures: a prepositional phrase (mostly possessive), a relative clause (including past participles)

PP Structure	*open*	*close/shut*	*turn*	*turn (var.)*	Total (205)
Prep + NP	10	30	50	6	96
Prep + NP + PP	8	13	43	1	65
Prep + NP + relative cl.	5	4	17	0	26
Prep + NP + *that*-cl.	4	4	1	0	9
Prep + *wh*-clause	3	2	3	0	8
Prep + NP + gerund	0	1	0	0	1

Table 4: Modifications of PP structure

or a *that*-clause (mostly introduced by *the fact that*). In a few cases, a *wh*-clause replaces the NP after the preposition. The examples of PP structures in Table 4 illustrate the types of modification.

The prepositional phrases describe what is either perceived or ignored according to the speakers. The following semantic classification is the result of an attempt to categorise the NPs contained in the PPs according to their meanings.[6] The classification was quite problematic because common features were difficult to establish across so many samples. Therefore the categories listed in Table 5 may seem arbitrary, yet the typical semantic contexts in which the expressions are used become visible. The NPs that could not be assigned to one of the categories were subsumed under the label "unspecified".

Category	*open*	*close/shut*	*turn*	Total
sth unlawful, violence	1	4	35	40
general truths, facts	9	7	2	18
political facts and problems	1	1	10	12
economic facts and problems	0	0	12	12
dangers or general problems	3	1	0	4
sb's activities or behaviour	0	0	14	14
persons	0	0	6	6
sth negative (general)	2	3	4	9
possibilities, opportunities	6	5	1	12
sth new/ different/ important	5	2	2	9
sth positive	2	2	3	7
unspecified	6	23	26	55
Total	35	48	115	198

Table 5: Semantic Categorisation of PPs

---

6 The variants of *turn a blind eye* were not considered here.

In the figurative samples of *open one's/sb's eyes,* the act of opening the eyes is normally viewed as something necessary and positive by the speaker or writer, as the use of modal auxiliaries like *must, may* or *can* also implies. The eyes are often opened to truths, realities or facts one has to face or wants somebody else to recognise. Someone has to become aware of something negative in order to avoid bad consequences, or of new possibilities and chances in order to profit. Whereas the opening of somebody's eyes is usually regarded as a positive act of becoming aware of something, the closing or shutting of one's eyes, i.e. the act of ignoring or pretending not to see something, is not approved of by the speakers in most samples, but considered unwise and short-sighted. The categorization shows that mostly unpleasant or problematic facts and terrible or unlawful activities or events are ignored. Only in relatively few examples do people refuse to take notice of opportunities or chances, supposedly to their disadvantage.

Similarly, in the vast majority of PPs that occurred with *turn a blind eye,* something rather negative or unpleasant is disregarded. In politics, economics and society in general, many illegal or violent activities, including human rights violations, minor and major breaches of the law, or the persons involved in them, are ignored, often by some kind of authority, as we shall see.

Semantic categorisation of subjects

The subjects of the verbs *open, close, shut* and *turn* reveal who or what either becomes aware of or ignores something. Table 6 shows the different categories of subjects. Apart from the purely grammatical subjects, the actual agents (persons or objects) referred to are listed. When no subject was used, *we* or *you* were often implied as subjects by the use of the imperative and the pronouns *our* and *yours.*

Whereas the subjects of *open one's eyes* are naturally persons, apart from *industry* (BNC CP2 126) as a kind of collective person, *open sb's eyes* is often used with the rather impersonal pronoun *it* or inanimate subjects like *this gripping novel* (BNC), *this first paper* (CC), *this reporting* (CC), *the project* (BNC), *a magic draught* (BNC), or *the convulsion of war* (BNC). Thus somebody can be induced to realise something by written materials, an experience or an activity, including working, thinking and travelling.

Most subjects of the verbs *close* and *shut* are personal pronouns that could not be further identified. Apart from *people* and personal names, mostly religious, political and legal authorities featured as subjects, a trend which will become more explicit with *turn a blind eye*. Impersonal subjects included *France* (CC), *London* (CC, referring to the Stock Exchange), and *arid formality* (CC).

The personal pronouns also form the largest group of subjects of *turn a blind eye*. The frequent use of *we* and *they* and of collective subjects like *people*, *most of us* or *some* indicates that often society as a whole or groups of people are said to ignore something. Still, a large number of subjects are (mostly male) individuals.[7] The remaining subjects often represent authorities of some kind, i.e. people who have a certain power or influence because they form part of political, legal, educational or religious institutions. The authority mentioned most frequently is the government, the highest political power in a country. It is often accused of turning a blind eye because it is felt to be responsible for many things that are happening or not happening. People or institutions that are responsible for enforcing the law also turn a blind eye on a lower level: the police, the security forces and legal institutions pretend not to see what is happening, and only rarely is this to a positive effect. In economics, directors,

---

7   In 33 samples, no subject could be identified because it was either contained in the verb (imperative) or because a passive, a gerund or an impersonal construction like *it is hard/easy to* was used.

industry or the market refuse to take notice of something, and in sports, small-scale authorities like coaches or referees ignore the players' bad behaviour.

Subjects	open sb's	open one's	close	shut	turn	turn (var.)	Total
personal pronouns	9	2	13	15	35	1	75
persons or organisations	3	1	3	3	31	4	45
religious authorities	3	0	2	0	3	0	8
political authorities, country, government	0	1	2	1	38	2	44
police, security forces	0	0	0	0	9	0	9
legal authorities	0	0	1	2	7	0	10
education, school, teachers	1	0	0	0	10	1	12
something written	3	0	0	0	0	0	3
activity	5	0	0	0	0	0	5
economy	0	0	0	1	6	0	7
sports	0	0	0	0	4	0	4
other	6	1	1	1	0	0	9
no subject	4	2	5	2	33	0	46
Total	34	7	27	25	176	8	277

Table 6: Categorisation of subjects/agents

Thus ordinary as well as powerful people can turn a blind eye, which is normally not approved of by the speakers, unless the unlawful activity is considered an excusable faux-pas that the authorities generously ignore. The use of inanimate or abstract subjects like *industry* or *rugby*, even if ultimately referring to people, shows that the physical dimension of seeing can be lost totally.

Conclusion

The samples collected from the BNC and the Collins Cobuild English Collocations CD-ROM have enabled me to illustrate the syntactic patterns and semantic status of the figurative expressions *open one's eyes*, *open sb's eyes*, *close one's eyes*, *shut one's eyes* and *turn a blind eye* in the typical contexts in which they are used by present-day speakers of English.

There are only few instances of syntactic variation for all expressions, mostly consisting of verb inflection, the use of different possessives and a few changes in word order. The great majority of samples are followed by a prepositional phrase (PP) with *to* that allows for a high degree of syntactic variation and therefore does not form part of the idiom core. Most lexical variation occurs with *turn a blind eye,* where the choice of a different adjective leads to a change in meaning and the creation of new metaphors.

The semantic analysis has shown that the literal use of the expressions *open one's eyes* and *close/shut one's eyes* refers to the physical dimension of seeing, although mental processes might already be involved. In the figurative examples, only the mental dimension of seeing normally remains as the eyes are opened or closed to something abstract. The choice of a preposition other than *to* is often accompanied by a tendency towards literalness.

According to the semantic classification of the PPs, people often ignore problematic, terrible and disquieting things rather than chances and possibilities. The subjects that (should) realize or (should not) ignore something are typically powerful political or legal authorities. The use of abstract objects and inanimate subjects illustrates the loss of the physical dimension of seeing in the figurative examples. The data support the view that the distinction between literal and figurative meaning is gradual and sometimes difficult to draw, especially if concepts are so closely linked mentally.

References

Bolinger, D. (1975). *Aspects of Language*. New York: Harcourt Brace Jovanovich.
Cruse, D. A. (1997). *Lexical Semantics*. Cambridge: Cambridge University Press.
Coady, J. & T. Huckin (1997). *Second Language Vocabulary Acquisition*. Cambridge: Cambridge University Press.
Cowie, A. P. & R. Mackin (1991). *Oxford Dictionary of Current Idiomatic English. Vol. 2: Phrase, Clause and Sentence Idioms*. Oxford: University Press.
Cowie, A. P. (1998). *Phraseology. Theory, Analysis and Applications*. Oxford: Clarendon.
Glucksberg, S. (2001). *Understanding Figurative Language. From Metaphors to Idioms*. New York: Oxford University Press.
Goatly, A. (1997). *The Language of Metaphors*. London: Routledge.
Lakoff, G. & M. Johnson (1980). *Metaphors We Live By*. Chicago and London: The University of Chicago Press.
Lewis, M. (1997). 'Pedagogical implications of the lexical approach'. In: Coady & Huckin (1997). 255-270

ALEXANDRA PUSCH & MICHAEL STUBBS

Frequent terms in linguistics:
A pilot corpus study for a pedagogical word-list

Corpus studies are typically highly cumulative, because later studies can build on earlier work, not only by using large computer-readable text collections with their access software (e.g. concordance programs), but also by using second-order data-bases (e.g. word-frequency lists) plus more specialized software (e.g. programs for comparing different corpora). It is the generosity of scholars who make available corpora, data-bases and software (often entirely freely) which allows such cumulative work, and which has led to the very rapid development of corpus studies since the mid-1990s. For example, large general corpora have been used to prepare word frequency lists for general English. These lists can be used to investigate which words are frequent only in specific text-types (e.g. written academic texts), and these lists can be used in turn to discover which words are frequent only in specific subject fields (e.g. linguistics).

Linguistic terms

This article illustrates a method of establishing the most frequent technical terms in English-language linguistics. It is a pilot study, based only on a small corpus, but the results are promising, and the study provides informal data on how large (or small) a corpus must be in order to give realistic results in this type of lexical study. It is therefore a study in terminology research. The large literature on the difference between words and terms is beyond the scope of our article. (See Pearson (1998) for a review and a differently designed corpus-study.) However, we illustrate a small terminology retrieval system, based on simple algorithms which can be used in other academic areas.

Beginning students of linguistics (especially non-native speakers) can experience difficulties with linguistic texts, due to unfamiliar content and terminology. Comprehension problems may also be due to complex academic syntax, and cannot be avoided merely by developing a list of technical terms, but a list can be used for developing teaching materials or study aids, and can help ensure that vocabulary does not pose an additional problem. If we are thinking of students who want to *understand* texts about linguistics, then we can regard terminology as predominantly lexical, and independent of morphology and syntax. If, however, they want to *produce* texts themselves, then they must also know the lexico-grammatical frames in which the terms are normally used: this topic is also beyond the scope of our article.

So, we illustrate a method of discovering technical terms which are both frequent and widely occurring. We describe the design of a small linguistic text collection (LTC), extract a frequency list from it using two different methods, describe the resulting linguistic word list (LWL), evaluate it in different ways, and suggest improvements.

Some of the original data for the paper, for which there is no room in the article, is available on a web-page at <http://www.uni-trier.de/uni/fb2/anglistik/Projekte/stubbs/lwl-data.htm>.

Specialized corpora: a linguistic text-collection (LTC)

First, we constructed a small corpus from texts available on the world-wide-web. It contained written professional (i.e. not popular) linguistic texts, written between 1970 and 2001, on phonetics and phonology, morphology and syntax, semantics, and miscellaneous topics (e.g. historical and applied linguistics, socio- and psycholinguistics, pragmatics, lexicography). For each topical category, we collected eight samples: one textbook chapter, three linguistic articles and four reviews of linguistic monographs. The main software used allows only 32 files to be processed at one time, and this set the limit on file-processing in this pilot study.

Our corpus contained around 230,000 running words. It is common nowadays for general corpora to consist of tens or even hundreds of millions of running words, but whereas general lexicography requires large corpora in order to capture a wide range of words, much smaller corpora may be sufficient to study high frequency vocabulary in restricted subject areas. Piotrowski (1984: 92) claims that, for analytical languages such as English, a corpus of 200,000 words is sufficient to cover 97 to 99 per cent of the vocabulary of academic and technical registers (see also Kennedy 1998: 56). Such rationales are not entirely convincing, and restrictions on size are almost always due to practical considerations, such as time and processing capacity. There is probably no real theoretical justification for setting an upper limit on corpus size, though it may well be that, above a certain size, the payoff is minimal and hardly worth the effort. It is therefore an empirical question as to how large a corpus must be to provide reliable results in different areas. We show that a small corpus can provide useful information. (For examples of special purpose corpora, see Ghadessy et al. (2001), on pedagogical analyses, and Zhu (1989), Faber & Lauridsen (1991), Vihla (1998), Pearson (1998), and Dodd (2000) for more general discussion and other specific examples.)

Certainly as important as the size of a corpus is its diversity, and much depends on what is sampled. A large number of smallish samples from independent sources guards against biases (e.g. from the idiosyncracies of individual authors), and is therefore better than a few long samples from a few sources. In compiling our linguistic word list, we used range as a first criterion, and frequency only as a second criterion, so it is unlikely that our results are biased towards any individual texts. A related issue is that not all linguistic features are distributed evenly over a text (Sinclair 1991: 19). We therefore used only full texts, all longer than 1,500 words (with their bibliographies removed).

Corpus compilers must respect copyright. All our texts were on the world-wide-web, so we assume that their authors wanted them to be read. Our data were collected only for a short-term project, not distributed to third parties, deleted on completion of the project, and no text extracts are reproduced here. Although the legal status of material published on the web is unclear, this avoids copyright problems: see Renouf (1987: 4), Atkins & Clear (1992: 4).

Method 1: 'keywords'

A simple method of extracting terminology from a topic-specific text collection is to use the 'keywords' software in WordSmith Tools (Scott 1997). This can compare a source corpus with a reference corpus, and calculate which words are significantly more frequent in the source corpus. We compared LTC with a 4-million-word corpus which combines the standard reference corpora of Brown, LOB, Frown and FLOB (i.e. written American and British English from 1961 and 1991). The top 50 keywords (omitting abbreviations), in descending significance (as measured by a log-likelihood test), were:

- language, is, phrase, semantic, lexical, words, syntax, movement, analysis, linguistic, syllable, downstep, phrases, languages, syntactic, chapter, semantics, german, english, structure, constraints, corpus, constraint, scope, meaning, syllables, phonological, grammar, vowels, haus, phonology, wen, lexicon, vowel, clause, theory, stechow, upstep, partial, structured, optimality, examples, noun, propositions, phonetic, are, speech, verb, word, iff, proposition

The success of retrieval methods is measured in terms of 'precision' and 'recall'. The method has a high degree of precision if a large percentage of what is retrieved is relevant: this is easy to check, since irrelevant terms are visible in the list. The method has a high degree of recall if a high percentage of relevant terms is found: this is difficult to check, since one cannot observe what is not found. Recall can be tested only by comparison with a different list which has been compiled with different data and/or different methods; for example, it could be compared with published lists of terminology (see below).

The list above certainly comprises mainly linguistic terms, with only a few non-linguistic items, and a full printout from the program gives additional information. Some words occur in LTC and not at all in the reference corpus (e.g. *phonological*) or only rarely (e.g. *semantics*: less than 2 per million running words). Other words are frequent in the reference corpus, either with approximately the same meaning (e.g. *language*) or with a different non-technical meaning (e.g. *scope*). (The list has, in fact, been improved manually, mainly by removing several abbreviations and isolated letters used in marking article sub-sections. For further details of the top 100 keywords, see the webpage.)

However, the "keywords" method uses only one criterion, relative frequency, and has corresponding limitations. The list includes several words which are not linguistic terminology: words which are amongst the most frequent words in the language (e.g. *is*, *are*), but merely more frequent in LTC; general academic words (e.g. *analysis*, *examples*); and foreign words from example sentences (e.g. *Haus*, *wen*). It also gives too much prominence to words (e.g. *upstep*) which are frequent in the corpus due to their high frequency in a single text.

Method 2: 'range' plus frequency

A better method combines frequency and range. This can identify words which occur in many different linguistics texts, but are absent or rare elsewhere. Here we have used software which can be used to create word-lists, to calculate the percentage of different texts covered by different word-lists, and to discover which words are shared by different texts or unique to a single text. This 'Range' software is written by Heartley & Nation (1996), described in detail by Nation (2001), and available at <http://www.vuw.ac.nz/lals/>.

'Range' can be used to compare the vocabulary of up to 32 different texts simultaneously. For each word in the texts, it provides the range (how many texts the word occurs in), a headword frequency figure (the total number of times the headword-type appears in all the texts), a frequency figure for each of the texts the word occurs in, and a family frequency figure (the total number of times the word and its family members occur in all the texts). Word families are, roughly, head-words plus their inflected and derived forms (Bauer & Nation 1993).

GSL, AWL and LWL

Three pre-defined lists are available with the software: the first and second thousand words of the General Service List (GSL1 and 2, below), and the Academic Word List (AWL). Since these lists contain the most frequent words of general and academic English, the remaining words are then good candidates for linguistic terms if they are both high in frequency and occur in several texts. It is therefore these words, after some manual post-editing, which form the Linguistic Word List (LWL).

The General Service List (GSL; West 1953) contains 2,000 frequent words of general English, with semantic and frequency information, drawn from a corpus of five million words. Strictly speaking, it is not a frequency list, since frequency was only one criterion used. Other criteria were: structural value (all structural words were included); subject range (no specialist items); definition words; word-building capability; and style (no colloquial or slang words). Howatt (1984: 256) summarizes the principles. Though compiled more than fifty years ago, it is still a valuable source of frequent words of general English.

The Academic Word List (AWL; Coxhead 2000) contains words which have both high frequency and wide distribution in academic texts, irrespective of subject area (excluding the 2,000 words in GSL). It comprises 570 word families: not just word-forms, but head-words plus their inflected and derived forms (see above), and therefore around 3,100 word-forms altogether, e.g.:

- concept: conception, concepts, conceptual, conceptualisation, conceptualise, conceptualised, conceptualises, conceptualising, conceptually

To construct AWL, Coxhead used a corpus of 3.5 million words, comprising texts from academic journals and university textbooks from four main areas: arts, commerce, law, and natural science. To be included in AWL, a word had to occur at least 100 times altogether in the whole academic corpus, at least ten times in each of the four sub-corpora, and in at least half of 28 more finely defined subject areas, such as biology, economics, history, and linguistics.

AWL gives very good coverage of academic texts, irrespective of subject area. Here it must be remembered that words are *very* uneven in their frequency. In a typical academic text, the single word *the* covers around 6 or 7 per cent of running text, the top ten words cover over 20 per cent, and the 2,000 most frequent words cover around 75 per cent. The words in AWL typically cover a further 10 per cent. The remaining 15 per cent will be specialized words which are specific to a given topic (and therefore of particular interest for LWL), plus proper names, etc.

Table 1 shows some summary statistics, produced by Range, for the whole of LTC:

WORD LIST	TOKENS	%	TYPES	%	FAMILIES
GSL1	159144	69.4	2606	18.0	950
GSL2	9342	4.1	1256	8.7	644
AWL	20913	9.1	1682	11.6	535
not in lists	39926	17.4	8946	61.7	???
TOTAL	229325		14490		2129

Table 1: Summary statistics for LTC

These simple statistics are already very revealing about the lexical make-up of LTC. In LTC (229,325 running words), over 70 per cent of the running word-tokens, and over 26 per cent of word-types, were in GSL1 and 2; and over 9 per cent of the running word-tokens, and nearly 12 per cent of word-types, were general academic vocabulary from AWL. Note in particular the importance of words from AWL. The percentage of AWL words is much higher than words from the second 1,000 words from GSL: after the first few hundred words of general vocabulary, lexis becomes very topic-specific. And note that 535 out of 570 word families from AWL are represented in the linguistic texts: these words occur frequently and evenly across many academic subject areas, and are essential for understanding texts on linguistics, in addition to linguistic terminology.

An algorithm for terminology retrieval

For LWL, it is the remaining 17 per cent of running word-tokens, and almost 62 per cent of word-types, which are of potential interest. In constructing LWL, we used range as the first criterion, and frequency as a second criterion, on the grounds that important words should be present in many texts rather than occur very frequently in few texts. So, words were extracted and post-edited in the following ways.

(1) All word forms which occurred in fewer than five texts were deleted. The list therefore includes only words which occurred either in more than half the texts of a sub-category or in more than four texts in more than one sub-category. (2) Words with a frequency of ten or lower were deleted. This criterion was, however, relaxed for word-families with only one member (e.g. *anaphora* <frequency 6>, *assimilation* <frequency 10> were not excluded: they still meet criterion 1). (3) The following categories were deleted: Roman numerals; abbreviations (e.g. *cf*, *etc*, *vs*); non-English words and first names (both often used in linguistic examples: e.g. *Haus*, *wen*, *John*, *Mary*) and place names (e.g. *Oxford*).

Names of linguists, names of languages, and linguistic abbreviations (with range greater than 4, and frequency greater than 10) were removed to subsidiary lists: presumably students should also know these:

- Austin, Chomsky, Grice, Lakoff, Searle
- American, British, Dutch, French, German, Germanic, Russian, Spanish
- NP, PP, VP

The remaining words were then split manually, on intuitive – and partly arbitrary – grounds (see below), into two lists: LWL itself, and other words which, although not necessarily linguistic terms, are particularly frequent in linguistic texts. We discuss LWL first.

LWL: the pilot linguistic word-list

The linguistic terms (word-forms) were sorted alphabetically, and grouped into lemmas and word-families (Bauer & Nation 1993). Nouns were usually used as the basic forms (e.g. *inflection* represents also *inflectional*, although *inflect* would be closer to the word stem). This is justified by the predominance of nouns and lack of verbs in LWL and linguistic glossaries in general (see below). Affixes were deleted (e.g. plurals were changed into singulars), and verbs were changed to their base form. In most cases this reduced distinct word-forms to one lemma. In cases such as *linguist* and *linguistics*, which left two nouns of the same family, the word with the wider range and higher frequency was taken (e.g. *linguistics* was included and *linguist* deleted). Words were lemmatized in this way only when there was more than one word-form in a potential word family. In cases where an adjectival form was much more frequent (e.g. *cognitive*), this was also not converted to a noun.

Using range as the first criterion and frequency as the second criterion, the list was then split into four groups, and each group was again ordered alphabetically:

Group 1: cognitive, consonant, dialect, discourse, generative, grammatical, lexicon, linguistics, morphology, phonetics, phonology, phrase, pragmatics, prosody, semantics, syllable, syntax, terminology, utterance, verbal

Group 2: adjective, collocation, corpus, deletion, dependency, derivational, diachronic, inflection, intonation, morpheme, node, optimality, phoneme, predicate, presupposition, pronoun, pronunciation, proposition, transcription, vocabulary

Group 3: acoustic, adjunct, affix, competence, comprehension, correlation, determiner, frequency, intuition, markedness, metaphor, mood, negation, quantifier, quantitative, schema, segment, sociolinguistic, synonymy, tone

Group 4: anaphora, articulation, assimilation, coda, connotation, paradigmatic, preposition, prototype, reference, reflexive, rhyme, singular, slot, synchronic, temporal, token, transformational, transitive, typological

The resulting list consists of 79 word families. Taking range as the first criterion, the top six words are *linguistics*, *lexicon*, *semantics*, *syntax*, *grammatical* and *phrase*. Taking raw frequency as the first criterion, the top six words are *semantics*, *phrase*, *linguistics*, *syntax*, *syllable* and *lexicon*.

(The full lists, with details of range and frequency, are on the webpage. In calculating frequencies, all members of a word family were added together. Range numbers could not be added together in this way, since several members of the same family often occurred in the same text, and this would have led to inflated numbers. Range was therefore calculated as the highest range figure of one member of the given word family. The range values are therefore minimum values, and possible underestimates.)

General academic words with high frequency in linguistics

Although the distinction between LWL and the following list is largely intuitive, it does have some quantitative basis. Only two of the "non-linguistic" words below *(overview* and *impression)* had a range greater than ten.

From a student's point of view, the difference between the two lists may, in any case, be unimportant. Some words in LWL above are arguably part of general academic vocabulary (e.g. *cognitive*), and some below have technical meanings which are not immediately derivable from their use in general English (e.g. *embedded, relational*), but students reading about linguistics need to know both sets. The first set below occurred in six texts or more, the second set occurred in five texts.

- attested, candidates, captured, embedded, default, encoded, entitled, impression, obligatory, overview, paradox, plausible, postulates, postulated, recall, relational, textbook, trivial, unclear, usage
- candidate, converge, generalization, genuine, handbook, henceforth, informative, overt, sketched, theoretic, vague, transparent

(These lists are unlemmatized. For further details of range and frequency, see the webpage.)

Some of these words are immediately recognisable as stylistic favourites of many linguists, especially of particular persuasions (e.g. *generalization, plausible, trivial, vague*)! Interesting cases – potentially confusing for students – are those words which have more precise meanings in linguistics than in general English (e.g. *usage*). In general, these two lists illustrate that there is no clear boundary between general academic and linguistic terms.

Text-coverage: GSL, AWL and LWL

The text-coverage provided by LWL could now be investigated with Range, using GSL (all 2,000 words), AWL and LWL as base lists. The results are given in Table 2. (There are 152 word-types for LWL, because base list three was not compiled on the basis of word families: this would of course have given a result of 79 types, since there are 79 word families in LWL.)

LWL accounts for just over 3 per cent of running word-tokens in the corpus, and for only one per cent of different word-types. These may seem small percentages, but mean that students might meet 15 linguistic terms (not all different, of course) on an average page. AWL accounts for much higher percentages: 9 per cent of running word-tokens, and 11 per cent of word-types, and emphasizes the importance of this vocabulary for reading linguistics texts.

WORD LIST	TOKENS	%	TYPES	%
One (whole GSL)	168486	73.5	3862	26.7
Two (AWL)	20913	9.1	1682	11.6
Three (LWL)	7847	3.4	152	1.0
not in the lists	32079	14.0	8794	60.7
TOTAL	229325		14490	

Table 2: Text coverage of linguistics texts

Perhaps rather surprising is that "other words" accounts for 14 per cent of running text and 61 per cent of types. But again we have to remember the *very* uneven distribution of words in texts. In an average text or small corpus, around half the words are hapax legomena: i.e. they occur only once. The occurrence of words in these different categories has general implications for vocabulary needed to read linguistics books and articles.

Method 3: 'keywords' plus 'range'

We can of course combine the results of methods 1 and 2. For example, we can look again at the output from method 1 to check whether method 2 has missed useful terms. Words (modified to their word-family base forms) which are not in the LWL are:
- analysis, chapter, clause, constraints, downstep, example, iff, language, meaning, movement, noun, scope, speech, structure, theory, vowel, word

This list seems to add relatively little to LWL. These are words in general English (e.g. *language, meaning*), words in the general academic vocabulary and therefore in AWL (e.g. *analysis, theory*), words which are arguably too specific and failed the range criterion for LWL (e.g. *downstep, iff*), or words which certainly do not belong in LWL (e.g. *chapter*). However, it does contain a couple of words which non-native speakers may not know (e.g. *clause, vowel*). For example, German-speaking students often attempt an English form such as "vocal" for *vowel*: the German is *der Vokal*.

Coverage of a general English corpus

In order to confirm that LWL contains words that really do occur frequently in linguistic texts, but infrequently elsewhere, we checked the percentage coverage of LWL in a general corpus of written British English, comprising over eight million running words. Here, only 0.2 per cent of the word-tokens, and 0.1 per cent of word-types, were in LWL, a much lower value than the 3.4 per cent in LTC.

WORD LIST	TOKENS	%	TYPES	%
One (whole GSL)	7025043	83.8	7688	6.0
Two (AWL)	352885	4.2	2893	2.3
Three (LWL)	14310	0.2	147	0.1
not in the lists	993138	11.8	117769	91.7
TOTAL	8385376		128497	

Table 3: Text coverage of mixed written texts

The very high percentage (over 90 per cent) of word-types which are not in any of the lists is a reminder of just how large the vocabulary of English is, and how much vocabulary depends on topic. Most of these words are rare and occur very infrequently (as word-tokens) in the corpus.

This provides a rough check on recall: LWL covers a much higher percentage of linguistic texts than of general written texts.

Comparison with linguistic glossaries

We can also compare LWL with published glossaries of linguistic terminology (which recognize the comprehension problems which motivated our attempt to set up LWL in the first place). Such glossaries are of course more extensive than the provisional eighty-entry LWL, and, we therefore examined only what percentage of LWL entries also occur in the glossaries: that is, we were here testing the precision of our results, not the level of recall.

First, we checked every entry in LWL against the glossaries in three introductory linguistics textbooks, one relatively old and two more recent: Crane et al. (1981), Finch (1998), and Weisler & Milekic (2000). An occurrence was marked positive if the word in the glossary belonged to the same word family as the respective LWL entry, or if the word in LWL was part of a multi-word item in the glossary (e.g. LWL entry *transformational* occurs in *transformational grammar*). Briefly: 44 per cent of LWL occurred in Crane et al., 52 per cent in Finch, and 49 per cent in Weisler & Milekic. The following LWL entries were in all three glossaries:

- assimilation, generative, lexicon, morpheme, morphology, phoneme, phonetics, phonology, phrase, predicate, synonymy, transformational

Altogether, 80 per cent of the LWL entries occurred in at least one of the glossaries, but the following LWL entries did not occur in any of the glossaries:

- articulation, comprehension, correlation, deletion, dependency, intuition, pronunciation, quantitative, schema, segment, singular, slot, temporal, token, transcription, typological, vocabulary

There are two reasons why the glossaries might not contain these words. First, even general introductions are not comprehensive, and their glossaries are biased towards the topics of the books. Second, their authors may have assumed that these are general words which require no explanation. This is questionable for terms such as *intuition* and *transcription*, and our list seems to identify gaps in these glossaries.

However, a better comparison might be with general dictionaries of linguistic terminology, and these show a much higher precision rate for LWL. We take as examples the first editions of two such books published in the early 1990s. Crystal (1992) contains almost all the terms identified in LWL (plus many more, of course). The few terms not in Crystal have mainly become current since the early 1990s, such as *optimality* (as in *optimality theory*), or *node*, *schema* and *token* (as used in corpus linguistics: Crystal does give *type-token density*). However, such comparisons require some caution. For example, Crystal gives *frequency*, but only in its use in phonetics *(fundamental frequency)*, and not with reference to frequency counts in quantitative linguistics. In turn, this use shows the impossibility of an absolute distinction between technical terms and general vocabulary, since there are many technical aspects of calculating word frequencies, but the meaning of the word is not essentially different from its everyday usage.

Trask (1993) claims to be a dictionary of grammatical terms, though it gives also more general terms such as *corpus* and *synchronic*. If we exclude the obviously phonetic and phonological terms in our list (e.g. *acoustic, articulation, phoneme, tone*), then, again, most of our terms are in Trask's list, but this time with some striking exceptions which reveal a bias in his list. Terms not given by Trask are *pragmatics, presupposition, prototype, quantitative, synonymy, token,* and *vocabulary*. These omissions reveal a view, certainly not accepted by everyone, that grammar can be neatly distinguished from lexis, semantics and pragmatics, and they reveal a bias away from certain approaches to linguistics (despite the claim in the blurb that the book "has few theoretical axes to grind").

So, published lists can be used to test the method: they confirm that we have identified genuine linguistic terms (precision). Conversely, the method can be used to test the lists: it allows us to check that the lists represent a balanced range of theoretical approaches, and that terms have not been missed. In addition, since they are based solely on the intuitions of their authors, and compiled without corpora, published lists of linguistic terms generally give no idea of the general importance of single glossary entries. Our method provides additional information on the frequency and range of terms, and therefore indicates how essential they are likely to be for beginning students.

The question of whether the definition of the terms in such glossaries represents their most frequent use in the literature is too large a topic for this article, but it would be a relatively easy task to concordance the terms we identify and to check on their use.

Limitations, problems and improvements

Our small text collection, of something under a quarter of a million running words, does not necessarily lead to unrepresentative data, but more complete lists would certainly need a larger corpus with a wider range of linguistic topics.

Since the Range software can handle only single words, no multi-word items occur in the LWL (e.g. the list includes *optimality* but not *optimality theory*). The glossaries used to evaluate the LWL do give multi-word items, such as *derivational morphology, synchronic linguistics, tone language* and *transformational grammar*. So, this is a clear limitation in our list, but also a major, and only partly solved, problem for lexicography in general (Cowie 1998) and for terminology extraction in particular (Chodkiewicz et al. 2002).

One method of finding multi-word units is to run a program on LTC which extracts all recurrent two- (or three-)word strings down to a specified minimum frequency. (For a detailed description of such software, see Stubbs 2002.) In this way, all two-word chains in the corpus, with a frequency of ten and greater, which consist of two content words, were extracted. This captured a large number of multi-word units which would certainly be good candidates for LWL. Precision is low (around 60 per cent of the list are genuine terms), but manual post-editing is very simple. Terms captured in this way (out of a total of around 50) include:

- applied linguistics, binding theory, Broca's area, lexical item, Middle English, native speaker, natural language, noun phrase, speech act

A similar run, looking for three-word chains, produced only *nuclear pitch accent*. (For a full list of the two-word chains, see the webpage.)

Finally, note that our method will not detect linguistic terms which occur in GSL or AWL. For example, the word *type*, frequent in the present article in its technical sense (as in *type-token ratio*) will be missed since it occurs in GSL.

Conclusions: applications and implications

Students reading linguistics have to cope with specialized linguistic terms, general academic words which occur across many subject areas, and academic words which are particularly frequent in linguistics. This paper provides a method of retrieving these different sets of vocabulary, and the basis of a text-independent glossary of linguistic terms. We have also illustrated other topics in text processing and vocabulary research, each of which could be considerably developed:

- Our algorithms for terminology retrieval can be used to identify terms in other academic disciplines.
- Our examples of the fuzzy borderline between general academic (sub-technical) vocabulary and specialist terminology require more detailed study.
- The lists of highly frequent general vocabulary (in GSL), academic vocabulary (in AWL), and technical terms (in LWL) can be applied to the analysis of specific texts, and used to study the nature and size of vocabulary required to read texts about linguistics.

Finally, the article itself is an example of how corpora, databases and associated software can give students the means of carrying out small but realistic research projects. The work was originally done as a term paper (by Pusch) and then developed slightly (by Pusch and Stubbs) into this article.

Acknowledgements

The "chains" program was written by Isabel Barth (as part of other undergraduate student work).

References

Atkins, S. & J. Clear (1992). 'Corpus design criteria'. *Literary and Linguistic Computing*. 7: 1-16.
Bauer, L. & P. Nation (1993). 'Word families'. *International Journal of Lexicography*. 6 (4) 253-79.

Chodkiewicz, C., D. Bourigault & J. Humbley (2002). 'Making a workable glossary out of a specialized corpus'. In B. Altenberg & S. Granger (eds.) *Lexis in Contrast*. Amsterdam: Benjamins. 249-67.

Coxhead, A. (2000). 'A new academic word list'. *TESOL Quarterly* 34 (2) 213-38.

Cowie, A. P. (ed.) (1998). *Phraseology*. Oxford: Oxford University Press.

Crane, L. B., E. B. Yeager & R. L. Whitman (1981). *An Introduction to Linguistics*. Toronto: Little, Brown & Company.

Crystal, D. (1992). *An Encyclopedic Dictionary of Language and Languages*. Oxford: Blackwell.

Dodd, B. (ed.) (2000). *Working with German Corpora*. Birmingham: University of Birmingham Press.

Faber, D. & K. M. Lauridsen (1991). 'The compilation of a Danish-English-French corpus in contract law'. In S. Johansson & A. Stenström, *English Computer Corpora*. Berlin: Mouton de Gruyter. 235-43.

Finch, G. (1998). *How to Study Linguistics*. Houndmills: Macmillan.

Ghadessy, M., A. Henry & R. L. Roseberry (eds.) (2001). *Small Corpus Studies and ELT*. Amsterdam: Benjamins.

Heartley, A. & Nation, P. (1996). *Range*. [Computer software]. Available at <http://www.vuw.ac.nz/lals/staff/paul_nation>. (accessed 6.2.2002)

Howatt, A. P. R. (1984). *A History of English Language Teaching*. Oxford: Oxford University Press.

Kennedy, G. (1998). *An Introduction to Corpus Linguistics*. London: Longman.

Nation, P. (2001). 'Using small corpora to investigate learner needs'. In M. Ghadessy et al., 31-45.

Pearson, J. (1998). *Terms in Context*. Amsterdam: Benjamins.

Piotrowski, R. G. (1984). *Text - Mensch - Computer*. Bochum: Brockmeyer.

Renouf, A. (1987). 'Corpus development'. In J. M. Sinclair (ed.) *Looking Up*. London: Collins. 1-40.

Scott, M. (1997). *WordSmith Tools*. [Computer software.] Oxford: Oxford University Press.

Sinclair, J. (1991). *Corpus, Concordance, Collocation*. Oxford: Oxford University Press.

Stubbs, M. (2002). 'Two quantitative methods of studying phraseology in English'. *International Journal of Corpus Linguistics* 7 (2) 215-244.

Trask, R. L. (1993). *A Dictionary of Grammatical Terms in Linguistics*. London: Routledge.

Vihla, M. (1998). 'Medicor: a corpus of contemporary American medical texts'. *ICAME Journal*. 22: 73-80.

Weisler, S. E. & S. Milekic (2000). *Theory of Language*. Cambridge, Ma: MIT Press.

West, M (1953). *A General Service List of English Words.* London: Longman, Green & Co.

Zhu, Q. (1989). 'A quantitative look at the Guangzhou petroleum English corpus'. *ICAME Journal.* 13: 28-41.

Nadja Nesselhauf

Transfer at the locutional level: an investigation of German-speaking and French-speaking learners of English

In a discussion of the different levels of word cooccurrence restriction, D. J. Allerton points out that there are

> restrictions on lexical cooccurrence, which are at best only partly explicable in semantic terms. In this type of case, the language simply seems to dictate, for no good semantic reason, that such-and-such a combination does, or does not, occur (1984: 28).

Allerton calls this level of cooccurrence restriction 'locutional', with reference to Saussure's 'locutions toutes faites' (1962: 172). The type of restriction at work at this level is also often referred to as 'arbitrary restriction' or 'phraseological restriction', and the combinations it results in are often referred to as 'collocations'. Locutional restriction seems to occur particularly often with prepositions and general verbs such as *do*, *get*, *give*, *have*, *make*, *put*, and *take*, and is best revealed by comparison of different languages (Allerton 1984: 30f):

English	*French*	*Italian*
in (the) summer (time)	en été	d'estate
in (the) winter (time)	en hiver	d'inverno
in (the) spring (time)	au printemps	in primavera
in autumn	à l'automne	in autonno

English	German	French
make a decision	*eine Entscheidung machen	*faire une décision
take a decision (only BrE)	*eine Entscheidung nehmen	prendre une décision
*hit a decision	eine Entscheidung treffen	*toucher une décision

Because of the arbitrariness of locutional combinations and the resulting difference between languages it can be assumed that they are difficult for language learners, and that when learners produce locutional combinations that are unacceptable in English, these are at least sometimes influenced by their first language (L1). So far, however, transfer at the locutional level has not been studied to any significant extent.

In this paper, I will investigate locutional combinations consisting of one of the two general verbs *make* or *take* and a noun, produced by two groups of advanced learners of English, one group with L1 German and one with L1 French. The different types of mistake the learners make will be identified and L1 influence on these mistakes will be analysed. More subtle influences of the L1 on the learners' production will also be identified, by comparing the overall use of locutional combinations with *make* and *take* in the two groups.

Previous studies of transfer at the locutional level

Transfer, which will be used in a loose sense here to refer to any kind of L1 influence on second language (L2) production, has only very rarely been studied at the locutional level of language. Most assessments found in the literature on the role of transfer in locutional combinations are largely speculative and also partly contradictory. Bahns (1997), for example, assumes that the great majority of collocational mistakes are due to transfer, while Dechert & Lennon (1989) assign a minor role to transfer and assume that L2 influences (such as blends of two existing expressions) are far more important. The few actual studies that have been carried out indicate that L1 influence is probably quite strong at the locutional level. Granger (1998), for example, in an investigation of learners of English with L1 French, finds that collocations that are congruent in L1 and L2 are used particularly frequently. Chi et al. (1994), who investigate the use of combinations with delexical verbs (such as *give an answer* or *make a statement*) in the English of Chinese-speaking learners, also find strong L1 influence. A study by Kellerman (1978) indicates that the more idiomatic an item, the less likely it is to be transferred, which means that locutional combinations can be expected to have a medium degree of L1 influence, between idioms (with a low degree of L1 influence) and free combinations (with a high degree of L1 influence). Gabrys-Biskup (1992), finally, compares the L1 influence on collocational mistakes of German and Polish learners of English and finds a significant difference between the two groups: the collocational mistakes of the German students were influenced by the L1 in about 20%, the ones by the Polish students in about 45% of the cases.

The data

The investigation will be carried out on the basis of three corpora.[1] The two corpora used primarily are slightly reduced versions of two subcorpora of the International Corpus of Learner

---

1 I would like to thank the coordinator of German ICLE, Gunter Lorenz, and the Centre for English Corpus Linguistics at the Université Catholique de Louvain, Belgium, for integrating me into the ICLE project at a late stage.

English (ICLE). ICLE consists of essays written by university students of English in their 2nd, 3rd or 4th year and contains a number of subcorpora consisting of data of different L1-groups. The ICLE-project also comprises a native speaker control corpus called LOCNESS, which consists of American and British student writing, and of which a slightly reduced version will also be used for some aspects of the present study. The essays contained in ICLE are mostly argumentative; a small proportion is descriptive. Typical essay topics include "Weekend traffic should be banned in the city centre", "Is there any point in being ecology-conscious?" or "My teenage idol." The size of the three corpora is displayed in Table 1; I will be referring to the corpora in their reduced form as GeCLE (German Corpus of Learner English), FreCLE (French Corpus of Learner English), and BAse (British and American Student Essays).[2]

corpus	number of words	number of essays
GeCLE (German ICLE)	154,191	318
FreCLE (French ICLE)	154,008	281
BAse (LOCNESS)	154,886 (BE: 72,542; AE: 82:344)	252

Table 1: Corpora used in the analysis

The analysis comprises all combinations of the verbs *make* and *take* with at least one object-noun, including verb-pronoun com-

---

[2] The corpora were slightly reduced in size to ensure direct comparison. Most importantly, essays written by A-level students (rather than university students) were taken out of LOCNESS and a number of essays on one specialised political topic ("Europe 92: loss of sovereignty or birth of a nation?"), which had apparently been prepared to some degree, was taken out of the French corpus.

binations if the pronoun refers to a noun, but disregarding the following structures:[3]

VOC (adj): *make sb angry,*

VOA (adv): *take sth/sb seriously,*

VO + bare inf.: *make sb cry.*

Therefore, structures included in the analysis are, for example, VO, VPO, VOO, VOPO, VO+to+inf; most locutionally restricted combinations were found in the following two structures:

VO: *make a decision,*

VOPO: *take sth into consideration.*

Methodology

After all combinations with *make* and *take* occurring in the relevant structures in GeCLE and FreCLE had been extracted, it was necessary to identify those that can be considered arbitrarily restricted. This means that a distinction had to be made between locutional combinations and idioms on the one hand, and, on the other, between locutional combinations and what have been called free combinations (e.g. Cowie 1994), where the restrictions on combinability are purely semantic. The following criteria were used to distinguish these three types of verb-noun combination:

Free combinations (vs. locutional combinations):

> The verb carries a meaning which can be defined without reference to the noun and which allows its combination with all nouns that semantically allow that verb.

---

3   These structures were excluded on the basis of the assumption that if restrictions occurred in them, they were more likely to occur between the verb and the adjective/adverb/verb than between the verb and the noun.

Locutional combinations (vs. idioms):
> The noun carries an identifiable part of the meaning of the whole combination.

According to these criteria, *take a book*, for example, is considered a free combination, as *take* in this sense can be defined without reference to the noun (unlike, for example, in the locutional combination *take pride in*) and can be combined freely on a semantic basis (cf. *take a pen, a guitar, a box*). *Take place*, on the other hand, is considered an idiom and not a locutional combination, as *place* does not carry an identifiable part of the meaning of the whole combination (whereas *pride* in *take pride in* does). Naturally, there is no clear dividing line between these three types of combination, so that decisions on what constitutes a locutional combination and what does not must remain arbitrary to a certain degree.

The locutional combinations with *make* and *take* that had been isolated in GeCLE and FreCLE were then judged as to their acceptability in English. Combinations were judged on the basis of dictionaries, native-speaker corpus data, and native speaker judgements. A combination was judged acceptable if it occurred in a dictionary (the *Oxford Advanced Learner's Dictionary*, the *Collins COBUILD English Dictionary* or *The BBI Dictionary of English Word Combinations*) or at least 5 times in the written part of the BNC (the British National Corpus)[4]. If this was not the case, it was presented – in context – to two native speakers, one of British and one of American English, who were asked to judge the combination acceptable, unacceptable or questionable and who were also asked to provide a correction. If either both native speakers judged a combination as unacceptable or one judged it as unacceptable and one as questionable, the combination was considered to contain a 'mistake' (or, in a few cases,

---

4 The written component of the BNC contains about 90 million words from a variety of text types; cf. <http://www.hcu.ox.ac.uk/BNC>.

several mistakes), which were identified on the basis of the corrections the informants had provided.[5]

Mistakes at the locutional level

Different types of mistake that the learners made with locutional verb-noun combinations can be distinguished and divided into three groups. First, a number of deviations in the form of the collocation occurs in the data (essay codes and corrections in brackets):[6]

- unacceptable verb: *make dreams* (FR-UCL-0024.3; *have dreams*)
- unacceptable noun: *make a trial* (GE-AUG-0053.3; *make an attempt*)
- unacceptable verb and unacceptable noun: *make science* (FR-ULB-0005.1; *do research*)
- unacceptable article or number or pronoun: *make profit* (e.g. FR-ULG-0010.1; *make a profit* or *make profits*); *take seats* (GE-AUG-0005.1; *take one's seats* or *take a seat*)
- unacceptable preposition: *take a look into [the newspaper]* (e.g. GE- AUG-0083.1; *take a look at*)
- multiple mistakes (other than unacceptable verb and unacceptable noun): *take one's responsibilities* (FR-ULB-0001.2; *take responsibility*)

---

5   No distinction will be made here between 'error' and 'mistake'; 'mistake' will be used with reference to British and American English, which are the common target varieties for German-speaking and French-speaking learners of English.
6   The essay codes have been slightly simplified. Their full form reads, for example, ICLE-FR-UCL-0002.1 for the French subcorpus and ICLE-GE-DR-0009.1 for the German subcorpus. "ICLE-" is omitted here.

A second group of mistakes consists of combinations which are correct in form, but which display a deviation in meaning, i.e. the apparently intended meaning (as it can be inferred from the context) would be conveyed by a combination different from the one used:

make a difference (FR-UCL-0021.1; *make a distinction*)

take measures (GE-SA-0004.3; *take measurements*)

A third group consists of what could be called 'invented collocations', as the combination used does not exist, and the meaning that the learner apparently tried to express is not expressed with a verb-noun collocation in English.

make digressions (FR-ULG-0007.1; *digress*)

make a shopping tour (GE-AUG-0014.2; *go shopping*)

type of mistake	number of mistakes	number of mistakes in GeCLE	number of mistakes in FreCLE
unacceptable verb	28	19	9
unacceptable noun	6	3	3
unacceptable verb and noun	3	2	1
unacceptable article, number, pronoun	10	4	6
unacceptable preposition	9	9	0
multiple mistakes	4	2	2
unintended meaning	23	11	12
invented collocations	10	3	7
Total	93	53	40

Table 2: Numbers of occurrence of the different types of mistake

Table 2 shows how often each of these types of mistake occur in GeCLE and FreCLE. Overall, more mistakes occur in GeCLE

(53, as opposed to 40 in FreCLE); the most frequent types of mistake are 'unacceptable verb' and 'unintended meaning'. In two categories, the difference between the number of occurrences in the two corpora is particularly striking: in the category 'unacceptable verb', there are 19 occurrences in GeCLE but only 9 in FreCLE, and an unacceptable preposition occurs 9 times in GeCLE, but never in FreCLE.

L1 influence on mistakes

In a study like the present one, it is of course not possible to determine whether L1 influence has actually occurred, so that everything that will be said about L1 influence should be taken to mean that L1 influence is considered likely. L1 influence was considered likely in the production of an unacceptable combination if what was actually produced by the learner resembles the corresponding L1-combination in form and/or meaning. For example, if *make an experience* (e.g. GE-AUG-0016.3) is used by a learner of L1 German instead of *have an experience*, this is assumed to have been influenced by the learner's L1, as the corresponding German combination is *eine Erfahrung machen*, and *machen* and *make* are often translation equivalents. *Make faults* (GE-AUG-0048.1; for *make mistakes*) was considered to have been influenced by the learner's L1 German because of the German equivalent for *mistake*, *Fehler*, which resembles *faults* phonologically. Table 3 shows in how many cases L1 influence on the different types of mistake is considered likely in the two corpora.

Overall, the percentage of L1 influence is extremely high: in more than three quarters (76%) of all unacceptable combinations, some kind of L1 influence seems likely. In FreCLE, L1 influence even seems likely in 88% of the unacceptable combinations, as compared to 68% in GeCLE. What is striking is that in spite of this, the category 'unintended meaning' is affected by L1 influence far more often in FreCLE than in GeCLE.

type of mistake	number of mistakes	L1 influence	GeCLE	FreCLE
unacceptable verb	28	25	18	7
unacceptable noun	6	5	2	3
unacceptable verb and noun	3	3	2	1
unacceptable article, number, pronoun	10	6	1	5
unacceptable preposition	9	4	4	0
multiple mistakes	4	4	2	2
unintended meaning	23	17	5	12
invented collocations	10	7	2	5
Total	93	71 (76%)	36 (68%)	35 (88%)

Table 3: L1 influence on the different types of mistake

L1 influence was also investigated in the combinations with *make* and *take* that were classified as free combinations and idioms. For free combinations, 37 mistakes were identified, of which 20 (or 54%) showed signs of L1 influence; for idioms, 9 out of 15 mistakes (60%) were probably influenced by the learners' L1. Therefore, it does not seem to be the case that transfer decreases with the degree of idiomaticity of a combination as Kellerman (1978) claims, but rather that locutional combinations – at least in the case of the verb-noun combinations with the two verbs investigated – are the type of combination that is most susceptible to transfer.

While investigating possible L1 influence on the learners' mistakes, it emerged that L1 influence was not the only factor responsible for what the learner actually produced. If a learner with L1-German produces *take care about* (e.g. GE-AUG-0084.3), for example, it seems likely that in addition to a possible L1 influence based on the frequent translation equivalence of *um* and *about*,[7] there is also what might be termed 'L2 influence', i.e. an influence of the similar combination *to care about* existing in English.

In Table 4, the extent of L2 influence is shown, i.e. the influence of an expression with a similar form and/or meaning on the production of unacceptable combinations. Although this influence occurs less frequently than L1 influence, it is still considerably strong: in more than half of the mistakes L2 influence seems likely.

type of mistake	number of mistakes	L2 influence	GeCLE	FreCLE
unacceptable verb	28	7	4	3
unacceptable noun	6	6	3	3
unacceptable verb and noun	3	3	2	1
unacceptable article, number, pronoun	10	1	1	0
unacceptable preposition	9	8	8	0
multiple mistakes	4	3	1	2
unintended meaning	23	22	11	11
invented collocations	10	3	1	2
Total	93	53 (57%)	31 (58%)	22 (55%)

Table 4: L2 influence on the different types of mistake

7   The German equivalent of *take care of sb.* is *sich um jmdn. kümmern*.

The L1 and L2 influences on mistakes interact in various ways. In a considerable number of the mistakes produced (52 out of 93), both L1 influence and L2 influence are discernable. Both types of influence are, for example, likely in *take charge of* (FR-ULB-0024.1; for *take care of*), which seems to have been influenced by French *prendre en charge* as well as by the fact that the meaning of *take charge of* in English is similar to the intended one of *take care of*. A further example is *take proportions* (FR-UCL-0009.4), which seems to have been influenced both by *prendre des proportions* and the English combination *take on proportions*. L2 influence without L1 influence only occurred in 7 mistakes, and mainly concerns prepositions. For example, *take care for* (e.g. GE-AUG-0048.3) is likely to be a blend of the target collocation *take care of* and the prepositional verb *care for*. In 27 combinations, L1 influence seems to have been at work exclusively. Such exclusive L1 influence is especially frequent with verbs, in particular delexical verbs: 19 out of 28 verb mistakes are influenced exclusively by the learner's L1; of these verbs, 13 are delexical. Examples are *make dreams* (for *have dreams*, influenced by *faire des rêves*; e.g. FR-UCL-0024.3) or *take changes* (for *make changes*, influenced by *Änderungen vornehmen*; GE-DR-0009.1). The category 'article, number and pronoun mistakes' is also particularly often affected by L1 influence only (6 of 9 mistakes). Examples are *make profit* (for *make a profit/ profits*, influenced by *faire profit*; e.g. FR-UCL-0018.3) and *take one's responsibilities* (for *take responsibility*, influenced by *prendre ses responsabilités*; FR-ULB-0001.2). Finally, in a small number of mistakes (7), neither L1 influence nor L2 influence are recognisable, for example in the production of *take a task* (for *carry out / perform a task*).[8]

---

8   A possible reason for the production of such a combination is the recognition by the learner that *take* can often be combined with a noun in order to denote action, such as in *take action, take a trip*; the combination is not considered to be subject to "L2 influence", however, as its production seems to rely on a quite general learner strategy rather than on the influence of a specific element that is very similar to the one intended.

Types of L1 influence

To support the assumption that L1 influence actually occurs, and in order to investigate whether there are more subtle types of influence than the type leading to mistakes, the locutional combinations with *make* and *take* in GeCLE and FreCLE were compared. Combinations that occurred at least three times more (or more precisely, in at least three more essays) in one corpus than in the other were analysed. Unfortunately, it turned out that some of the differences in the number of occurrence were most likely due to an imbalance in the distribution of topics in the two corpora. Two types of imbalance had to be considered. First, there is a number of essays in GeCLE (but not in FreCLE) with rather more personal and concrete topics, such as "The pleasures of cycling" or "I don't know exactly when I started to hate body building". Secondly, in the French corpus two topics dominate, namely: "The generation gap: a real problem or a fantasy?" and "Some people say that in our modern world, dominated by science and technology and industrialisation, there is no longer a place for dreaming and imagination. What is your opinion?". I used two criteria to eliminate those combinations in which the difference in the number of occurrence is probably due to one of these types of imbalance: the distribution of the collocations over topics (i.e. whether a collocation occurs mainly in essays with one of the topics predominant in the French corpus) and the number of occurrences of the noun (and its derivations) of a combination in the two corpora. For example, the lexeme *friend* with all its derivations occurs 50 times in FreCLE and 234 times in GeCLE, so that the difference in the use of *make friends* (6 times in GeCLE and never in FreCLE) is most likely related to that imbalance and was thus disregarded. Similarly, the combination *make progress*, which was used 18 times in FreCLE and only twice in GeCLE, was excluded from further consideration, as it was almost exclusively used in essays on the topic on the modern world and imagination in FreCLE.

For all combinations for which the difference in occurrence did not seem due to the topic imbalance in the two corpora, the possibility of L1 influence was considered. While for a number of the combinations the difference does not seem to be due to the learners' different first languages (such as for *make a mistake*, which occurs six times in FreCLE and twice in GeCLE), for many of them this seems to be the case, albeit in different ways.

The most obvious type of influence that emerges from the comparison is where the L1 leads to the use of a combination that does not exist in the L2. For example, the combination *make part of* (for *be part of*) is only used by speakers of L1 French (in 3 essays), and is most likely modelled on French *faire partie de* (where German, like English, has *Teil sein von*). One example of its use is: "The generation gap [...] is a real problem: it makes part of the reality of life" (FR-UCL-0010.4). Interestingly, the combination *make an experience* (for *have an experience* or *to experience*) is also only used by one of the two groups of learners, occurring 6 times in the GeCLE and never in FreCLE. As there is no significant difference in the occurrence of the lexeme *experience* and its derivations in the two corpora, it can be assumed that this difference is not primarily due to the fact that the essays in GeCLE tend to be more personal. Instead, it seems that the frequency of the L1 combination plays a role: whereas German exclusively has the combination *eine Erfahrung machen* to express the concept in question, French has both *faire une expérience* and *avoir une expérience*.

A further type of L1 influence that emerges is where the L1 leads to the use of an existing collocation with an unintended meaning, because the two (related) meanings are expressed by the same combination in the learner's L1. The combination *make a difference*, for example, is used 8 times in FreCLE and 4 times in GeCLE. In FreCLE, in 7 of the 8 occurrences of the combination, what seems to be intended is not *make a difference* but *make a distinction*, as for example in the following sentence: "television [...] plays such an important role in our everyday life that some people cannot make the difference anymore between fiction and reality" (FR-ULB-0014.1). In GeCLE, this mistake is only made once, the reason probably being that whereas German has a different combination for the two concepts *(einen Unterschied machen* for *make a difference*, and *eine Unterscheidung treffen* for *make a distinction)*, French has *faire une différence* to express both meanings.

In addition to L1 influences leading to mistakes, two other types of L1 influence emerge from the comparison of combinations in GeCLE and FreCLE. One type is an influence on the selection from two (or more) possible L2 collocations, where one combination is preferred over another (or several others) because it is also used in L1 while the other is not. Such is the case with the combination *take a decision*, which occurs 6 times in FreCLE and only once in GeCLE. If we look at the use of *take a decision* in English, we find that it occurs almost exclusively in British English, where it is used alongside but less frequently than *make a decision*:[9] FROWN (a corpus of American English with one million words of different written text types) yields 57 occurrences of *make* and only one of *take*, the British equivalent FLOB yields 25 occurrences of *make* and 16 of *take*; the American part of BAse yields 13 occurrences of *make* and none of *take*, the British part 16 of *make* and 6 of *take*. The reason for the comparatively frequent use of *take a decision* by the French-speaking learners (in comparison: they use *make a decision* twice) is therefore likely to be the influence of the French equivalent *prendre une décision*; German-speaking learners, on the other hand, orient themselves towards what they have probably been predominantly exposed to, namely *make a decision* (which they use 7 times), as their L1 (which has *eine Entscheidung treffen*) does not lead to the preference of either of the two existing combinations.

A final type of L1 influence is the frequent use of collocations which are congruent in L1 and L2, i.e. word-for-word equivalents of each other. This seems to be the case with the

---

9   A possible semantic and/or stylistic difference between the two combinations will not be considered here.

combination which differs most strikingly in its number of occurrences in the two corpora: *take into account* occurs 30 times in FreCLE versus only 5 times in GeCLE (and also only 5 times in BAse). This overuse by the French-speaking learners is probably caused by the fact that a word-for-word equivalent is used in French (*prendre en compte*), whereas German does not have such a word-for-word equivalent (German has *in Betracht ziehen*, with *ziehen* corresponding to *draw*). Although none of the uses of this combination in FreCLE was considered unacceptable by the native speaker judges, some of the occurrences might be on the borderline between overuse and misuse. In one essay, for example, it is used thus at the beginning: "The generation gap is a vast subject that can be viewed under different aspects. I will take into account two situations [...]" (FR-UCL-0016.4). A similar, though not as striking, case of overuse apparently due to the learners' L1 is *make a choice*, which is used 7 times in FreCLE and twice in GeCLE (and 3 times in BAse) and which is likely to have been caused by the fact that French has the word-for-word equivalent *faire un choix* while German has *eine Wahl treffen*. A further similar case is *make use of*, which is used 10 times in FreCLE and never in GeCLE and BAse. Like in the case of *take into account*, the overuse does not lead to mistakes, but sometimes it leads to somewhat awkward sentences, as in: "The use we want to make of TV depends exclusively on us" (FR-ULB-0015.2). The situation is slightly different in this case, however, in that both French and German have word-for-word translation equivalents: French has *faire usage de* and German *Gebrauch machen von*. The difference is, however, that the French combination, unlike the German one, is phonetically similar to the English combination. If we look at the other examples discussed, this is also the case there (cf. *choice – choix, account – compte*), so that it seems likely that combinations that are phonetically similar in L1 and L2 are used particularly frequently in the L2.

Conclusions

Before drawing conclusions, it should be pointed out that the database, although large for a study of learner language, is of course too small for all the results to be completely reliable. Further studies will be needed to confirm them, and the results are clearly to be regarded as preliminary – even more so as they are only based on the analysis of certain locutional combinations and of certain groups of learners. Nevertheless, a number of interesting tendencies have emerged which may well be valid beyond the type of data and the type of learner investigated. First of all, the L1 influence on locutional combinations in the English of advanced learners seems to be considerable: about three quarters of all collocational mistakes are probably at least partly due to transfer. The influence of the L1 seems to be even greater at the locutional level of language than for free combinations and idioms. Second, French-speaking learners of English seem to rely more on transfer than German-speaking learners in the production of collocations. Possible reasons for this (such as language distance or teaching methodology) will need to be investigated; what also requires investigation is how this can be related to Gabrys-Biskup's observation that German learners rely less on transfer than Polish learners. A third important result is that very often (in about 2/3 of the mistakes), L1 influence interacts with L2 influence. This means that learners mainly transfer L1 collocations if the expression they intend to produce is supported by the existence of a similar expression in the L2. Fourth, elements seem to be particularly prone to L1 influence if they do not carry much lexical meaning (i.e. articles, pronouns, number and delexical verbs; prepositions seem to be an exception to this, however). Fifth, L1 influence apparently manifests itself not only in mistakes but also in more subtle ways, in particular in the overuse of certain combinations. Finally, certain combinations seem to be transferred more easily than others, namely those that are more frequent in the L1, and those that are phonetically similar in the L1 and L2. It is hoped, therefore, that

– despite the tentativeness of the results – the present study has demonstrated the importance of investigating transfer at the locutional level of language and indicated some directions for further research.

References

Allerton, D. J. (1984). 'Three (or four) levels of word cooccurrence restriction'. *Lingua* (63) 17-40.
Bahns, J. (1997). *Kollokationen und Wortschatzarbeit im Englischunterricht*. Tübingen: Narr.
Benson, M., E. Benson, & R. Ilson (1997). *The BBI Dictionary of English Word Combinations*. (Rev. ed. of *BBI Combinatory Dictionary of English*, 1986.) Amsterdam: Benjamins.
Chi, M. L. A. & P. K. Wong (1994). 'Collocational problems amongst ESL learners: a corpus-based study'. *Entering text*, ed. L. Flowerdew & A. K. Tony. Hong Kong: University of Science and Technology. 157-165.
Collins COBUILD English Dictionary (1995). London: Harper Collins.
Cowie, A. P. (1994). 'Phraseology'. In: R. E. Asher (ed.). *The Encyclopedia of Language and Linguistics*, Oxford: Pergamon. 3168-3171.
Dechert, H. W. & P. Lennon (1989). 'Collocational blends of advanced second language learners. A preliminary analysis'. In: W. Oleksy (ed.) *Contrastive pragmatics*. Amsterdam: Benjamins. 131-168.
Gabrys-Biskup, D. (1992). 'L1 influence on learners' renderings of English collocations. A Polish/German empirical study'. In: P. J. L. Arnaud & H. Béjoint (eds.) *Vocabulary and applied linguistics*. London: Macmillan. 85-93.
Granger, S. (1998). 'Prefabricated patterns in advanced EFL writing: collocations and formulae'. In: A. P. Cowie (ed.) *Phraseology. Theory, analysis, and applications*. Oxford: Clarendon. 145-160.
Kellerman, E. (1978). 'Giving learners a break: native language intuitions as a source of predictions about transferability'. *Working Papers on Bilingualism* (15) 59-92.
Oxford Advanced Learner's Dictionary (2000). Oxford: Oxford University Press.
Saussure, F. de (1962). *Cours de linguistique générale*. 3rd ed. (1st ed 1915). Paris: Payot.

CORNELIA TSCHICHOLD

Error analysis and lexical errors

Collecting and describing linguistic data is typically the starting point for research in linguistics. Given the – at least apparently – messy nature of linguistic data, the task of describing and classifying is not always an easy one. But it is a step that is clearly necessary before any further analysis, aiming at an explanation for the data on a psychological or cognitive level, can be achieved. Any reasonably large set of linguistic data is likely to contain a certain number of mistakes, most of them performance mistakes, errors that the producer of the utterance would recognize and be able to correct, but some competence mistakes (often called 'errors' in contrast to 'mistakes' arising from performance restrictions) might also appear.

Errors are thus a consistent part of linguistic data, but they are not often at the centre of attention of theoretical linguists. In psycholinguistics and other more applied branches of linguistics on the other hand, errors have always been a major source of data. Thanks to aphasic patients and the linguistic problems they show, we know more about the normal brain, and thanks partly to children's early utterances, we can observe them going through the various stages in the acquisition of their first language. Those applied linguists interested in the teaching and learning of foreign languages have always shown a certain concern for errors as well, even if errors made by learners of a second or foreign language were seen in a less favourable light than those made by children. Language teachers have a tendency to interpret errors as evidence of failure, either students' failure to learn properly, or possibly their own failure to teach properly. In a teaching context, errors are most typically seen as language in need of marking and correction.

Since Chomsky, syntax has been at the core of linguistic studies, at least in theoretical linguistics. Following this trend in theoretical linguistics, the field of applied linguistics put the emphasis firmly on syntactic aspects of language – including errors of syntax – as well. Consequently, the lexicon was treated with relative disregard for a long time. Researchers in applied linguistics were interested in the (transformational-generative) grammar rules violated by the sentences produced by learners. From this perspective, errors deriving from lacking or deviant lexical knowledge did not seem to promise any linguistic insight.

Error analysis, one of the methods used in applied linguistics, is a case in point. Corder (1973: 257) recognized errors as "probably the most important source of information about the nature of [the learner's] knowledge". However, many exponents of error analysis kept their attention firmly on those aspects that fell within the range of contemporary linguistic fashion and have a clear focus on the learner's evolving grammatical system and the resulting grammar errors.. These errors could be explained by the learner's imperfect mastery of the target language grammar system, e.g. cases of overgeneralization of a particular rule, because, according to Corder (1973: 278), "[r]elations, categories and rules are what are learned, not 'words' or other items, as such".

Grammar vs. lexicon

While research on syntax both in theoretical and applied linguistics is still thriving and the classic type of (syntax) error analysis has never totally died out (James 1994), the pendulum today seems to swing in the direction of the lexicon. The compilation of large corpora and the computational tools to investigate them has made it possible for linguists to investigate words and their patterns of usage to an extent unthinkable before the electronic age. The concominant rise of interest in the lexicon in general and in phraseology in particular has resulted in a number of developments in applied linguistics as well, possibly the most important being a change of perspective as documented in publications on the lexicon such as Lewis (1993) and Nation (2001), among many others. Still more recent is the interest in lexical and phraseological aspects of *learner* language (e.g. Granger 1998, Singleton 1999; see also Nesselhauf, this volume).

The new findings in these areas raise questions about the relationship between the lexicon and the syntax components of our linguistic system. In this context Sinclair's (1991) hypothesis offers a model of language that combines the so-called 'open choice principle' with the 'idiom principle' in an attempt to overcome the neat, but simplistic, division into grammar on the one hand, and vocabulary on the other. His model priviledges the idiom principle, the use of prefabricated stretches of language, for linguistic processing in most communicative situations. Evidence for native speakers' use of the two principles and their combination can be found in the performance data in the large corpora available today. The challenge for language learners is to find the proper balance between the two principles, something they often seem to have problems with, as Wray (2002: 148-149) posits:

> Establishing and maintaining a balance between formulaicity and creativity seems to be essential for successful acquisition, but in taught adults, this is difficult to achieve, with the learner most often erring on the side of too much creativity.

If the typical taught adult she has in mind was taught by a typical teacher, the emphasis in teaching will have been on grammar rules. Successful teaching of these rules allows learners to make use of linguistic creativity. As long as learners only have a vocabulary of a few hundred words, this strategy allows them to communicate in the foreign language, albeit on a rudimentary level and certainly not in any way free of errors. At a later stage in the language learning process, however, this emphasis on the mastery of grammar rules becomes more and more problematic, as Lennon (1991: 184) points out:

> At the advanced level highly localized morphological error is less prevalent than error involving usage, lexical choice, stylistic appropriacy, and various sorts of global discourse error. It is precisely such errors that traditional error analysis is ill-equipped to deal with [...].

At this level, learners differ from native speakers not so much with respect to their knowledge and application of grammatical rules, but rather in their choice of words and phrases, which somehow is not native-like. Traditional error analysis, as we have seen, is mostly concerned with grammar errors and does not provide any insight as to the role of lexical errors or the relationship between lexical and grammatical errors. Besides these more academic studies, however, there have always been published compilations of common errors, publications which might have provided some input for studies in the field of error analysis even before the age of the electronic corpus. In the next section, two such collections of common errors will be examined with respect to the amount of lexical errors they contain.

Common errors

In the light of the revived interest in the lexicon, I have attempted a re-analysis of some typical learner errors, as they can be found in popular collections such as Allison (1992) and Fitikides (2000). My assumption was that most teachers are so strongly influenced by the long-prevailing emphasis on grammar that they sometimes have problems recognizing their students' errors as lexical rather than grammatical, especially if the linguistic problem is on the level of usage or phraseology rather than that of an individual word.[1] A quotation from Allison (1992: 4) illustrates this phenomenon:

> Viele dieser "unenglischen" Ausdrücke sind *strenggenommen keine grammatikalischen* Fehler. Es ist beispielsweise nicht falsch zu sagen: "I have too little time" oder "He has too much money". Aber beides klingt sehr fremd, und Engländer würden es normalerweise so formulieren: "I haven't got enough time" und "He's got a lot of money". [...] Die in Klammern stehenden Zahlen hinter den 'Oxford English'-Sätzen verweisen auf die entsprechenden Erklärungen im *Grammatikteil* am Ende des Buches.[2] (my emphasis)

The 'grammar part' at the end of the book is a simple list of all the 'horror mistakes' the exercises in the book are meant to help eradicate. Of these 333 mistakes, the majority are of a lexical nature; only about a fifth of them are either truly grammatical problems or errors related to grammatical words. Table 1 below shows a classification of the errors into simple types of lexical and grammatical errors. (The authors do no classify the errors at all.) In my classification I have tried to adhere to a more restrictive definition of 'lexical error' than that proposed in Lewis (1993: 171), who analyses *the wife to my brother* as a gap in the learner's lexical knowledge, i.e. the absence of *sister-in-law*. Traditionally, such a phrase would more likely be corrected to *my brother's wife*, a corrected grammar error. As I relied on the corrections given in the books, this type of error would still be classified as a non-lexical error in my system. A more radical approach in the spirit of Lewis (1993) would therefore presum-

---

1   One exception to this 'lexicon-blindness' are the so-called 'false friends', e.g. German *bekommen* – English *become*, a phenomenon teachers are well aware of and one that gives rise to numerous jokes.
2   Strictly speaking, many of these "un-English" expressions are not grammatical errors. It is not wrong to say: "I have too little time" or "He has too much money". But both sentences sound very foreign, and English speakers would normally say "I haven't got enough time" or "He's got a lot of money" instead. Numbers in brackets following the "Oxford English" sentences refer to the grammar part at the end of the book. (my translation, CT)

ably give even higher figures for lexical errors than those given in Table 1.

Error type	Number
Verb-related lexical errors *When did you marry?	61
Noun-related lexical errors *I'm not working in the moment.	57
Lexical errors related to other word classes *The garage is a great building.	38
Phraseological errors *When was the last strong winter?	95
other (mistranslations, etc.) *It gives four theatres in the town.	15
Grammatical errors, incl. errors related to grammatical words *That's the car from the boss.	67
TOTAL	333

Table 1: Lexical vs. grammatical errors in Allison (1992)

Allison (1992) is a book written in German, published in Germany and therefore clearly aimed at German-speaking learners of English. One might speculate that German-speaking learners and their teachers are particularly fond of grammar and therefore package as much of what needs to be learned as possible in terms of grammar rather than vocabulary. For comparison, let us therefore have a look at another collection of errors. Fitikides (2000) is a new edition of perhaps *the* classic collection of errors frequently made by learners of English as a foreign language. It was first published in 1936 and has seen numerous (slight) revisions and editions since then. Its author uses a very simple classification system for the several hundred mistakes listed. The five parts of his classification comprise one part each on "incorrect omissions", "incorrect additions", and "incorrect word order". The remaining two parts concern "misused forms", a rather mixed category, and "confused words", sorted by part of speech.[3]

Part I ("Misused forms") opens with a section on verbs, adjectives and nouns followed by wrong prepositions, e.g. *afraid from* (4), *believe to* (10).[4] It also includes collocational errors (where a preposition is involved) of the type *travel with the train* (13), which might be more usefully classified under the noun rather than the verb. All 75 errors listed in this category can be seen as errors arising from lack of knowledge on specific lexical items. The second section covers the "misuse" of the infinitive. Of the 29 errors listed there, the large majority, i.e. 27 errors, can be said to be lexically conditioned, e.g. *capable *to V* (77), *mind *to V* (91); and the remaining two cases concern prepositions, i.e. *without *to V* (75), and *instead of *to V* (76). The third section, "Use of the wrong tense", seems to be a clearly syntax-related category, but even here we can find a few errors that would more easily be dealt with in a lexical perspective, i.e. **I would wish to know more English* (129) for *I wish (that) I knew more English*.

These and all remaining classes of Fitikides are given in Table 2 below, with my own classification into errors that could ('lexical') or could not ('non-lexical') be more usefully treated in a lexical framework of error analysis.

---

[3] Corder (1973) proposes a similarly simple classification into omission, addition, selection, and ordering for each of the three linguistic levels phonology/orthography, grammar and lexicon as the first step of analysing errors. Lennon (1991) criticizes such criteria as inadequate, being based on a superseded linear, non-hierarchical model of language where words in a sentence are added one after the other, like beads on a string.

[4] Numbers in brackets refer to the numbering in Fitikides (2000).

Part	Section	non-lexical	lexical	% lex
I Misused forms	1 Using the wrong prep.	0	74	100
	2 Misuse of the infinitive	2	27	93
	3 Use of the wrong tense	27	4	13
	4 Miscellaneous	35	15	30
	5 Un-English expressions	0	37	100
II Incorrect omissions	1 Omission of prepositions	0	19	100
	2 Miscellaneous	29	13	31
III Unnecessary words	1 Words	0	17	100
	2 Propositions	6	14	70
	3 Articles	5	6	55
	4 Miscellaneous	13	8	38
IV Misplaced words	1 Adverbs	7	0	0
	2 Miscellaneous	16	3	15
V Confused words	1 Prepositions	0	17	100
	2 Verbs	3	56	95
	3 Adverbs	0	10	100
	4 Adjectives	9	14	61
	5 Nouns	7	59	79
	6 Confusion of number	32	32	100
	7 Parts of speech	7	22	76
TOTAL		198	415	68

Table 2: Lexical vs. grammatical errors in Fitikides (2000)

Again, we see that the large majority of the errors listed are of a lexical nature. The exact difference in percentages of lexical vs. non-lexical errors for Allison (1992) and Fitikides (2000) is not relevant here because – in such a purely numerical exercise – we need to take into account the fact that we are dealing with individual sentences, each one illustrating one particular error. Errors concerning lexical items, of which there are potentially thousands even in the lexicon of relative beginners, can thus quite easily be compiled into long lists. A book on errors need not list dozens of sentences illustrating the same subject-verb agreement error, but can very easily list hundreds of different collocational errors. We could interpret this as a particular case of the question whether it is more useful to count types or tokens, a question which will not be pursued here, as the point is simply to show that a clear majority of errors in such collections are of a lexical nature. While not changing the data they collected from their students, the compilers of such lists seem to have a tendency to adopt the vocabulary of a particular linguistic perspective, even if it does not fit their data very well.

Error taxonomies and error gravity

A more useful question than that about bare numbers in this context concerns error gravity. Both Allison (1992) and Fitikides (2000) have learners and possibly teachers as their target audience, probably not linguists. They do not attempt to grade the errors they list according to gravity or seriousness. Error gravity is a measure of reaction by native speakers (or sometimes non-native teachers) to language learner errors. The aim of error gravity studies is to find out which type of errors hinder communication most, or irritate native speakers most. In case of teacher judges, error gravity can also refer to the marking scales used by these teachers. In his review of studies on error gravity, James (1998) shows that lexical errors are judged to be the most severe errors, i.e. the errors that constitute the greatest hindrance to successful communication. In apparent contradiction to this, McCretton & Rider (1993) found that lexical errors were judged by native and non-native teachers of English to be the least severe errors, but their sample included only lexical errors of word class confusion, e.g. *The trip was very pleasant except for the long waiting at Customs*. It is not surprising that teachers judge a verb form error such as *Did you frightened them off?* as being a more serious error than the type of word class confusion. Such a hierarchy is certainly also influenced by the teachers' training and the syllabus they have to adhere to. Verb forms have been taught, therefore students are expected to master this part of English grammar. Errors of a more clearly lexical nature were not included in McCretton & Rider's (1993) study.

The apparent contradiction makes two problematic aspects of many studies in error analysis evident: firstly, the fact that the errors used for testing are often constructed by the researchers specifically for the purpose of the study and are not taken from a corpus of errors produced under realistic conditions by real learners.[5] The second problem is that the labels for the categories of errors used in each study are not easily matched with those in other studies on similar research topics, so that comparison becomes very difficult.

Two more recent studies on error gravity at least steer clear of the first of these problems. Dordick (1996) claims that his results, which show that lexical errors are the most serious errors, are consistent with a number of previous studies, but also points out that there are some methodological weaknesses (of the kind just mentioned) in these studies. His own study tested comprehension of a version of a reading passage that contained a certain number of errors. The passage was taken from a genuine student essay and subsequently manipulated to contain only one error type (of half a dozen types) or a mix of the errors the student had made.

---

[5] James (1998: 14-15) hypothesizes that some of the errors cited by researchers in the field were invented especially for the purpose of illustrating the violation of a particular rule and are too unlikely to have come from learner data.

Cutting's (2000) study on advanced learners also used 'real' errors. It shows that vocabulary is by far the most important source of error for non-native learners studying at a British university. These students have only marginally more problems with grammar than their native speaker peers, but they do still struggle with vocabulary problems; and it is their lack of lexical knowledge that keeps them from getting higher marks.

Lexical errors in applied linguistics

Some researchers have also made an attempt at finding an explanation for the learners' errors they analysed. Liu & Shaw (2001) show that their sample of (Chinese) learner language contains comparatively few compounds of the type *decision-maker*, a fact they attribute to the learners' lack of qualitative lexical and collocational knowledge. They hypothesize that the fact that learners know a translational equivalent might hide this lack of depth in their lexical knowledge.

Nation's (2001: 186) findings seem to point in a similar direction. He found that in students' essays most errors occur with high-frequency words, i.e. the 1000 most frequent words in English. Words of lower frequency (in general English) are typically used correctly. Given that the most frequent words are also those with the highest number of subsenses, the highest frequency of multiple word class membership, and the highest number of occurrences as parts of multi-word units, such an error pattern would confirm the hypothesis that learners lack depth of knowledge for many of the words they have learned and that are assumed to be known (by their teachers and by themselves).

The popular fallacy that students 'know' a word as soon as they are able to recognize and produce it in one of its subsenses is also shared by applied linguists. Bogaards (2001) questions the related assumption by many linguists (including Nation) working on the acquisition of the lexicon that learners can be assumed to know a word as soon as they have learned the base form of a word family. He calls for the replacement of the notion of 'word' as it is often used in the assessment of vocabulary knowledge by the notion of 'lexical unit', a term suggested by Cruse (1986). A lexical unit in this context is a word or multi-word unit with a single sense. Bogaards shows that learners need to learn new senses for known words, i.e. that they do not automatically understand the sense of the word *party* in (1) if they are known to understand it in (2).

(1) The lawyer refuted the arguments of the other *party*.
(2) Our neighbours are throwing a *party* tonight.
    (after Bogaards 2001: 324)

The two uses of *party* in (1) and (2) constitute two different lexical units and thus have to be learned separately according to Bogaards. His results show that learners find it easier to add a new sense to a word form they already know than to learn a completely new word. This is precisely the reason why Nation and others advocate teaching the core, often highly abstract, sense of a polysemous word. In the case of *party,* this core would have to cover the two senses illustrated above, plus a number of other senses. Each of these subsenses of the word has its own phraseological pattern, which also needs to be acquired by the learner. Whether Nation's or Bogaards' approach to the problem is the more appropriate one needs to be investigated, but it seems clear to me that error analysis would benefit greatly from taking a fresh look at learners' errors. Just as "recognition of the centrality of lexis in language readily suggests that the teacher's response to student error may need to be lexically rather than grammatically oriented" (Lewis 1993: 172), so applied linguists can only profit from taking such a different perspective. Learning vocabulary is not just prior to learning the grammatical system of a language, it is prior, simultaneous, *and* subsequent to grammar learning.

References

Allison, G. & P. (1992). *Englisch mit Oxford: 333 'Horror' Mistakes*. Berlin: Cornelsen & Oxford University Press.

Bogaards, P. (2001). 'Lexical units and the learning of foreign language vocabulary'. *Studies in Second Language Acquisition* 23, 321-343.

Corder, S. P. (1973). *Introducing applied linguistics*. Harmondsworth: Penguin.

Cruse, D. A. (1986). *Lexical semantics*. Cambridge: Cambridge University Press.

Cutting, J. (2000). Written Errors of International Students and English Native Speaker Students. In G. M. Blue (ed.) Assessing English for Academic Purposes. Bern: Peter Lang.

Dordick, M. (1996). 'Testing for a hierarchy of the communicative interference value of ESL errors'. *System* 24 (3) 299-308.

Fitikides, T.J. (1936, 2000). *Common mistakes in English*. London: Longman.

Granger, S. (ed.). (1998). *Learner English on Computer*. London: Longman.

James, C. (1994). 'Don't shoot my dodo: On the resilience of contrastive and error analysis'. *IRAL* 32 (3) 179-200.

James, C. (1998). *Errors in Language Learning and Use*. London: Longman.

Lennon, P. (1991). 'Error: Some problems of definition, identification, and distinction'. *Applied Linguistics* 12 (2) 180-196.

Lewis, M. (1993). *The lexical approach: The state of ELT and a way forward*. Hove. LTP.

Liu, E. & P. Shaw (2001). 'Investigating learner vocabulary: A possible approach to looking at EFL/ESL learners' qualitative knowledge of the word'. *IRAL* 39 (3) 171-194.

McCretton, E. & N. Rider (1993). 'Error gravity and error hierarchies'. *IRAL* 21 (3) 177-188.

Nation, I. S. P. (2001). *Learning Vocabulary in Another Language*. Cambridge: Cambridge University Press.

Sinclair, J. (1991). *Corpus, Concordance, Collocation*. Oxford: Oxford University Press.

Singleton, D. (1999). *Exploring the Second Language Mental Lexicon*. Cambridge: Cambridge University Press.

Wray, A. (2002). *Formulaic Language and the Lexicon*. Cambridge: Cambridge University Press.

ALLAN TURNER

Fronting in Tolkien's archaising style and its translation

Ever since Tolkien's fantasy romance *The Lord of the Rings* appeared almost half a century ago it has divided both critics and ordinary readers into two camps: those who see it as a work of genius, and those who would prefer to deny it any merit whatsoever.[1] A feature which has frequently come under attack is his archaising style, characterised by early reviewers as "Boys' Own" and "Brewer's Biblical" (Shippey 1992: 159).

Tolkien defended his linguistic and stylistic usage in a draft of a letter to a young correspondent, Hugh Brogan, (Tolkien 1981: 215f.), who had criticised in particular the chapter "The King of the Golden Hall", calling the style 'Ossianic' and agreeing with a critic who had dismissed it as 'tushery'.[2] The main points of the draft may be summarised as follows:

- 'Tushery' is properly applied only to bogus attempts by writers without specialist knowledge to create temporal colour by using incidental expletives such as 'pish' and 'tush'.

- Even using words that are still used, or at least known passively by educated people, it is possible to create two levels of archaism, a strong and a moderated form; the chapter in question makes use of moderated archaism.

---

1 A detailed survey and attempted explanation of the critical response can be found in Curry (1999).
2 In the event Tolkien did not send the letter, but wrote Brogan a short note indicating that the question of archaism would take too long to debate in a letter and would have to wait until their next meeting.

- The language represents a mode of thought corresponding to the culture in which the story is set, just as the description of clothes, weapons and other artefacts will use words appropriate to the technology. Therefore to make a character from a 'heroic' culture express himself in modern categories would produce a clash far worse and more insincere than the use of archaic language in modern times.

- There is a legitimate place in literature for genuine archaic English, which is terser than the modern idiom. It is a mistake of the 20th century to imagine that its usages are more valid than those of any other period simply because they are 'contemporary'.

Tolkien focuses on one short sentence from the text (completed here in order to make clearer what is changed in the modern paraphrase) to illustrate what he means by terseness and the linguistic resources by which it can be obtained:

> 'Helms too they chose[, and round shields]' is archaic. Some (wrongly) class it as an 'inversion', since normal order is 'They also chose helmets' or 'they chose helmets too'. (Real mod. E. 'They also picked out some helmets and round shields'.) But this is not normal order, and if mod. E. has lost the trick of putting a word desired to emphasize (for pictorial, emotional or logical reasons) into prominent first place, without addition of a lot of little 'empty' words (as the Chinese say), so much the worse for it.

Tolkien is expressing his linguistic ideas here in an informal manner, since he was not writing for publication, but clearly what he is referring to is the syntactic and stylistic device of fronting. There is no doubt that it is a characteristic feature of his archaising style: in the chapter in question, some twenty pages in length, examples of fronting as defined below occur no less than 79 times. This article will examine the types of fronting used and attempt to analyse the literary effect that they create. It will not pass any judgement on the quality or appropriateness of Tolkien's writing, since that is a task for literary criticism or aesthetics rather than linguistics, and it is unlikely to change the minds of those who believe that there is no place in modern literature for the re-creation of ancient cultures, real or imagined. However, for readers who enjoy the effects created it may give an indication of what exactly it is that they enjoy, and provide linguistic material for a literary debate.

Translation is an important analytical tool in this article. In fact it had its origin in research into the problems of translating Tolkien,[3] so a section is devoted to the treatment of Tolkien's fronting in two of the published translations. *The Lord of the Rings* has proved popular throughout the world; Hammond & Anderson (1993) list 20 languages into which it has been translated, although some languages have more than one translation, and further translations have been made since the publication of their bibliography (including two into Chinese), while the release of the trilogy of films directed by Peter Jackson could create a demand for even more. However, every translation must depend on an interpretation, and on the basis of Robert Frost's famous dictum that "poetry is what is lost in translation", published translations may provide a useful aid to literary criticism, particularly where that is founded on a linguistic analysis.

The translations chosen here are German[4] as a representative of the Germanic languages, and French to represent Romance. Shippey (1992) has demonstrated in detail that Tolkien drew a large part of the inspiration for his creative writing from his professional activity as a philologist, and undoubtedly he had the expertise in Old and Middle English to reproduce the genuinely archaic style that he advocates in his letter to Brogan. As a general rule, it may be said that the earlier the stage of English

---

[3] A rudimentary version was presented with the encouragement of David Allerton at a joint postgraduate seminar of the Universities of Basel and Strasbourg in 1994.

[4] The older Carroux translation has been used in preference to the new one (2000) by Wolfgang Krege, since firstly the new translation has not yet established its superiority, and secondly the older one, first published in the same year as the French translation, offers a more fitting parallel because it represents the same stage in the history of the critical reception of Tolkien.

under consideration, the more similarities it will show to other Germanic languages in its lexis and syntax. So far there has been no full-scale study of Tolkien's use of language, but even a cursory examination will show that in the archaising sections he makes extensive use of the Germanic element in English lexis, reducing Romance-derived vocabulary to a minimum. However, neither of the two target languages has the choice of two contributory streams in making decisions about stylistic aspects. It is true that in its lexis German sometimes has a stylistic choice between *Fremdwörter* and native derivations, but this is on a limited scale and applies mostly to certain areas of scientific vocabulary, e.g. *Myopie* and *Kurzsichtigkeit,* where the former term belongs to a restricted technical register. Here it will be seen that Tolkien's privileging of Germanic extends to syntax too. An examination of the translations will show the extent to which the German and the French translators have found it desirable or possible to reproduce, with the resources of the target languages, Tolkien's stylistic exploitation of one particular syntactic feature. This in turn will help to identify what is peculiar to the source text.

Fronting may be considered a typical Germanic structure, since it is found, with regular inversion of subject and verb, in the earliest extant forms of all the Germanic languages. It is common in modern German, and is not restricted to any particular register; it can be seen in any newspaper article, very often in its linking function, just as well as it can in the sober style of Duden: "Falsch ist es auch, ein Relativpronomen [...] durch ein Personalpronomen zu ersetzen." The commoner a structure is, the less it will appear stylistically marked in any way. Therefore it may be hypothesized that translation into German will preserve a large part of the syntactic structures of fronting, but this will result in a stylistic levelling and will not in itself convey a sense of archaism. In French, fronting is much less common. It is always dangerous to attempt to characterise a language, but French has a reputation for clarity, which suggests an emphasis on clear informational structures, and since both lexis and syntax are regulated by the Académie Française to achieve standardisation, there has been little encouragement for authors to create a recognised archaising style. Therefore it may be hypothesized that the translator will tend to restore an unmarked order of Subject Verb [Object Complement Adjunct] and preserve end-focus.

Form and function of fronting in English

Greenbaum & Quirk (1990: 397) offer the following definition: "Fronting is the term we apply to the achievement of marked theme by moving into initial position an item which is otherwise unusual there." This is useful for the conceptual fields that it implicitly draws together: first, it links the syntactic structure of the sentence or clause with its informational structure (theme/rheme); second, by drawing attention to what is unusual, it points to Jakobson's (1969) 'poetic function' of language, in which the linguistic form draws attention to itself over and above the informational content. Greenbaum & Quirk's account of fronting will be followed here, and the terminology used will be theirs except where specifically noted.

Fronting can be carried out on three sentence elements: object, complement and adverbial adjunct. In the case of adjuncts, only predication adjuncts will be considered here. It is perfectly usual to find sentence adjuncts in initial position, therefore they do not satisfy the condition of unusualness in the definition above. Examples of the three types, with some variants, would then be:

(1) That much I knew already. [object]
(1a) What that means I simply can't imagine. [object noun clause]
(2) A right fool I felt! [complement]
(2a) Mary they called her. [complement after complex-transitive verb]

(3) To that extent I agree with the thrust of your argument. [adjunct]

(3a) Round the corner came a fire engine. [adjunct with subject-verb inversion]

But as we have seen from the definition, a list of forms is not enough. We must also consider the communicative dynamism of these sentences, that is the variation in communicative value between their different parts. An unmarked sentence usually shows a progression in information value from beginning to end; it has end-focus:

(4) John will finish the article next week.

Here a standard syntactic unit (subject-verb-object-adjunct) corresponds to a standard information unit (theme-rheme), and also to a standard tone unit (with an intonational nucleus on *week* denoting the new information). Fronting changes this progression by removing at least some of the focus to the element in sentence-initial position. Paradoxically, this can either remove the end-focus or strengthen it. Examples (1) and (1a) demonstrate a typical discourse-structuring use of fronting, where the marked theme resumes something that has already been said, or at least is implicit; this is known as the linking function. Here the main focus remains on the final position, and the nucleus falls as expected on *already* and *imagine* respectively. In (3a) the marking provided by the fronting and the inversion functions as a postponement of the new information contained in the subject, giving even more prominence to final position; this is the presentational function. These are perhaps the most common types of fronting in English.

In (2) and (2a) on the other hand, the fronted complement contains the new information and therefore receives a strongly marked focus, while the element in sentence-final position loses all prominence. In (2a) the nucleus falls on *Mary*, leaving the remaining elements unstressed, while in (2), which perhaps has the most emotive force, the nucleus falling on *right* serves to underline the idiomatic nature of the phrase. Examples of this kind certainly occur in everyday English, but they must be regarded as more stylistically marked than either the linking or presentational use, and are less common. The relatively high frequency of their use by Tolkien in the chapter under consideration will be seen to be a typical feature of his poetic diction.

Example (3) also demonstrates the linking function, but it is dependent upon context for the interpretation of its communicative dynamism. If it falls at the end of a turn in the discourse structure, it could well have the structure of (1) and (1a), with some prominence remaining on *argument* in final position. If it is followed by another sentence in which the speaker restricts his agreement, then contrastive focus could fall on *agree* or *thrust*. However, if the focus is on THAT extent alone, with a low rising intonation spread over the whole sentence, so that the restriction of agreement is implicit, we are left with a string of syntactic elements without any clear communicative dynamism. Such sentences will be designated here as 'bumpy' sentences.

Examples of fronting in Tolkien

Examples will be considered in order of markedness, that is to say the extent to which the balance of focus is moved from the usual end position to initial position.

The presentational use, as has been demonstrated, normally strengthens the end-focus by putting new information in final position. Sentence (5) is a straightforward example, where the first two elements are short and the subject gains end-weight from the alliterating patronymic. The effect is weakened in (6), syntactically by the addition of two short adverbials, and informationally because "Rohan" in the context is known.

(5) There dwells Théoden son of Thengel [...]
(6) Thus spoke a forgotten poet long ago in Rohan [...]

Such sentences (ignoring the choice of lexis) can be considered quite usual in literary usage.

Next come examples of the linking function, where the new information remains in final position, while the fronted element refers back to information that is known, or at least implicit from the preceding discourse. This occurs frequently in the chapter, although there is no example where the link is quite so direct as in examples (1), (1a) and (3):

(7)   [...] for better help you will not find.

(8)   How far back his treachery goes, who can guess?

(9)   But upon one form the sunlight fell [...]

In the context of (7) the topic[5] of help has already featured in the discourse; the adjective *better* receives the main stress within the fronted element, since this is the new information. In some cases the information contained in the fronted element may have been so implicit that it appears almost as a new discourse topic:

(10) [...] but any weapon that you bear, be it only a staff, you must leave on the threshold.

In cases of fronting which cannot be easily related to either the presentational or the linking function, the balance between initial position and end position is more even. Where there is little in the way of new information in later elements, end-focus can be maintained by other means, which can be seen increasingly as typical stylistic features:

(11) Hours of my precious time he has wasted already.

(12) No counsel have I to give to those that despair.

(13) Weapons they have laid at your doors that are worth many a mortal man [...]

---

5   Greenbaum & Quirk use 'topic' only to note it as an alternative term for 'theme'; here it is used in the context of discourse structure, and would answer the question "What are they talking about?".

(14) Many long lives of men it is since the golden hall was built.

In (11) the final element is an adverb, as in (1). Since adverbs are short and contain relatively little information, in spite of their prominent position, more of the sentence focus may be seen to have passed here to the fronted element in both cases. In (12) the end-weighting comes from the post-modifying relative clause. In (13) too there is a balancing relative clause, but its antecedent is the fronted object itself, so that there is discontinuity. Discontinuity of this kind is another of Tolkien's archaising stylistic devices, and can be found in (14) too.

We come now to the relatively large number of sentences in this chapter which have the focus entirely on initial position, as in examples (2) and (2a) above. This happens particularly with intransitive and copular verbs. In (15) to (17) the fronting removes the focus from the verb even though it falls in a prominent position, reinforcing the impression of stylistic marking. Example (17) is formed on the pattern of (2a), throwing the name into even sharper relief than if it had been in the usual sentence-final position:

(15) Quickly now Gandalf spoke.

(16) A witless worm have you become.

(17) Háma is my name.

There are a number of other sentences similar to (17), since names, their significance and their linguistic form take a particularly important place in Tolkien's writing (see Shippey 1992: 50 and *passim*); there are well over a thousand names of beings and places in the index to *The Lord of the Rings*. They are often accentuated by stylistic devices such as the discontinuous gloss in (18), or the parallelism in (23):

(18) *Láthspell* I name you, Ill-news [...]

(19) Edoras those courts are called [...] and Meduseld is that golden hall

Another type of linguistic and stylistic patterning similar to the parallelism of (19), in which both clauses display fronting, is chiasmus, which has fronting only in one clause, while the other gives a mirror image with its normal SV[OCA] word order:

(20) it is thatched with gold. [...] Golden, too, are the posts of its doors.

(21) Swords you do not need, but there are helms and coats of mail

(22) Very fair was her face, and her long hair was like a river of gold.

(23) Old and weary you seem now, and yet you are fell and grim beneath, I deem.

When the example which Tolkien chose to comment upon in his letter is set in its context, it is also seen to be a part of such linguistic patterning, a discontinuity:

(24) Helms too they chose, and round shields

Finally, there are some examples of the 'bumpy' sentences as seen in (3), that is sentences with a number of syntactic elements in which the communicative dynamism is unclear, that is to say it is not clear from the immediate context (unfortunately not available in short extracted examples of the kind used here) exactly what the new information is and where the focus falls. In (27) the presentational use seems to have been deliberately sabotaged by rejecting the expected inversion and leaving the verb, short and weightless, completely without focus in a normally prominent position:

(25) And this sword your master himself gave into my keeping.

(26) Some reward you have earned at least.

(27) There men in bright mail stand.

The strangeness of these sentences will be made clear by the ways in which translators have dealt with them.

Treatment in translation

Translations of a selection from the examples above will show that in many cases the hypothesis in Section 1 is substantially correct. The German translator does in fact preserve the fronting in a large number of cases, while the French translator normalises it to SV{OCA}:

(7) for better help you will not find.

(7g)[6] denn bessere Hilfe werdet Ihr nicht finden.

(7f) car vous ne sauriez trouver de meilleure assistance.

(11) Hours of my precious time he has wasted already.

(11g) Stunden meiner kostbaren Zeit hat er bereits verschwendet.

(11f) Il a déjà gâché des heures de mon précieux temps.

(13) Weapons they have laid at your doors that are worth many a mortal man

(13g) Waffen haben sie an Eurer Tür abgelegt, die so manch einen sterblichen Mann […] wert sind

(13f) Ils ont déposé à votre porte des armes qui valent maints hommes mortels

(16) A witless worm have you become.

(16g) Eine einfältige Schlange seid Ihr geworden.

(16f) Tu es devenu un serpent sans intelligence.

(24) Helms too they chose, and round shields

(24g) Auch Helme wählten sie und Rundschilde

---

6 Examples in German translation will always be designated with g, and in French with f. This is no indication of ordering; the example which is closest in structure to the source text will usually appear first. Paraphrases are denoted by the prime sign (').

(24f) Ils choisirent aussi des heaumes et des boucliers ronds

However, in German there are some subtle changes to the distribution of information because of the requirements of German word order. One of these is that fronting in German always produces inversion of subject and verb, whereas in English the requirement varies, and sometimes there is a stylistic choice to be made: in (16) the word order could just as well have been "you have become". Also, although the discontinuity of the last example is preserved, it is possible that the stylistic effect of discontinuity in general could be less in German because of the standard syntactic feature of bracketing (Verbklammerung), which regularly sends such informationally significant elements as infinitives and past participles to the end of their clause; a normalised version of (13g) would therefore still display discontinuity:

(13g') Sie haben an Eurer Tür Waffen abgelegt, die [...]

The familiarity of this type of construction may make discontinuity appear less stylistically marked in German anyway than it would in English. It also makes impossible the focus on the adverb in final position in (11).

There is one other change of word order which is dictated by the rules of German grammar, namely that only one adverbial may come before the verb. This applies to two sentences from the chapter; in (28) *evil tidings* is understood as given information:

(28)   Yet in two ways a man may come with evil tidings.

(28g) Dennoch mag ein Mann auf zweierlei Art mit schlechten Nachrichten kommen.

(29)   For a moment still as stone she stood [...]

(29g) Einen Augenblick stand sie reglos wie ein Stein [...]

In (28) the conjunct *yet* is given priority, since it is a part of the discourse structure, which operates at a higher level than the syntax of the individual sentence, so that what in English is the stylistically marked fronting of the adjunct *in two ways* is normalised in German. In (29) both a sentence adjunct (*for a moment*) and a predication adjunct *(still as stone)* precede the subject. But since in Greenbaum & Quirk's definition only the predication adjunct counts for fronting, again the German translation must be viewed as a normalisation.

Apart from the changes required by German grammar, it can be taken as read that in all the examples above for which a translation has not been provided here, the syntax of the German translation follows that of the source text. However, in French there are more exceptions to be noted. In (13f) the object is postponed to appear as antecedent directly in front of the relative pronoun, so that there is a smooth progression from one clause to the next:

(13) Weapons they have laid at your doors that are worth many a mortal man

(13f) Ils ont déposé à votre porte des armes qui valent maints hommes mortels

In French the principle of end-focus can be seen to be particularly important, so that end-weight is regularly achieved in object relative clauses by the inversion of subject and verb, the 'inversion d'élégance':

(30) Dites-moi ce qu'a fait votre ami.

Therefore it is not surprising that object fronting, which tends to displace end-focus, is encountered far more rarely in French than in either English or German. Dupriez (1984), a standard students' reference work of literary devices, gives (under the entry 'Inversion') only one example, from James Joyce, without apparently seeing any significance in the fact that it is taken from a translation. It is not found in our French target text, although complement fronting is occasionally preserved:

(31) Dark have been my dreams of late

(31f) Sombres ont été mes rêves depuis quelque temps

(20) it is thatched with gold. [...] Golden, too, are the posts of its doors.

(20f) qu'il soit couvert d'or. [...] Dorés aussi sont les montants de ses portes.

In (20f) the chiasmus is kept, but that is not the case with the other occurrences of this figure. Complement fronting is evidently a construction to be used sparingly, since it is not preserved in (32), which in its form is very similar to (25):

(32) Dark is the hour.

(32f) L'heure est sombre.

Similarly, it is not thought appropriate to duplicate a parallelism of fronting, even though it is retained for the first half. The contrast underlined by the syntactic structure of the English is made explicit in the translation by a lexical marker, "en même temps":

(33) Slender and tall she was in her white robe girt with silver; but strong she seemed and stern as steel.

(33f) Mince et élancée apparaissait-elle dans sa robe blanche ceinte d'argent; mais elle était en même temps forte et dure comme l'acier.

Presentational fronting of adverbials is not uncommon in French, since it helps to create end-focus, and it is represented here, again with a normalising postponement of the subject for the sake of end-focus:

(6) Thus spoke a forgotten poet long ago in Rohan

(6f) Ainsi s'exprimait jadis en Rohan un poète oublié

However, in the other example of the presentational function a different procedure is followed, namely clefting, where the relative clause allows for the typical inversion which maintains end-focus:

(5) There dwells Théoden son of Thengel

(5f) C'est là que réside Théoden fils de Thengel

Clefting as a means of drawing attention to information at the beginning of the sentence, while leaving the desired weighting at the end, is common in French, which typically uses syntactic devices to mark focus, rather than stress as is often the method used in English. There are two further examples of its use in this chapter to replace English fronting; in (34) the front focus is strongly marked, whereas in (35) it is very light, fulfilling the linking function in a sentence which postpones for effect the name of an important character:

(34) Not West but East does our doom await us.

(34f) C'est à l'Ouest et non à l'Est [sic] que notre destin nous attend.

(35) Thus Aragorn for the first time in the full light of day beheld Éowyn, Lady of Rohan

(35f) C'est ainsi qu'Aragorn vit pour la première fois à la pleine lumière du jour Eowyn, Dame de Rohan

Clefting is of course also used in English, though less frequently than in French. It is seldom used in German, although the pseudo-cleft is more common. There are in fact only two cleft sentences in the source text, and it may be that Tolkien deliberately avoided this structure in his archaising style, since it uses the "little 'empty' words" referred to above; apparently he preferred the "terser" (and more Germanic) stylistic device of fronting. In (36), the clefting forms part of a chiasmus, which is not retained in either target text; (36f) converts it to a parallelism, while (36g) uses the characteristic German fronting here too. Example (37) compensates for the theoretically more modern syntax by the older use of the present simple where nowadays the progressive form would be expected. In fact it does not give an impression of modernity or fluency at all. It is another 'bumpy' sentence, the communicative dynamism of which is made clearer by the modern paraphrase (37'). The French translation retains the fronting, whereas in German the structure is changed (and thereby stylistically neutralised, in spite of the compensatory dative -*e*):

(36) It is orc-necks I would hew, not shave the scalps of Men

(36g) Orkhälse möchte ich abhauen, nicht die Schädel von Menschen scheren

(36f) Je voudrais tailler des cous d'Orques et non raser des cuirs chevelus d'Hommes

(37) and it is to Mundburg that he goes.

(37') and in fact he *is* going to Mundburg.

(37f) et c'est à Mundburg qu'il se rend.

(37g) und er ist auf dem Wege nach Mundburg.

Another device which is used in the French translation to replace fronting in its linking function is left dislocation. A topic which has already been mentioned, or at least is implicit, is reintroduced at the beginning of the sentence; however, unlike a fronted element, it appears as syntactically separate, followed in writing by a comma, and is then taken up as a pronoun in the following clause:

(38) That I would call aid.

(38f) Cela, ce serait de l'aide

(39) That I knew already

(39f) Cela, je le savais déjà

Finally, we shall consider what happens to the remaining 'bumpy' sentences. In (25f), the French translator levels out the bumpiness using both left dislocation and clefting. In German the fronting is retained as expected, but the communicative dynamism is smoothed by the insertion of an (unstressed) indirect object before the subject and the normal movement of the past participle to sentence-final position. This compulsory bracketing also neutralises the adverbial in sentence-final position in (26), while for (27) both translations restore the normal presentational word order (again compulsory in German grammar):

(25) And this sword your master himself gave into my keeping.

(25f) Et cette épée, c'est votre maître lui-même qui m'en a confié la garde.

(25g) Und dieses Schwert hat mir dein Herr selbst zur Aufbewahrung gegeben.

(26) Some reward you have earned at least.

(26g) Einigen Lohn hast du zumindest verdient.

(26f) Vous avez au moins mérité une récompense.

(27) There men in bright mail stand

(27g) Dort stehen Männer in schimmernder Rüstung

(27f) Là se tiennent des hommes en mailles brillantes

The stylistic significance of these 'bumpy' sentences and how they are normalised in translation will be seen in the following section.

Commentary

The examples have shown that Tolkien's archaising style displays a high proportion of linguistic patterning, or "verbal art", as it is styled by Fabb (1997), to which fronting makes a significant contribution. In spite of what early critics may have thought, it is certainly not an indiscriminate use of the Victorian and Edwardian generic poetic diction to which there was such a strong reaction amongst modernists in the 20th century. Certainly Tolkien did make use of a specifically literary diction and avoided the gritty language of the streets which was in vogue during his lifetime, but the style is not uniform. In fact it is highly nuanced, with varying degrees of literariness being used to differentiate characters and cultures.

In the present case of a strongly archaising style, it is made clear in Appendix F of *The Lord of the Rings* that the Rohirrim are calqued on the Anglo-Saxons, while Shippey (1992) has demonstrated that the chapter under consideration here is closely modelled on *Beowulf*, both in individual motifs (the challenge by the guard, the description of the hall, the hostile counsellor) and in the sententious dialogue. In that case it follows that the archaic style of the language used is intended to contribute to this depiction of an antique society, with even the details of syntax finely calculated to convey the impression of pre-modernity.

The frequent use of fronting is an obvious Germanic characteristic that is being used here. The verbal art, the use of chiasmus, parallelism and discontinuity, may suggest poetry, and particularly a pre-modern epic style. Lexis has not been considered here, though it could be seen to fit in with this interpretation; it is anyway the most frequent indicator of an archaic setting, even at the level of mere "tushery". Grammatical features not examined here include the non-standard position of adverbs and the use of non-assertive forms in positive sentences. But an important part of Tolkien's archaism comes not from what he puts in, but from what he leaves out, and it is here that the translations may act as an indicator. We have seen the tendency to smooth out the discontinuities and the irregularities of focus in French, while what is stylistically marked in the word order of the source text is neutralised in German translation because it corresponds more to the regular German syntax. In particular French has sought to restore a modern communicative dynamism with a clear end-focus, of the type that is demonstrated in (4). But it is precisely this modern fluent, rational, post-Enlightenment presentation of ideas that Tolkien is trying to avoid, as is shown also by his avoidance of the "little 'empty' words" which are typical of the modern style. We could paraphrase some 'bumpy' sentences into a more contemporary idiom to demonstrate that; for (38) it has already been done above:

(25) And this sword your master himself gave into my keeping.
(25') And anyway, it was your master himself who gave me this sword to keep for him.

(28) Yet in two ways a man may come with evil tidings.
(28') But there are two ways in which a man may come with evil tidings.

Examples (25') and (28') make use of clefting in the French manner, while (25') and (37') show the use of conjunctional discourse markers to make the text cohesive. Tolkien deliberately avoids these, so that his characters speak in rough-hewn syntactic blocks in which fronting almost takes the place of explicit cohesion. It is perhaps not too fanciful to hear in this an echo of the Old English alliterative long line with its discontinuities and parallelisms, and the regular insertion of paraphrases which seem gratuitous to the modern mind used to a regular communicative dynamism. In it we see a significant part of the "terseness" to which he refers in the letter quoted above. Although it cannot be demonstrated adequately from a short study of one syntactic feature, this forms a part of a deliberate strategy to reproduce a pre-modern discourse structure, the strangeness of which in combination with the lexis and the subject matter gives an impression of an archaic society which goes far deeper than the merely decorative temporal colour of writers such as Robert Louis Stevenson, or the self-mocking style of Jeffery Farnol. Tolkien had both the linguistic skill and the philological insight to do what he regarded as essential: to make the language congruent with pre-modern modes of thought.

It is clear by now how translation can be used at least in one way to identify "poetic" language in the source text. But to show what the published translations fail to capture is not to be taken as any criticism of the translators' work. It is perhaps inevitable that in all translation there tends to be a degree of normalisation, a levelling of certain characteristic features, because it is the translator's task to take that which is unfamiliar and inaccessible and render it into a form accessible to the target culture. Moreover they have to write according to the expectations of the target culture (concerning genre, for example) and use the resources of the target language. It must be said that both translators are aware of at least the more obvious archaising features and attempt to capture at least some of the effect by using markedly literary language or compensatory devices such as additional alliteration (in German). But Beowulf is not part of their target culture – the references probably go unnoticed by most English readers anyway – and there is a limit to what can be demanded when language refers to its own history as it frequently does in Tolkien. We are dealing here with matters on the very limits of translatability.

References

Curry, P. (1999). 'Tolkien and his Critics: A Critique'. In: Th. Honegger (ed.), *Root and Branch - Approaches towards understanding Tolkien*, Zurich and Berne: Walking Tree Publishers.
Dupriez, B. (1984). *Gradus: Les procédés littéraires*. Paris: Editions 10/18.
Fabb, N. (1997). *Linguistics and Literature*. Oxford: Blackwell.
Greenbaum, S. & R. Quirk (1990). *A Student's Grammar of the English Language*. Harlow: Longman.
Hammond, W. G. & D. A. Anderson (1993). *J. R. R. Tolkien: A Descriptive Bibliography*. Winchester: St. Paul's Bibliographies/ New Castle, Delaware: Oak Knoll Books.
Jakobson, R. (1969). 'Linguistics and Poetics'. In: T. Sebeok (ed.). *Style in Language*. Cambridge, Massachusetts: MIT Press. 350-77.
Shippey, T. A. (1992). *The Road to Middle Earth* (second edition, first edition 1982). London: HarperCollins.
Tolkien, J. R. R. (1981). *The Letters of J. R. R. Tolkien*, ed. Humphrey Carpenter. London: George Allen and Unwin.
Tolkien, J. R. R. (1996). *The Peoples of Middle-Earth*, ed. Christopher Tolkien. London: Harper Collins.

Texts

Tolkien, J. R. R. (1992). *The Lord of the Rings*, second edition, one volume paperback. London: HarperCollins (first edition in three volumes 1954-5. London: George Allen and Unwin).

Tolkien, J. R. R. (1972). *Le Seigneur des Anneaux: Tome I La communauté de l'anneau, Tome II Les deux tours, Tome III Le retour du roi*, trans. F. Ledoux. Paris: Christian Bourgeois.

Tolkien, J. R. R. (1972). *Der Herr der Ringe: Band I Die Gefährten, Band II Die zwei Türme, Band III Die Rückkehr des Königs*, trans. M. Carroux and E.-M. von Freymann. Stuttgart: Klett-Cotta.

Kevin McCafferty

Language contact in Early Modern Ireland: the case of *be after V-ing* as a future gram

The *be after V-ing* construction is a well-known feature of Irish English (hereafter IE). It is exemplified in the sentence 'She's after telling him the news', which translates into Standard English as 'She's just told him the news' (Harris 1984b). Following McCawley's (1973) survey of the semantic range of the perfect in English, it has been known as the 'hot-news perfect' (e.g. Harris 1984a, 1984b, 1991; Kallen 1989, 1990, 1991), while other terms used are '*after* perfect' (Filppula 1999) and 'immediate perfective' (Hickey 2000).[1]

This construction is assumed to be a clear case of direct transfer from Irish to IE (Harris 1984a, Hickey 2000, Odlin 1997), being a calque on the Irish construction with '*be after* + verbal noun', as in *Tá sí tréis an bád a dhíol*, lit. 'Is she after the boat selling' (Harris 1984a: 319). The Irish structure emerged by the 12th century (Greene 1979, 1980; Ó Corráin 1997: 28 fn), while the earliest IE examples date from the late 17th century (Bliss 1979). Beyond Ireland, the construction is encountered only where there has been IE input into local English, as in Newfoundland (e.g. Shorrocks 1997) and Prince Edward Island (Pratt 1988), or in English vernaculars influenced by another Celtic language substrate, as in the Hebrides (e.g. Filppula 1999: 106-7).

---

1 However, the hot-news sense appears to be giving way to a wider range of perfect-tense meanings in both present-day IE (Kallen 1989, 1990, 1991; Fieß 2000; McCafferty forthcoming a) and Gaelic (Greene 1979; Ó Corráin 1997).

However, in early texts, *be after V-ing* carried future meanings (Bliss 1979, Kallen 1991). Moreover, both future and perfect uses were common in the 18th and 19th centuries, both meanings can be found in the language of individual writers in the 19th century (Filppula 1999, McCafferty 2002), and the relative strengths of future and perfect-tense usage display the kind of S-curve development typical of language change, with one spreading at the expense of the other (McCafferty 2002).

This paper assesses the data in Bliss (1979) in terms of a crosslinguistic model of the development of the future (Bybee et al. 1994). This model makes sense of the puzzling instances of the construction in the texts as uses of a typical future gram. It is proposed that language contact may explain the use of the structure as a future gram in early IE and that it represented a compromise between native English-speaking colonists and Irish learners of the colonial language, with Irish providing the syntactic structure and English the semantics.

Explanations

Bliss' (1979) anthology remains a major source of data on the early stages of IE. The texts are literary representations of IE and their authenticity has been queried (e.g. O'Maolain 1980). Future uses of *be after V-ing* have been used as evidence for dismissing such texts as 'Stage Irish', i.e. misrepresentations of IE for purposes of caricature or satire. A typical conclusion is that "laboured Hibernicisms like 'will you be after having a drink?' have no basis in the English of Ireland" (Greene 1966: 49). Bliss was well aware of the issue of his texts' validity, but argued in relation to future uses of *be after V-ing* that it was more profitable to seek an explanation than to ridicule or dismiss such usage (Bliss 1979: 300). Some subsequent treatments are reviewed here.

Kallen (1990) suggests that *be after V-ing* in early IE merges anterior and non-actual meanings as a result of universally motivated principles of tense, mood and aspect categorisation in a situation of language contact and creolisation; later, the construction became restricted to perfect-tense use only, as a result of decreolisation (Kallen 1990: 131-2). However, the non-actual meanings Kallen cites do not seem relevant to the construction. Nor was the contact situation in Ireland a likely setting for creolisation: only two languages, Irish and English, were in contact, and throughout 300-400 years of language contact, increasing bilingualism and eventually language shift, Irish people acquiring English (or creating IE) could always fall back on a shared native language (Irish Gaelic).

Another approach is to view examples like (1) and (2) as equivalent to the modern sentence in (3), i.e. as expressions of the future perfect (Hickey 1997: 1003f., 2000: 100f.).

(1) You will be after being damn'd.

(2) He **will not be after hanging** his Countrymen. (Bliss 1979: 299f.)

(3) If you don't hurry up, they**'ll be after leaving** by the time you get there. (Hickey 2000: 101)

Hickey (1997: 1003) attributes this view to Bliss, but the latter discounts future perfect readings, as they "would not suit the context" (Bliss 1979: 300). As we will see, it makes more sense to read (1) and (2) as conveying future meanings: 'You will be/are going to be damned' and 'He is not going to/is not about to hang his countrymen'.

Filppula (1999: 99-107) observes that a change occurred in the '*after* perfect' so that older future uses were replaced by a newer perfect-tense semantics by about the 1830s. Filppula also notes future uses in the writings of William Carleton and John Banim, who were both born in the 1790s, while these did not occur in late 19th-century letters. McCafferty's (2002) diachronic survey also shows that future and perfect senses co-existed over a long period.

The occurrence of *be after V-ing* with future time reference has led to consideration of whether this use might be rooted in

British varieties of English. However, there is little reason to believe that *be after V-ing*, with either future or perfect meaning, has ever been widely used in British English. A search of the Chadwyck Healey database *Literature On Line* for the period 1500-1700 produced not a single instance of the construction in texts that were not written by Irish or Anglo-Irish authors. For traditional dialects, there is little evidence relating to its use in British English, none of it earlier than the late 19th century. There are some dictionary citations (e.g. EDD, OED, Pratt (1988) s.v. *after*), but most sources have Irish connections. And the EDD examples seem to have been the only basis for Kelly's (1989) argument that future-tense uses originated in dialects of Great Britain. For modern British English, I know only of one example (4), cited by Harris (1984a) from an interview with a Tyneside speaker.

(4) He wants to cut up to 1,500 jobs – that's what *he's after doing*. (1984a: 308 fn.4)

In the absence of evidence for a grammaticalised source in British dialects, future uses of the construction must be assumed to be an innovation that arose in Ireland as a result of language contact.

The process involved in calquing the IE construction on the Irish Gaelic hot-news perfect is adequately dealt with elsewhere (e.g. Hickey 1997: 991). Learning strategies typical of untutored second-language acquisition are the means by which the construction was transferred into IE (e.g. Odlin 1997). The likely mechanism has been termed 'negative transfer' (Odlin 1989), 'gap-filling' (Thomason 2001) or a search for 'categorial equivalence' (Hickey 1997). Adopting this kind of strategy, learners of a second language fall back on L1 structures and transfer them to L2 in order to fulfill functions expressed in L1 for which they do not know the L2 equivalents. This accounts adequately for the transfer of *be after V-ing* from Irish Gaelic as a perfect-tense gram, explaining why modern IE has a direct equivalent of the Irish hot-news perfect construction. But it does not explain the future uses of the construction at earlier stages.

Emergence of future uses

The idea that the hot-news perfect was transferred into IE with its Gaelic semantics intact assumes that IE evolved in a situation in which its speakers had little or no interaction with speakers of superstrate Englishes. While that may have been the case in the 18th and 19th centuries (Odlin 1994, 1997), this situation was less common in the earlier stages of contact, in which mutual interference – 'negotiation'[2] in Thomason's terms – between emerging IE and British English superstrate varieties was more likely.

We may invoke the uniformitarian principle (Labov 1994: 21-3) to suggest how future-tense readings might have emerged in the contact situation. We know that *be after V-ing* is frequently misunderstood by non-Irish speakers of English, who often take it to be a future tense. Kallen (1990: 131), for instance, observes that:

> In fact, it is the interpretation of 'future desire' which, in my experience and in that which I have heard reported, is generally given to the Hiberno-English perfect form by speakers of United States English. Since the usages in [6, below] are entirely unfamiliar in American English, the future interpretation in this case cannot be seen as an example of dialect borrowing, but rather must be taken as an interpretive strategy arising from more inherent features of English *after*.

The strength of the perfect reading in modern IE *versus* future (mis)interpretations by British English speakers is indicated by Harris' (1982: 111) report on the choices of two groups of listener-judges – native speakers of IE and British English – the results of which are displayed in Table 1. A full 98.6% of IE speakers interpreted the test sentence as conveying hot news (and it had past-time reference for the others too), while 81% of

---

2 'Negotiation' is unconscious approximation to what are believed to be the patterns of another language or dialect (Thomason 2001: 142).

British English speakers opted for the future reading. The remaining 19% gave the hot-news meaning, but many identified it as an IE construction that they would not use.

Misinterpretation of this type may have produced the future semantics of the construction in early IE. Thus, *be after V-ing* with future time reference was an innovation that occurred as a result of interaction between native speakers of British English and Irish-speaking learners of English: the latter provided the syntactic structure as a calque on their Gaelic hot-news perfect construction, while the former supplied the future semantics. As bilingualism spread, interaction in English was increasingly between Irish bilinguals (with imperfect command of English) rather than between bilinguals and speakers of English with little or no knowledge of Irish (Odlin 1989, 1994, 1997). In this situation, the perfect-tense reading based on the semantics of the Irish construction could establish itself as the norm.

Meaning	IE	%	BrE	%
a) I had a cup of tea a couple of minutes ago.	143	98.6	12	19
b) I had a cup of tea last week.	2	1.4	-	-
c) I want to go for a cup of tea now.	-	-	51	81
TOTAL	145	100	63	100

Table 1: Someone said "I'm after getting a cup of tea". What do you think they meant? (after Harris 1982: 111)

Dolan (1998) provides a historical anecdote that illustrates of the kind of confusion that might arise when the IE construction is used by a speaker of Irish and/or IE who intends a perfect-tense meaning to an English interlocutor who interprets the utterance as a future:

> An Englishman who had settled in Ireland once related to me a conversation which he had with an Irish servant. 'Mary,' he said, 'will you please light the fire in my study?' 'I'm just after lighting it,' she replied. 'Then do it at once,' he said. 'Don't I tell you, sir,' she said, 'that I'm just after doing

it?' (Birmingham, *The lighter side of Irish life*, 1912: 170; cited in Dolan 1998, s.v. *after*)

The modern example in (5) is from a play written by Martin McDonagh, who was born in London of Irish parents. In (5), the writer's knowledge of the IE structure combines with his British English interpretation to produce a future-tense usage:

(5) I suppose a sup would you be after?
(McDonagh, *A Skull in Connemara*. In *Plays I*, 1999: 112)

If this can happen today, it could have occurred in early IE as well. In fact, the Tyneside example in (4) might be a case of accommodation by the interviewee to a perception of what Harris (himself from Ireland) would intend if he used the construction. As we will see, interpretation of *be after V-ing* as a future gram is supported by the semantics of its lexical source, the preposition or adverb *after*, which gives rise to this kind of interpretation.

Be after V-ing as a future gram

Crosslinguistically, verbs conveying meanings of DESIRE, OBLIGATION, or MOVEMENT towards a goal are the most common lexical sources for the formation of the future (Bybee et al. 1994: 253). British English exemplifies all three types in the future morphemes *will* (DESIRE), *shall* (OBLIGATION), and *be going to* (MOVEMENT). For present purposes, it is important that *after* can express both DESIRE and MOVEMENT. A further, less common, source of future grams identified by Bybee et al. (1991) is the use of temporal adverbs, to which category *after* belongs in one of its uses. Thus, *after* may be regarded as a prime candidate for development into a future gram, because it is capable not only of "indicating a time after the moment of speech or a reference time" (Bybee et al. 1991: 19), but also of expressing both DESIRE and goalward MOVEMENT.

Surveying the future in 76 languages, Bybee et al. (1991: 19) note that the prototypical use of future grams is "to signal that *an assertion about future time* is being made, or in other words, to signal a *prediction*". While PREDICTION may be the core meaning of 'the future', this sense emerges only at a late stage of grammaticalisation. Typological surveys show that the core future meaning of PREDICTION develops from meanings of INTENTION, which in turn derive from verbs of DESIRE, OBLIGATION or MOVEMENT. Bybee et al. (1991: 25ff., 1994: 279) postulate four stages in the semantic development of future grams, which they call *future ages* (or FUTAGEs). These FUTAGEs specify the uses grams may have in addition to the core sense of PREDICTION. The stages may, of course, overlap in what Hopper & Traugott (1993: 124-6) call 'layering'. The process of future-tense grammaticalisation is presented in Table 2.

futage 1	futage 2	futage 3	futage 4
desire >	intention, willingness >	future/ prediction >	imperative, complements, protases
movement >	intention, immediate future >	future/ prediction >	imperative, complements, protases

Table 2: FUTAGEs for grams derived from modal DESIRE and MOVEMENT

In the case of *be after V-ing*, we are not dealing with a verb, which is the most frequent source of tense and aspect forms (Bybee et al. 1991), but with a complex construction that includes a preposition or adverb that originally referred to location but also carries temporal meanings (OED, s.v. *after*). Following Heine et al. (1991), we may assume that the concrete, locative meaning ('farther off / behind') predates the more abstract temporal one ('later'), and that the latter derives from the locative meaning by metaphorical extension in the well-known way that time relations often come to be expressed in spatial terms.

As Kallen (1990) observes, *after* can refer to both 'prospective' and 'anterior' situations, as in (6a) and (6b), respectively:

(6) Ambiguity of *after*

    a) Prospective:

        Business people are always after more money.

        The cops are after you, Charley!

        Lucinda is always after the boys.

    b) Anterior:

        After the break, we all went back to work.

        This book was written after the writer's long illness.
        (after Kallen 1990: 131)

This is not just a matter of temporal reference, however. In (6a) *after* refers to 'a state of desire relative to the future', while in (6b), *after* "fixes a reference point anterior to the primary state of affairs" (Kallen 1990: 131). The prospective senses derive from the meaning "following with intent to overtake, pursuing, in pursuit of" (OED, s.v. *after*), i.e. MOVEMENT towards a goal. Thus, in addition to past-time reference, *after* manages to combine no fewer than three of the categories frequently grammaticalised as future grams. This polysemy prepares the way for *after* to become a marker of the future: it is a temporal adverb ('later') that also denotes DESIRE and MOVEMENT in the direction of a goal, while *after* used in the sense of 'pursuit' links both meanings.

The path by which *after* developed into a future marker is traced in (7). As a locational proposition, 'X is after Y' refers to physical location 'behind', but also to 'following', denoting either location or movement. Following on from this, we have 'pursuit' (MOVEMENT), which refers to sequences that are either locational or temporal (or both). From 'pursuit' we can derive 'desire', which leads to the core FUTURE interpretations of *be after V-ing* – i.e. uses conveying PREDICTION, which are thus derived from 'behind', via senses like 'following', 'pursuit', 'desire', 'intention', 'willingness' and 'proximative' meanings.

(7) Development of *after* as a future marker:

after: behind (location) > following (location + movement) > pursuit (movement) >

desire > intention/willingness/proximative (time) > future/prediction (time) >

imperative/complement/protases

Below we will see that the IE data from the 17th and early 18th centuries covers the full range of grammaticalised senses (bold type) in this future chain.

Early Irish English

The data for the present study is taken from the representations of IE contained in Bliss' (1979) anthology. These texts, dating from 1600 to 1740, contain only 21 examples, the earliest of which is from a text dated c. 1670. In some examples, the nominalised verb is not in the present participle, as it invariably is in modern IE. We encounter a number of verbs in the infinitive (8), and there are hybrid forms that combine elements of *be after V-ing* and the English perfect: *have been after* + preterite/past participle (9), and *have been after* + present participle (10). Example (8f) may consist of either *be after* + infinitive, or *be after* + preterite/past participle.

(8) *be after V*

    a) And fate, when **he** [my father] **was after dee,** / Vas give it charge to come to see [...]. (Anon., *The Irish Hudibras*, 1689; Bliss 1979: 129)

b) She cannot hold one touch, butt **itching / She's after bee** to run a-bit[c]hing! (Anon., *Purgatorium Hibernicum*, 1670-75; Bliss 1979: 118)

c) der fell be no Waacancy, unless **I be after buy** de Plaash (Michelburne, *Ireland Preserved*, 1705; Bliss 1979: 146)

d)/e) **I fill be after dig** my potato, / **And drink** my good Bonny Clabber. (Michelburne, *Ireland Preserved*, 1705; Bliss 1979: 273)

f) First come, first sherv'd, His Graash de Lord *Tirconnel* has great kindness for dose dat **be after first come**. (Michelburne, *Ireland Preserved*, 1705; Bliss 1979: 146)

(9) *have been after V-ed/-en*

but what do dee say to Chests full of Plaat, Barrels of de Money, dat **have been after hid**, dare is Treasure upon Treasure in *Darry*. (Michelburne, *Ireland Preserved*, 1705; Bliss 1979: 147)

(10) *have been after V-ing*

fait Joy, **he has been after wearing** dem himself (Michelburne, *Ireland Preserved*, 1705; Bliss 1979: 146)

Apart from (9) and (10), (11) is the only other example in the data of a perfect-tense meaning. In fact, (11) is the only instance that parallels the modern IE use as a hot-news perfect.

(11) Deare Catolicks, you shee here de cause dat **is after bringing** you to dis. (John Dunton, *Report of a sermon*, 1698; Bliss 1979: 133)

Given the functional overlaps between these variants, they are here regarded as instances of the same construction (cf. Bliss 1979: 302-3). This is unproblematical, since overlap in the use of the present participle and infinitive in the progressive in early IE was noted by Bliss (1979: 294ff.; cf. also Ronan 2000: 51), so that vacillation between them in early instances of *be after V-ing* is also to be expected. Furthermore, as Ronan has also pointed out (2000: 51f.), the Irish verbal noun translates variably into English as either an infinitive or a present participle.

We can now examine the rest of the data in Bliss (1979) in relation to the model of the future outlined above. The distribution of the data across Bybee et al.'s (1991, 1994) FUTAGEs (cf. Table 2) illustrates how well-developed a future gram *be after V-ing* was in the 17th and early 18th centuries.

At FUTAGE 1, future grams tend to express either agent-oriented modalities like DESIRE, OBLIGATION and ABILITY, or MOVEMENT. In the case of *be after V-ing*, the modal sense of DESIRE is relevant, and in the early IE data, we find it used in this sense. However, it is difficult to separate DESIRE (FUTAGE 1) from INTENTION and WILLINGNESS, which belong to FUTAGE 2. At the latter stage, agent orientation remains important, but has typically been generalised from the source meanings. At FUTAGE 2, Bybee et al. (1991: 27) suggest that the development of this meaning is due to the inference that someone who *wants* to do something both *intends* and is *willing* to do so. Since these categories are difficult to keep apart, they are combined here, so that the examples in (12) illustrate the combined FUTAGE 1/2 category of DESIRE / INTENTION / WILLINGNESS.

(12) DESIRE / INTENTION / WILLINGNESS:

a) She cannot hold one touch, butt **itching / She's after bee** to run a-bit[c]hing! (Anon., *Purgatorium Hibernicum*, 1670-75; Bliss 1979: 118)

b) Art thou in love Joy? by my shoule dou dosht Comitt fornicaation; I vill tell you it is a veniall Sinn, and **I vill be after absolving** you for it (Thomas Shadwell, *The Lancashire witches*, 1681/82; Bliss 1979: 122)

c)/d) der fell be no Waacancy, unless **I be after buy** de Plaash, and I have a Shoul to be shaved, **I fell be after keeping** my Cow and my Seep, and twenty Ewe Lamb (John Michelburne, *Ireland preserved*, 1705; Bliss 1979: 146)

- e) Dere be none, **dat be after coming** in de Nort, but get dat worth deir laubour axshept my own shelf Joy. (John Michelburne *Ireland preserved*, 1705; Bliss 1979: 147)
- f) First come, first sherv'd, His Graash de Lord *Tirconnel* has great kindness for dose dat **be after first come**. (John Michelburne *Ireland preserved*, 1705; Bliss 1979: 146)
- g) An **will you be after giving** me the Moidore indeed, and by my Shoul now? (Susanna Centlivre, *A wife well managed*, 1715; Bliss 1979: 151)
- h) Be St. *Patrick*; and I did confess nothing; and you have no Evidensh here but this Gentleman, and **he will not be after hanging** his Countryman. (John Durant Breval, *The Play is the* Plot, 1718; Bliss 1979: 157)
- i) Well, **fat will you be after Drinking** good Countryman? (John Durant Breval, *The Play is the* Plot, 1718; Bliss 1979: 155)

For a gram derived from a MOVEMENT source, FUTAGE 2 may additionally include IMMEDIATE FUTURE or PROXIMATIVE meanings, as in (13), which refers to situations that will (or would) take place in the immediate or near future. Such uses, being semantically richer and more specific than straightforward futurity, are classified as belonging to this early stage. (13) can be paraphrased as 'when he was about to die'.

(13) PROXIMATIVE:

And fate, **when he** [my father] **was after dee**, / Vas give it charge to come to see (Anon, *The Irish Hudibras*, 1689; Bliss 1979: 129)

At FUTAGE 3 the agent orientation of grams is eroded and they typically carry the core future meaning of PREDICTION, as in (14). Here too, it can be difficult to distinguish this prototypical sense from others, so that we also find sentences that combine core futurity with DESIRE/INTENTION/WILLINGNESS, as in (15). Overlaps of this kind are to be expected in grammaticalisation, as new stages will not entirely replace the preceding stages (Hopper & Traugott 1993: 35-8).

(14) PREDICTION:

    a) No vonder do' it be deare, in trote, / Fen pole bushell is vort a groat! / Fen beggars **must be after chooseing!** (Anon., *Purgatorium Hibernicum*, 1670-75; Bliss 1979: 120)

    b) and de Caatholicks do shay, dat **you vill be after being damn'd** (Thomas Shadwell, *The Lancashire witches*, 1681/82; Bliss 1979:122)

(15) PREDICTION + DESIRE / INTENTION / WILLINGNESS:

    a) Cozen *O'Sulivan*, **I'll bee after telling** dee de Raison, de *Irish* Brogue carry de ill smell wid dem; [...]. (John Michelburne *Ireland preserved*, 1705; Bliss 1979: 146)

    b) No Body spaake, but day did ferry fell for demshelves, and **I fill be after doing** fell for my shelf. (John Michelburne *Ireland preserved*, 1705; Bliss 1979: 146)

    c) Who-bub-boo, **I can be after maaking** twenty thirty of my fadders and my followers, dat fell go wid me tro de World. (John Michelburne *Ireland preserved*, 1705; Bliss 1979: 146)

    d) de Priest **fill not be after give** us de Absolushon widout dem, and must show dem every time we go to de mash. (John Michelburne *Ireland preserved*, 1705; Bliss 1979: 148)

    e)/f) **I fill be after dig** my potato, / **And drink** my good Bonny Clabber. (John Michelburne *Ireland preserved*, 1705; Bliss 1979: 273)

In Bliss (1979) there are no instances of *be after V-ing* used in the FUTAGE 4 contexts of IMPERATIVE or as the PROTASES of conditional clauses, though these uses can be documented at this time from other sources (McCafferty forthcoming b). However, that

FUTAGE 4 has been reached is shown in this data by the use of the construction in COMPLEMENT clauses, of which there are examples in (12), (13) and (14), indicating how highly developed a future gram *be after V-ing* was in early IE. Bybee et al. (1991: 28) regard this as a late development, since future grams are used in main clauses before they appear in subordinate clauses.

On this evidence, *be after V-ing* has been polysemous from the earliest stages of IE, with perfect senses constituting a minority semantics at first. In Bliss' period (1600-1740), the gram was already used across the full range of future time reference. While no significance can attach to percentages, given the small numbers involved here, at this time, *be after V-ing* was most frequent in contexts conveying the FUTAGE 1/2 senses of DESIRE / INTENTION / WILLINGNESS (n = 9, or 43%) and the FUTAGE 3 sense of PREDICTION (n = 8, or 38%). There is also a single instance of PROXIMATIVE use (5%), giving a combined total for futurity of 18/21 (86%), while 3 perfects (14%) account for the remaining data. A striking feature of the perfects is that, in 2 of 3 cases, we are dealing with the hybrid forms in (9) and (10). It is also remarkable that only a single perfect-tense form is precisely equivalent to the paradigmatic modern sense of the hot-news perfect (11).

Conclusions

The uses of *be after V-ing* in the 17th and early 18th centuries accord well with the pattern of future-tense development outlined for English and a number of other languages. In this earliest documentary evidence of IE, future senses dominate, and the construction covers the full range of semantic nuances that we might expect to find in a future gram. *Be after V-ing* was prime material for use as a future gram, because *after* conveys so many of the senses that tend to be so grammaticalised – DESIRE, goalward MOVEMENT, and temporal relationships, the latter ambiguous as to whether reference is to the future or the past. Both future and perfect-tense senses rest, as Kallen (1990) has observed, on the inherent semantic ambiguity of the word *after* itself, which supports both past and future time reference. Hence, the semantics of English *after* conspired to make it likely for *be after V-ing* to be used to convey futurity. But the Irish Gaelic sense (hot-news perfect) meant that it could simultaneously grammaticalise in another direction as well – as a perfect-tense – even though such meanings are relatively rare in the early period studied here, as they were to remain until about 1850 (cf. McCafferty 2002, forthcoming b).

I have suggested that this situation was the result of a process of polygrammaticalisation by which *be after V-ing* came to be used in two senses, one originating in Irish, the other in British English interpretations of the calqued Irish construction as a future gram – and, of course, in the interaction between the structure and the semantics of *after* in English. It is suggested that future senses emerged in the language used between British and Irish speakers in the early stages of IE as a consequence of 'negotiation' (Thomason 2001), with speakers of emerging varieties of IE providing the structure and British English speakers the semantics. Thus, *be after V-ing* as a future gram became part of the target language aimed at by subsequent generations of IE speakers alongside its use as a perfect-tense gram. Interpreting the Bliss data in this way helps to explain why the construction was used with future meanings well into the 19th century, as shown by Filppula (1999) and McCafferty (2002).

References

Bliss, A. J. (1979). *Spoken English in Ireland 1600-1740*. Dublin: The Dolmen Press.

Bybee, J. L., W. Pagliuca & R. D. Perkins (1991). 'Back to the future'. In E. C. Traugott & B. Heine (eds.), *Approaches to grammaticalization. Volume II. Focus on types of grammatical markers*. Amsterdam: John Benjamins.17-58.

Bybee, J. L., R. Perkins & W. Pagliuca (1994). *The evolution of grammar. Tense, aspect, and modality in the languages of the world*. Chicago: Chicago University Press.

EDD. *English Dialect Dictionary* (Vol. I, 1898). Oxford: Oxford University Press.

Dolan, T. P. (1998). *A dictionary of Hiberno-English*. Dublin: Gill & Macmillan.

Dolan, T. P. and D. Ó Muirithe (1996). *The dialect of Forth and Bargy, Co. Wexford, Ireland*. Dublin: Four Courts Press.

Fieß, A. (2000). 'Age-group differentiation in the spoken language of rural East Galway'. In Tristram (ed.), 188-209.

Filppula, M. (1999). *The grammar of Irish English. Language in Hibernian style*. London: Routledge.

Greene, D. (1966). *The Irish language*. Dublin: The Cultural Relations Committee of Ireland.

Greene, D. (1979). 'Perfects and perfectives in Modern Irish'. *Ériu* 30: 122-41.

Greene, D. (1980). 'Perfect and passive in Eastern and Western Gaelic'. *Studia celtica* XIV/XV:87-94.

Harris, J. (1982). 'The underlying non-identity of English dialects. A look at the Hiberno-English verb phrase'. In J. Milroy, L. Milroy, J. Harris, B. Gunn, A. Pitts & L. Policansky, *Sociolinguistic variation and linguistic change in Belfast*. Report to the Social Science Research Council. Grant No. HR 5777. 85-117.

Harris, J. (1984a). 'Syntactic variation and dialect divergence'. *Journal of linguistics* 20: 303-27.

Harris, J. (1984b). 'English in the north of Ireland'. In P. Trudgill (ed.), *Language in the British Isles*. Cambridge: Cambridge University Press. 115-34.

Harris, J. (1991). 'Conservatism versus substratal transfer in Irish English'. In P. Trudgill & J.K. Chambers (eds.), *Dialects of English. Studies in grammatical variation*. London: Longman. 191-212.

Heine, B., U. Claudi & F. Hünnemeyer (1991). 'From cognition to grammar. Evidence from African languages'. In Traugott & Heine (eds.), 149-87.

Hickey, R. (1997). 'Arguments for creolisation in Irish English'. In R. Hickey & S. Puppel (eds.), *Language history and linguistic modelling, volume I: language history.* Berlin: Mouton de Gruyter. 969-1038.

Hickey, R. (2000). 'Models for describing aspect in Irish English'. In Tristram (ed.), 97-116.

Hopper, P. J. & E. C. Traugott (1993). *Grammaticalization.* Cambridge: Cambridge University Press.

Kallen, J. L. (1989). 'Tense and aspect categories in Irish English'. *English world-wide* 10: 1-39.

Kallen, J. L. (1990). 'The Hiberno-English perfect. Grammaticalisation revisited'. *Irish university review* 20/1: 120-36.

Kallen, J. L. (1991). 'Sociolinguistic variation and methodology. *After* as a Dublin variable'. In J. Cheshire (ed.), *English around the world. Sociolinguistic perspectives.* Cambridge: Cambridge University Press. 61-74.

Kelly, P. (1989). *'Afterthoughts on AFTER + DOing'*. Paper presented at joint meeting of Linguistics Association of Great Britain/Irish Association for Applied Linguistics, Belfast.

Labov, W. (1994). *Principles of language change, volume 1: internal factors.* Oxford: Basil Blackwell.

McCafferty, K. (2002). 'Sure how would the (imminent) future ever be after becoming the (recent) past? Change in the Irish English *be after V-ing* construction'. *ERIC Database of Educational Documents.* Washington DC: ERIC Clearinghouse on Languages and Linguistics, CAL.

McCafferty, K. (forthcoming a). 'English in the north of Ireland'. In D. Britain (ed.), *Language in the British Isles.* Cambridge: Cambridge University Press.

McCafferty, K. (forthcoming b). "I'll bee after telling dee de raison [...]': *be after V-ing* as a future gram in Irish English'. In Tristram (ed.), *The Celtic Englishes III.* Heidelberg: C. Winter. 1601-1750.

McCawley, J. D. (1973). 'Tense and time reference in English'. In J. D. McCawley (ed.), *Grammar and meaning. Papers on syntactic and semantic topics.* Tokyo: Taishukan Publishing. 257-72.

McDonagh, M. (1997/1999). *A skull in Connemara.* In *Plays 1.* London: Methuen. 61-126.

Ó Corráin, A. (1997). 'Spatial perception and the development of grammatical structures in Irish'. In F. Josephson (ed.), *Celts and Vikings.* Göteborg: Meijerbergs Institutt vid Göteborgs Universitet. 89-101.

O'Maolain, S. (1980). Review of A. J. Bliss, *Spoken English in Ireland 1600-1740. English world-wide* 1: 139-40.

Odlin, T. (1989). *Language transfer.* Cambridge: Cambridge University Press.

Odlin, T. (1994). 'A demographic perspective on the shift from Irish to English'. In C. A. Blackshire-Belay (ed.), *The Germanic mosaic. Cultural diversity in society.* Westport, Connecticut: Greenwood Press. 137-45.

Odlin, T. (1997). 'Hiberno-English. Pidgin, creole, or neither?' *CLCS occasional paper* 49. Dublin: Centre for Language and Communication Studies, Trinity College Dublin.

OED. *Oxford English Dictionary* (2nd ed., 1989). Oxford.

Pratt, T.K. (1988). *Dictionary of Prince Edward Island English*. Toronto: University of Toronto Press.

Ronan, P. (2001). 'Observations on the progressive in Hiberno-English'. In J. M. Kirk & D. P. Ó Baoill (eds.), *Language links. The languages of Scotland and Ireland*. Belfast: Cló Ollscoil na Banríona. 43-58.

Shorrocks, G. (1997). 'Celtic influences on the English of Newfoundland and Labrador'. In H.L.C. Tristram (ed.), 320-61.

Thomason, S. G. (2001). *Language contact. An introduction*. Edinburgh: Edinburgh University Press.

Thomason, S. & T. Kaufman (1988). *Language contact, creolization, and genetic linguistics*. Berkeley: University of California Press.

Traugott, E. C. & B. Heine (eds.) (1991). *Approaches to grammaticalization. Volume I. Focus on theoretical and methodological issues*. Amsterdam: John Benjamins.

Tristram, H. L. C. (ed.) (1997). *The Celtic Englishes*. Heidelberg: C. Winter.

Tristram, H. L. C. (ed.) (2000). *The Celtic Englishes II*. Heidelberg: C. Winter.

Paul Skandera

Start doing or *start to do*:
Is the gerund spreading in American English?

With the help of various passages in Shakespeare's dramas, Potter (1975) attempts to prove that, in British English, the gerund has been increasingly used since the 17th century in contexts that had previously been reserved for the infinitive, and indeed, in all of the citations he presents, the infinitive would nowadays usually be replaced with a gerund (1975: 134). Also a recommendation by H. W. Fowler (1926: 215) on the use of the two non-finite verb forms might point to the spread of the gerund in British English, namely when he writes that "there is very little danger of using the gerund, but much of using the infinitive, where the other would be better". In the linguistic literature on American English, there is no mention of a shift in the distribution of the non-finite verb forms in favor of the gerund. On the contrary, Follett (1966: 180), prescriptivist and author of a widely-read usage book, speaks of the opposite tendency to prefer the infinitive to the *-ing* form. Many prescriptivists, however, direct their criticism not so much against such a development in general as against the choice of the non-finite form in specific constructions. Follett, for example, regards the use of the infinitive after *be welcome to* and *be accustomed to* as a "mangling" of idiomatic constructions, and demands the use of the gerund in both cases (1966: 180).

The construction most frequently commented on is undoubtedly the combination of *convince* with an infinitive (*convince sb to do sth*) in place of a prepositional object introduced by *of*, which can be realized by both a gerund (*convince sb of doing sth*) and a noun phrase (*convince sb of sth*), or in place of a subordinate clause introduced by *that (convince sb that...)*. Prescriptivists also complain here about the semantic differentiation of the verb that goes hand in hand with the new syntactic pattern: *convince* no longer refers solely to the act of convincing, but can now also imply an action that results from the act of convincing, in the sense of 'persuade.' The controversy surrounding this usage was presumably first kindled in 1958 by a comment in Bernstein's *Watch your language*. In *The careful writer* from 1965, Bernstein refers to it as a "nonuse" (1965: 120), and Follett, too, closes his eyes to the linguistic reality when he insists that *convince* refuses to combine with *to* (1966: 111). In a detailed entry on this phenomenon, the authors of *Webster's dictionary of English usage* write that the use of *convince* plus infinitive in printed language probably first occurred in the middle of the 20th century, and has gradually spread since then. The earliest citation of this construction in the citation files of the Merriam-Webster publishing company dates back no farther than 1952, and the construction is not mentioned in *Webster's third new international dictionary* because, at the time of publishing in 1961, the verb was followed by an infinitive in merely 3 citations whereas it was followed by a *that*-clause in 61 citations. Of all the citations gathered between 1961 and 1969, however, nearly 60 percent showed the infinitive construction (297f.). The increasing acceptability of *convince* plus infinitive in present-day American English is also reflected in the responses from the 166 members of a usage panel appointed by William and Mary Morris (1985), of whom a surprising 71 percent tolerate the use of *convince* instead of *persuade* "in the speech of others" (139f.).

In Potter's view, the gerund emphasizes the course of an action while the infinitive simply names the action. Despite this semantic differentiation, however, he lists a number of expressions which he assumes are followed by both forms in free variation. Furthermore, the author shows, by using the sentence *That needs explaining / to be explained* as an example, that the gerund behaves neutrally with respect to the distinction between active and passive voice. Yet as a reason for the possible spread of the gerund he merely mentions its ability, in contrast to that of the infinitive, to form the complement of a preposition (1975: 134-135). The semantic differentiation between the gerund and the infinitive postulated by Potter is put forward in a similar way in almost all descriptive grammars. Yet at the same time, there is some doubt in most of these works as to the practical relevance of this differentiation, even in contexts in which both forms are generally permitted and used. Quirk et al. (1972: 835), for instance, concede that the difference in meaning may in practice be of little importance, but the same authors describe in Quirk et al. (1985: 1191) to what extent modal factors seem to be at least partially responsible for the distribution of the non-finite forms:

> Where both constructions [...] are admitted, there is usually felt to be a difference of aspect or mood which influences the choice. As a rule, the infinitive gives a sense of mere 'potentiality' for action, as in *She hoped to learn French*, while the participle gives a sense of the actual 'performance' of the action itself, as in *She enjoyed learning French*.

The authors exemplify this rule once again with the complementation of *try*, and go so far as to speak here of the double meaning of the verb. But even in this later work, they then come to the conclusion that the difference between the gerund and the infinitive in combination with other verbs is more subtle, and may well be neutralized by the meaning of the superordinate verb. Jespersen (1909-49) emphasizes right from the outset the semantic similarity between both forms, but he also reminds his readers that the speaker often does not really have a choice:

> When we come to speak of the use of infinitives as primaries – i.e. as subject or predicative of a sentence, as object of a verb or of a verbal phrase – we unavoidably come to deal with the gerund, too, for the two forms are here used for virtually the same purposes. There is a good deal of overlapping, though in many cases idiomatic usage allows only one construction. (V, 162)

Thereafter, he shares his assessment of the difference in meaning between the gerund and the infinitive, but he does so merely in small print:

> Some grammarians say that the gerund is more abstract, the infinitive more concrete or lively; others that the aspect of the gerund is imperfective and that of the infinitive perfective. Both definitions contain some truth and fit some instances, but neither is really to the point and applicable to all cases. (V, 162)

Curme (1931), too, repeats the usual hypotheses, but then follows his perception of actual language use when he simply denies that a semantic differentiation between both forms exists:

> Attempts have been made to prove that there is a differentiation of meaning between gerund and infinitive where the two forms compete with each other. It has been claimed that the gerund is preferred in stating a general fact, while the infinitive is used in referring to special circumstances of a particular individual act [...]. Actual usage knows nothing of this distinction. (1931: 491f.)

Finally, Quirk (1974: 166f.) sums up the uncertainty surrounding the two constructions as follows:

> There ought to be a big award for anyone who can describe exactly what makes him say 'I started to work' on one occasion and 'I started working' on another.

A comprehensive study of the distribution of both non-finite verb forms would have to include all contexts in which both constructions would in principle be conceivable. The aim of the present study, however, is not quite so ambitious. The study is confined to a possible shift in the distribution of the gerund and the infinitive in the syntactic function of an object complementing a set group of verbs. (Non-finite forms in object function complementing nouns and adjectives, and non-finite forms in subject function are not taken into account.) The investigation is based on a comparison of two machine-readable text collections containing texts that were written 31 years apart: the Brown Corpus (henceforth Brown) and the Freiburg-Brown Corpus (henceforth Frown). These two corpora are structured along the same lines, and form representative cross sections of printed, edited American English from the years 1961 and 1992, respectively. Brown and Frown have been sufficiently described in the linguistic literature, for example in the accompanying manuals by Nelson & Kučera (1989) and Hundt, Sand & Skandera (1999). They will therefore not be elaborated on here.

While Curme's (1931) rigorous denial of any semantic nuance of the non-finite forms clearly does not do complete justice to the linguistic reality, the following examples from Brown and Frown do indeed call some of the above-mentioned hypotheses about a semantic differentiation into question:

(1) A fascinating letter has just reached this desk from a correspondent who *likes to receive* so-called junk mail. (Brown B07.169f.)
(2) Ask any older child: a younger sibling just *loves to mess up* a big event. (Frown A33.126f.)

Although it can be assumed that the writer of the letter likes receiving advertising leaflets, handouts, etc. repeatedly, and that younger siblings love spoiling big events in general – rather than on a concrete, individual occasion – in both cases the relevant finite verb is complemented by the supposedly perfective infinitive. Thus the present study is grounded on the assumption that a possible difference in aspect or mood between the gerund and the infinitive in combination with the following verbs is usually perceived to be so marginal that both complements are virtually in free variation, and that such constructions therefore explicitly reveal a general preference for one non-finite form or the other:

> *bear, begin, cease, continue, deserve, hate, intend, love, prefer, propose, start.*[1]

Despite the careful selection of the verbs, an attempt was made, while counting the citations in the two corpora, to circumvent

---

1 This list does not claim to be exhaustive, nor is it assumed that the choice of verbs meets with unqualified approval. Potter (1975:134-135), for instance, perceives the infinitive after begin as an expression of an action that has not yet started whereas the gerund, for him, marks a definite starting point. By contrast, he does not recognize the widely observed difference between the two non-finite forms in combination with like.

further factors that presumably influence the choice between the gerund and the infinitive. Mair (1990: 103ff.), for instance, points out that an infinitival complement does not commonly designate an action that occurred prior to the action designated by the superordinate verb whereas most of the matrix verbs possessing a meaning that is directed toward the future *only* take the infinitive. If such verbs, like *remember* or *regret*, are not exclusively used in a futural sense, then an infinitival complement lends them this meaning. Citations representing the contexts just described were therefore left uncounted in this analysis. Furthermore, Mair notes that a number of other verbs, when they occur in the conditional form together with *would*, can take on a futural character and, as a result, are then usually also complemented by an infinitive.[2] In the case of *would like*, Mair draws attention to a semantic difference that goes beyond the temporal reference: a combination with the infinitive usually expresses the frequently used concept of an unfulfilled wish, while a gerundial construction signifies the less frequently occurring notion of conditional joy.[3] As it can be assumed, then, that the choice of the non-finite complement after verbs in the conditional form is influenced by semantic factors, citations in which the matrix verb is modified by *would* or the contracted form -*'d* were also left uncounted. Mair sees a further semantic difference between the gerund and the infinitive in the complementation of verbs of liking (or disliking) in negative contexts. With the example sentence *I didn't like telling / to tell them*, he

---

2   It is the nature of corpus linguistic work that even clearly recognizable tendencies are often seemingly called into question by a number of counterexamples, such as the following: *The announcement that U.S., British and French planes would begin enforcing the no-fly zone south of the 32nd parallel to protect dissident Shiite Moslems had been slated for today* [...] (Frown A05.99ff.). Counterexamples do not necessarily refute a rule, but they remind the linguist of the heterogeneity of language.
3   Mair illustrates the latter use with the example sentence *I know I'll never have the time, but speaking in purely theoretical terms I think I would like learning a few languages* (1990: 109).

demonstrates that the gerund here expresses a completed, or in other cases a habitual, action while the infinitive leaves the question of the actual performance of the action open. For that reason, citations of the verbs *hate*, *love*, and *prefer* in negations were, once again, not included in the count. Finally, all citations of matrix verbs in the progressive were excluded as well because of the likelihood that a speaker chose an infinitival complement solely for stylistic reasons: whereas a succession of two *-ing* forms does not occur a single time in the constructions analyzed, concatenative verbs show that a series of two or more infinitives is quite common in English.

In combination with the eleven matrix verbs listed above, within the limitations mentioned, Brown contains 126 citations of gerundial and 478 citations of infinitival complements. Thus the gerund was chosen in 21 percent of the cases in which both non-finite verb forms can be regarded as quasi free variants. Frown, on the other hand, contains 231 citations of gerundial and 474 citations of infinitival complements. Thus the authors of the various texts chose here a gerundial construction in 33 percent of the cases. The numbers show that, while there is generally a clear preference for the infinitive, the overall distribution of the non-finite complements has shifted marginally in favor of the gerund. A closer look at the complementation behavior of the individual matrix verbs reinforces these findings. Virtually all matrix verbs examined, with the sole exception of *start*, prefer the infinitive to the gerund in both corpora, but not a single one shows a clear shift still further toward the infinitive. On the contrary, the complementation behavior of seven of the matrix verbs – *bear*, *cease*, *continue*, *deserve*, *intend*, *prefer*, and *propose* – has remained relatively stable whereas that of the remaining four – *begin*, *hate*, *love*, and *start* – has clearly shifted toward the gerund. As a complement of *start*, for example, the gerund was able to increase its lead over the infinitive from 55 percent in Brown to 74 percent in Frown. The numerical data for four of the matrix verbs were singled out in order to exemplify these developments, and are shown in Table 1.

		begin	*continue*	*intend*	*start*
Brown (1961)	total number of citations	275	119	29	106
	gerundial complements	54	5	0	58
	infinitival complements	221	114	29	48
	preference in percent	80% for infinitive	96% for infinitive	100% for infinitive	55% for gerund
Frown (1992)	total number of citations	276	170	29	151
	gerundial complements	96	7	0	112
	infinitival complements	180	163	29	39
	preference in percent	65% for infinitive	96% for infinitive	100% for infinitive	74% for gerund
	tendency	shift toward gerund	stable	stable	shift toward gerund

Table 1: Distribution of the gerund and the infinitive as complements of verbs in Brown and Frown

The controversial infinitive after *convince* occurs only once in Brown and 11 times in Frown whereas the construction with *of* plus gerund, preferred by prescriptivists, is not attested in either of the corpora. Since these low frequencies, or absences, do not provide sufficient evidence of a possible (diachronic) shift in the complementation of the verb, an attempt was made, by using samples from the *Miami Herald* from 1992 on CD-ROM, to draw inferences about the (synchronic) distribution of both constructions in the American English of the early 1990s: of 100 randomly selected citations of *convince* with a non-finite complement, every single one contained an infinitive. There should be no doubt, therefore, that *convince sb to do sth* is now an integral part of Standard American English.

In conclusion, it may be generalized from the foregoing that the majority of the matrix verbs complemented by both non-finite verb forms without much difference in meaning probably prefer the infinitive to the gerund. Furthermore, the use of the infinitive in many of these constructions can be assumed to be quite stable. If, however, a shift in the complementation behavior of a matrix verb becomes discernible, it is likely to be a shift toward the gerund. The numerical data for the verbs *begin* and *start* in particular point to a gradual spread of the gerund in object function, which means that Potter's (1975) hypothesis regarding British English, referred to at the beginning of this paper, might also be true of American English. Since neither of the two non-finite verb forms is usually considered stylistically better than the other, it seems improbable that the choice of the complement is influenced by the formality of the communicative situation. There is no reason, therefore, to assume that the tendencies observed in Brown and Frown are restricted to printed, edited language, and do not manifest themselves in spoken and unedited text types as well. Thus a possible overall increase in the use of the gerund would contradict Follett's (1966) claim, also referred to at the beginning of this paper, that the choice of the non-finite verb form in American English more and more often falls on the infinitive. Finally, that a syntactic shift of the type discussed here may well be a grammatical innovation is proven by the first citation of *convince* with the infinitive found in the Merriam-Webster citation files from 1952, and the rapid spread of this construction since then.

References

Bernstein, T. M. (1958). *Watch your language*. Great Neck, NY: Channel.
Bernstein, T. M. (1965). *The careful writer: A modern guide to English usage*. New York: Atheneum.

Curme, G. O. (1931). *Syntax*. Boston: D. C. Heath. [vol. III of the *Grammar of the English language*]

Follett, W. (1966). *Modern American usage: A guide*. New York: Hill and Wang.

Fowler, H. W. (1926). *A dictionary of modern English usage*. Oxford: Oxford University Press.

Francis, W. N. & H. Kučera. (1989). *Manual of information to accompany a standard corpus of present-day edited American English, for use with digital computers*. 4th ed. Providence, RI: Department of Linguistics, Brown University. [1st ed. 1964]

Hundt, M., A. Sand & P. Skandera. (1999). *Manual of information to accompany the Freiburg-Brown Corpus of American English ("Frown")*. Freiburg: Englisches Seminar der Universität.

Jespersen, O. (1909-49). *A modern English grammar on historical principles*. Vol. I-VII. Heidelberg: C. Winter.

Mair, C. (1990). *Infinitival complement clauses in English: A study of syntax in discourse*. Cambridge: Cambridge University Press.

Morris, W. & M. Morris. (1985). *Harper dictionary of contemporary usage*. 2nd ed. New York: Harper and Row.

Potter, S. (1975). *Changing English*. 2nd ed. London: Deutsch. [1st ed. 1969]

Quirk, R. (1974). 'Our knowledge of English.' In: R. Quirk (ed.) *The linguist and the English language*. London: Arnold. 164-176.

Quirk, R., S. Greenbaum, G. Leech & J. Svartvik. (1972). *A grammar of contemporary English*. London: Longman.

Quirk, R., S. Greenbaum, G. Leech & J. Svartvik. (1985). *A comprehensive grammar of the English language*. London: Longman.

Webster's dictionary of English usage. (1989). Springfield, MA: Merriam-Webster.

LYNDON HIGGS

Has *shall* become extinct?

For the last two years, I have been in charge of teaching a course entitled "English grammar" to (mostly French) students studying[1] at Marc Bloch University, Strasbourg. Inevitably, a significant part of the course deals with a description of modal auxiliaries. While most grammar sources agree to a large extent on the uses and functions of, for example, *may* or *can*, the same cannot be said for *shall* (and, in particular, its distribution with respect to *will*). The fact that the vast majority of occurrences of *shall* or *will* appear in their identical reduced form *'ll* does nothing to reduce the confusion. Thus, in the preparation of my course, I have been confronted with a problem that is two-fold: firstly, many grammar sources appear to differ in their description of the uses of *shall*, and secondly, I have been under the increasingly uncomfortable impression of teaching something that may be becoming irrelevant to today's student of English, since it would appear that many native English speakers no longer include certain functions of *shall* in their active English use.

In this article, I will attempt to provide a brief overview of the (sometimes contradictory) descriptions of *shall* in some grammar sources, before moving on to describe my own preliminary research into the use of *shall* by a) some dialect speakers of English, and b) a selection of native standard English speakers.

---

1   The course is designed for first and second year students studying for a two-year degree *(Diplôme d'Etudes Universitaires Générales)* in English.

shall: a grammatical overview

Probably one of the most complete descriptions of *shall* is to be found in Leech (1971), and this can be used as a useful base for my overview. In his section on *will* and *shall*, Leech decides to separate their modal functions from their 'future auxiliary' functions, whilst recognizing that these two categories are very closely connected: the nature of futurity itself means that we cannot be as certain of future events being realised as we can when we talk about past or present events. Thus, in all future utterances, the speaker's judgement or attitude towards the probability of the event being realised is inevitably present – and therefore, as Leech points out, all future utterances contain a hint of modality. Quirk & Greenbaum (1973) agree with this analysis, adding, however, that *shall* and, particularly, *will* still remain the closest approximations to a colourless, neutral future.

Beginning with the "future auxiliary" functions, Leech maintains that both *will* and *shall* express the same basic value of prediction, although he adds that this neutral predictive meaning is only compatible with *shall* when combined with a first person pronoun as subject, as in example (1).

(1) I shall/will be thirty next week.

He remarks that with first person pronouns, many English speakers feel that *shall* is the correct form, and therefore use it when on their best linguistic behaviour. Quirk & Greenbaum (1973) add that while *will* can be used in all persons throughout the English-speaking world, *shall* appears to be restricted to first person usage in southern British English.

Other grammar sources are less specific; Swan (1980) merely indicates that *shall* is used as the first person future auxiliary, mentioning that *will* can be used instead of *shall* in most cases. Thomson & Martinet (1980) choose not to separate explicitly the two functions of *will* and *shall* (i.e. future auxiliary vs. modal auxiliary), but comment that although *shall* is still used as a first person auxiliary in formal English, *will* is preferred in conversation. Ogée & Boucher (1997) claim that *will* has replaced *shall* in all persons, and has become the only future auxiliary. Berland-Delépine (1974), another popular reference grammar used in France, is much more specific, remarking that while in America and Scotland *will* has become the only future auxiliary, *shall* is still preferred in England as a first person auxiliary when there is a total absence of choice or willingness on the part of the grammatical subject, as is the case when we express obligations *(have to)* or involuntary intellectual operations, as in examples (2) and (3):

(2) We shall have to walk.

(3) I shall always remember your visit.

All of the grammar sources mentioned above agree that *shall* is still used (in British English) in the interrogative, as question tags with *let's* and in suggestions, requests for orders or instructions (see examples (4), (5) and (6)):

(4) Let's leave, shall we ?

(5) Shall I open a window?

(6) What shall I do with this?

Moving on to Leech's second category, i.e. *will* and *shall* as modal auxiliaries, we see that Leech divides *shall* "modal auxiliary" into three uses: willingness ("weak volition"), insistence ("strong volition") and intention ("intermediate volition"). Contrary to *will*, he says, *shall* indicates that the volition is on the part of the speaker, and not that of the grammatical subject. Examples (7), (8) and (9) illustrate these three uses:

(7) You shall stay with us as long as you like.
("willingness on behalf of the speaker")

(8) He shall obey my orders!
("strong volition on behalf of the speaker")

(9) I shall go tomorrow.
("intermediate volition on behalf of the speaker").

Leech (1971: 81) points out that while the first two uses are restricted to second and third person subjects, the third use is restricted to first person subjects. He adds that all three uses of *shall* are relatively rare. For the first one (example (7)), he explains that it can have "an unpleasant connotation of condescension" and is only heard "in address to pets or young children". The second use, illustrated in (8), he says, is equally rare, since it carries "strong overtones of imperiousness".

The third use, seen in (9) is the most interesting, since it seems to overlap with the use of *will* in the first person: indeed, Leech maintains that these two modal auxiliaries are interchangeable in the first person, explaining that this is perfectly understandable since the first person pronoun means that the grammatical subject and the speaker are one and the same.

Quirk & Greenbaum (1973) establish the same categories for *shall* "modal auxiliary", adding "legal and quasi–legal injunction" within the category of "insistence" (equivalent to Leech's "strong volition on behalf of the speaker"):

(10) The customer shall pay within 30 days.

Quirk & Greenbaum go on to say that while the first two uses are rare, the third use, i.e. first person intention (Leech's "intermediate volition on behalf of the speaker") is still widely used in British English.

Bouscaren & Chuquet (1987) have a theoretical standpoint which is slightly different to that of Leech and Quirk & Greenbaum. They maintain that like all modal auxiliaries, *will* and *shall* can establish two different types of relations. The first is a relation between the speaker and the whole of the predicative relation (i.e. the subject and the predicate); they explain that *will* and *shall* both establish the same relation: that of prospective validation. In other words, *will* and *shall* indicate that the speaker believes that the event expressed by the verb will take place. This is very similar to Leech's definition of a "future auxiliary" expressing predictability.

The second type of relation that *will* and *shall* can establish is between the grammatical subject and the predicate. They maintain that *will* establishes a relation of volition or willingness, while *shall* establishes a relation of "non-autonomy of the grammatical subject". This roughly corresponds to Leech's "modal auxiliary" definition. However, their standpoint is different in that they prefer not to make a distinction between "modal auxiliary" and "future auxiliary" uses. Indeed, they say that the particularity of *will* and *shall* (contrary to other modal auxiliaries such as *may* or *can*) is that very frequently, both relations (i.e. the relation between the speaker and the predicative relation *and* the relation between the grammatical subject and the predicate) exist simultaneously. For instance, in example (11), there is clearly a future prediction on behalf of the speaker, but at the same time we have negative volition, or refusal, on behalf of the grammatical subject:

(11) He won't go to Paris next week.

Another interesting point in Bouscaren & Chuquet's work is that the notion of "non-autonomy of the grammatical subject" allows us to explain all occurrences of *shall* without having to resort to three sub-categories (as is the case with Leech's description). Consider examples (12) to (15):

(12) You shall go to the ball!

(13) You shall obey!

(14) I shall have to leave.

(15) Shall I open a window?

In each case, by using *shall*, the speaker simply states that the grammatical subject is in a position of non-autonomy; the deontic source (i.e. the origin of the obligation) of this non-autonomy is not necessarily identified as the speaker (although clearly, in examples (12) and (13) this is the case). In example (14), the grammatical subject is the speaker. Since the semantic content of the verb, *have to*, is incompatible with a notion of volition, it seems logical that the speaker would use *shall*, indicating that (s)he is in a position of non-autonomy. In example (15), the speaker adopts a non-autonomous position with respect to the addressee, who is the deontic source.

Now that we have seen a brief overview of the uses of both *shall* "future auxiliary" and *shall* "modal auxiliary", it would appear that there is a clear contradiction in one aspect of the descriptions: on the one hand, most grammar sources tell us that *shall* can be used as a "colourless" first person future auxiliary, where there is a total absence of volition on behalf of the speaker, as in (16):

(16) I shall be thirty next week.

On the other hand, some grammar sources tell us that *shall* can be used as a first person modal auxiliary, where it expresses "intermediate volition on behalf of the speaker" (see example (17)).

(17) We shall overcome.

In this context, it would appear that *shall* can be replaced by *will*:

(18) We will overcome.

Few grammar sources deal with this apparent ambiguity in any detail; however, Thomson & Martinet (1980: 176) refer in passing to *shall* "intermediate volition on behalf of the speaker" as "a new function of determination", and explain that while determination is normally expressed by *will*, some speakers feel that to express strong determination, "they should use another word, a 'heavier' word, a word not normally used much, and so they use *shall*".

Bouscaren & Chuquet's theory of non-autonomy, however, appears to adopt a rather different approach. While example (18) clearly indicates volition on behalf of the grammatical subject, example (17) indicates that the grammatical subject is in a position of non-autonomy with respect to destiny; i.e. the predicative relation <we-overcome> will be validated simply because destiny says that it will be so. This would explain why – as Thomson & Martinet so rightly said – some native speakers still feel that (17) expresses a "stronger determination" than (18).

Dialect use of *shall*

On the use of *shall* in dialects of English, Trudgill & Hannah (1985: 48) comment:

> *shall* is rarely used in North American English, except in legal documents or very formal styles, and is replaced by *will* (or *should* in questions with first person subjects). The negative form *shan't* is even rarer in U.S. English.

Trudgill (1984: 42) further comments:

> The use of the auxiliary *shall*, already absent from Scottish English and unusual in North American English, is becoming increasingly rare in Standard English also. Instead, *will* or the reduced form *'ll* is used. *Shall* survives most strongly in first person interrogatives: *Shall I turn out the light?*

In my research (Higgs 2003) into grammatical features and their variation in the Black Country dialect,[2] however, it is immediately apparent that the distribution of *shall* is very different to that of Standard English described above by Trudgill. In the research, samples of natural speech of 27 informants, aged between 14 and 84, were analysed. Twenty two cases of the use of *shall* (as opposed to the reduced form *'ll*) were recorded in the data, in eleven subjects' samples. These were found in all age groups. Ten of the eleven used *shall* as a constant (i.e. they never used *will*, although, of course, the reduced form *'ll* was used), and only one subject occasionally used *will/won't*. One example of the negative form, *shan't*, was recorded: (19). There was also one example of its dialect form, *shor*, used by the same subject: (20).

(19) I shan't play any more

---

[2] The Black Country dialect is spoken by inhabitants of an area falling within the four metropolitan boroughs of Wolverhampton, Walsall, Dudley and Sandwell, England.

(20) and if it goes wrong, I shor say, I shall ring the bell

Upon closer analysis of the examples of *shall* found in the data, it is interesting to note that there were no examples of *shall* with second or third person pronouns. This supports the information given in our overview of grammatical sources: utterances such as example (21) have disappeared from modern English.

(21) You shall marry him!

Apart from two cases of first person interrogatives asking for confirmation (see example (22)), the others were all of the declarative type *I shall* or *we shall*. Approximately half of these seemed to belong to the category *shall* "future auxiliary" (i.e. 'colourless' prediction), since they were followed by verbs whose semantic content is incompatible with the notion of volition. See examples (23) to (27).

(23) and I goes: shall I do it? He goes: yes.

(24) Fanny says: I shall be glad when I've had enough

(25) I shall be with different people.

(26) I shall have my own group to work with.

(27) I don't know whether I shall be able to keep it up.

The other half of the examples seemed to express "intermediate volition on behalf of the speaker" (i.e. *shall* "modal auxiliary") (see examples (28) and (29)). Interestingly, example (29) was the conclusion of a rather dramatic anecdote where the speaker explains that having been upset by her father's persistent criticisms of her piano-playing, she decided to abandon it for ever. In this context, it is easy to reconstruct the idea of 'destiny' mentioned earlier.

(28) I shall have to try me some of those.

(29) If I see him again I shall run off.

(30) I put down the lid [of the piano] and I said I shall never play it again, and I never did.

It would appear, then, that in the Black Country dialect (as is the case in many other dialects of English), *shall* is still present – much more so, it seems, than in Standard English. Clearly, further research into who uses *shall*, and into its distribution with respect to *will*, would be useful.

Preliminary research into the use of *shall* by some Standard English speakers

Having briefly studied the use of *shall* in one dialect of English, I decided to ascertain to what extent *shall* still figures in some standard English speakers' written production. I created a short written questionnaire to be sent via email to fifty native English speakers. In research of this type (i.e. a written questionnaire), email has several important advantages: it allows the researcher to access people all over the world, and generally gives a higher response rate than traditional mail. The questionnaire asked the reader to recreate the "full forms" of ten reduced auxiliary forms, all in context. Figure 1 gives the ten items.

As can be seen, five of the ten sentences were distracters; only questions 2, 4, 6, 8 and 10 involved choosing between *will* and *shall* (although question 1 involved choosing between *would* and *should*; in reality, 100% of the answers received gave *would*.) The instructions I sent with the questionnaire simply explained that I was conducting a linguistic survey. I asked my subjects to complete the sentences with the appropriate full forms, to add their sex, age and nationality, and to return the email to me. I also offered to explain the purpose of the survey if they so desired, but only once the email had been returned. In all, 38 questionnaires out of 50 were completed.

Firstly, a brief explanation of how I chose my subjects: as in all linguistic research, there are two main alternatives in sampling methodology. On the one hand, the researcher can work with a random sample. This has the advantage of ensuring that the speakers chosen are representative of the community as a whole, and the disadvantage of requiring large numbers of participants. On the other hand, the researcher can decide in advance, on the basis of careful observation, about which informants would best suit the study in question (often referred to a 'judgement sample'). The latter is becoming more and more popular, partly because linguistic behaviour seems to be more homogenous than other kinds of social behaviour, so that increased data handling brings diminishing analytical returns, and partly because of the immense practical difficulties in working with large samples. In this preliminary study, I decided to adopt a type of judgement sample; my informants were quite simply friends, or friends of friends. This had the immense advantage that I knew the linguistic background of each informant, allowing me to choose only people I considered to be speakers of Standard English of their country of origin (I eliminated so-called non-standard dialect speakers). Although my main objective was to study Standard English as spoken in England (26 of the 38 subjects were English), I also included 2 Australian, 4 Irish, 1 Scottish and 5 American informants. Ages ranged from 28 to 76.

1. <I'd> go, if I were you.
2. Whether you like it or not, <you'll> do as I say!
3. You <can't> do that.
4. <I'll> be disappointed if he fails the exam.
5. <I'd> rather you came later.
6. <We'll> have to save some more money.
7. <I'd> never seen such a sight !
8. Next month <I'll> be thirty !
9. <I'd> better go now.
10. <I'll> leave at noon because my bus leaves ten minutes later.

Fig. 1: The questionnaire's items

The five *shall-will* sentences were chosen to test informants' sensitivity to some of the functions of *will* and *shall* (as discussed earlier). Item 2 in Figure 1 suggested the use of *shall* "strong volition on behalf of the speaker". Items 4, 6 and 8 suggested the use of *shall* as a "colourless" future auxiliary; i.e. the nature of their predicates excluded any notion of volition. Item 10, on the other hand, suggested the use of *will* as a modal auxiliary of volition.

Before examining the results obtained from the survey, it is important to mention the limitations and short-comings of the present research. Firstly, as mentioned above, the sample is very small and is not intended to be representative for any particular country: under no circumstances can one Scottish informer be considered to represent the use of *shall* in Scotland! As already stated, it is merely a first indication of the use of *shall* by some speakers of Standard English.

Secondly, a written questionnaire – by definition – is testing informants when on their best linguistic behaviour. This, in itself, is not a problem, if the objective of the research is, indeed, to ascertain if *shall* still functions in formal written English. However, an additional problem presents itself in this type of study: the targeted nature of the questionnaire (even with a certain number of distracter items) still raised some informants' curiosity as to the real objective of the research (especially when – as is the case – several of the informants are specialists in the field of language teaching and/or linguistics!). Indeed, two informants added comments (see below) at the end of their questionnaire to this effect. In retrospect, a gap-fill questionnaire may have better disguised the real purpose (although this would inevitably have produced many reduced forms – of no interest for the present research – among the answers).

Thirdly, once the responses had been returned and I had explained the real purpose of my research, two informants commented on the fact that for phonetic reasons, the reduced form *'ll* probably has a much stronger association with *will* than with *shall*. I would argue, however, that if this is the case, it is simply because *will* is used in a much larger number of contexts than *shall*. After all, it could be argued that *I'd go* (question 1) has a stronger phonetic association with *I had* than with *I would*, yet no informant chose the former.

Turning now to the results of the research, it would seem useful to study them with respect to the following variables: nationality, age, and the items themselves. Firstly, nationality: as could be expected from comments in various grammar sources, *all* American, Scottish, Irish and Australian informants used *will* as a constant. Only English informants (9 out of 26) used *shall*. This confirms previous research into the use of *shall* outside England.

Secondly, age: contrary to what might have been expected, no correlation between the use of *shall* and the age of the informant can be made. The number of occurrences of *shall* among younger informants (22-40) is roughly the same as that of the older informants (40+). This would seem to suggest that age is not the deciding factor, even though several of the informants who commented on the research agreed that *shall* seems to be an "old-fashioned" element of the English language.

Thirdly, the items themselves (see figure 2): the most conclusive result is certainly that only one informant out of 38 chose *shall* for item 2 *(Whether you like it or not, you'll do as I say!)*; it could be argued, then (bearing in mind the limitations of the research mentioned above), that second person use of *shall* as "strong volition on behalf of the speaker" has virtually disappeared from modern Standard English.

Item	shall	will
2: Whether you like it or not, you'll do as I say!	1	37
4: I'll be disappointed if he fails the exam.	8	30
6: We'll have to save some more money.	7	31
8: Next month, I'll be thirty.	4	34
10: I'll leave at noon because my bus leaves [...]	6	32

Fig. 2: Results of the survey

Item 10, *(I'll leave at noon because my bus leaves ten minutes later)*, gave an interesting result in as much as six informants chose *shall*, which was virtually the same as for items 4, 6 and 8. This result suggests two possible explanations: either the informants who chose to use *shall* with first person pronouns applied this general 'rule' everywhere, regardless of the presence or absence of the notion of volition. (This seems to be partially disproved, however, by the fact that out of the 9 informants who used *shall* at least once, only 3 used it all 4 times. The other 6 informants chose to use *will* for certain items). The second explanation is that the item itself was ambiguous and suggested two interpretations. Either: *I will leave at noon because I want to leave (if not, I shall miss my bus)*. Or a "colourless" future auxiliary interpretation: *The timetable of my actions is established: I shall leave at noon, regardless of my wishes*. In retrospect, it would have been more interesting to choose an item whose interpretation was exclusively volitional.

Items 4, 6 and 8 all seemed to suggest a total absence of volition due to the semantic content of their predicates, yet the results show that this is not the case. While items 4 *(I'll be disappointed if he fails the exam)* and 6 *(We'll have to save more money)* received virtually identical results (8 and 7 occurrences of *shall* respectively), item 8 *(Next month, I'll be thirty)* only received 4 occurrences of *shall*. An explanation for this discrepancy is difficult to find, bearing in mind the especially strong similarity between items 4 and 8, (both items include *be*, and both items have predicates *[being disappointed* and *turning thirty]* that are clearly non-volitional). One possible explanation is that while item 8 *(Next month, I'll be thirty)* is factual, item 4 *(I'll be disappointed if he fails the exam)* is conditional. Any further research into the phenomenon of *will - shall* should include a study of this factor.

One final aspect of the results needs to be mentioned: the linguistic background of the informants. Upon closer study of the 9 informants who used *shall*, a high proportion received what could be described as a more classical education in England (the older informants in this category all attended grammar school;

the younger informants nearly all attended private schools). Indeed, one informant (who used *will* throughout) made this comment, which seems to confirm this tendency:

> And yes, I am interested in an explanation as to what you are exploring here. I asked an older, perhaps more classically educated, colleague of mine to do it as well. He tended to use *shall* in some of the examples, so I was wondering if this was the point you were exploring.

Another informant, who used *shall* in items 4, 6, 8 and 10, commented:

> I supposed your study was something to do with *shall* and *will*, and I suppose it's relevant that you asked for our age. I even hesitated between *you will do as I say* and *you shall do as I say*, as it really should be *shall* if I remember correctly what my teachers taught me, but I rebelled at the last minute and put *will*.

It is particularly revealing that this informant refers to "rebelling" when she chooses *will*. This implies that while the informant realises that the second person use of *shall* is no longer a feature of Standard English, her adherence to "correct grammar rules" learnt at school – especially in formal written production – is still important for her.

Conclusion

In conclusion, it would appear that further research needs to be carried out into two areas. Firstly, the use of *shall* in other dialects of English: does this use correspond to that of the Black Country dialect? Does there seem to be a preference for *shall* "colourless future" or for *shall* "modal auxiliary of volition"?

The second area of research would be to extend the preliminary study of standard English speakers to a larger sample, paying particular attention to the informants' linguistic background. Does the use of first person *shall* – at least in written production – suggest a certain educational or social background? Does *shall* exist equally in their casual speech? Is the distinction "volition/non-volition" relevant?

My final point will be a response to the question raised in my introduction. In a modern grammar course designed for students of English, should we be teaching *shall* ? Certainly, in view of the results obtained from my preliminary research, second and third person *shall* need only be taught from a historical perspective. Furthermore, it is probably fair to say that students can safely use *will* instead of *shall* as a first person auxiliary in both spoken and written English. However, I would maintain that it is important for any student of English to understand the fundamental values of *shall* (prospective validation and non-autonomy of the grammatical subject) since it allows a logical connection to be made with *should*: it seems interesting to be able to explain that *should*, the past form of *shall*, still maintains this notion of non-autonomy, albeit slightly attenuated. When we use *should* in utterances such as example (30), the basic value of non-autonomy has simply been "reduced", by virtue of the past form, to one of advice or reproach.

(31) You should make less noise!

In this way, the student can better understand the similarity between *shall* and *should* and other modal auxiliaries such as *may* and *might*: again, the past form, *might*, simply attenuates the basic value of *may* (bilateral possibility) to one of reduced logical possibility.

Hopefully, therefore, a description of *shall* can allow a better understanding of the complete modal auxiliary system of English.

References

Berland-Delépine, S. (1974). *La Grammaire Anglaise de L'Etudiant*. Paris: Editions Ophyris.

Bouscaren, J. & J. Chuquet (1987). *Grammaire et Textes Anglais. Guide pour l'analyse linguistique*. Paris: Ophyris.

Higgs, L. (2003). *A Description of Grammatical Features and their Variation in the Black Country Dialect*. International Cooper Series in English Language and Literature. Basle: Schwabe.

Leech, G. N. (1971). *Meaning and the English Verb*. London: Longman Group.

Ogée, F. & P. Boucher (1997). *Grammaire Appliquée de l'Anglais*. Editions SEDES.

Quirk, R. & S. Greenbaum (1973). *A University Grammar of English*. London: Longman.

Swan, M. (1980). *Practical English Usage*. Oxford: Oxford University Press.

Thomson, A. J. & A. V. Martinet (1980). *A Practical English Grammar*. Oxford: Oxford University Press.

Trudgill, P. (ed.) (1984). *Language in the British Isles*. Cambridge University Press.

Trudgill, P. & J. Hannah (1985). *International English. A Guide to Varieties of Standard English*. London: Edward Arnold.